THE FIRST SUBURE

CHINATOWN

IN THE SERIES

Asian American History and Culture

EDITED BY

Sucheng Chan

TIMOTHY P. FONG

The First Suburban Chinatown

THE REMAKING

OF MONTEREY PARK,

CALIFORNIA

Temple University Press

Philadelphia

Temple University Press, Philadelphia 19122
Published 1994
Printed in the United States of America

The paper used in this publication meets the minimum requirement of
American National Standard for Information Sciences—Permanence of
Paper for Printed Library Materials,
ANSI Z39.48-1984 ∞

Library of Congress Cataloging-in-Publication Data
Fong, Timothy P.
     The first suburban Chinatown : the remaking of Monterey Park,
California / Timothy P. Fong.
          p.   cm. – (Asian American history and culture)
     Includes bibliographical references and index.
     ISBN 1-56639-123-7
     1. Chinese Americans—California—Monterey Park—History.
2. Chinese Americans—California—Monterey Park—Social conditions.
3. Monterey Park (Calif.)—History. 4. Monterey Park (Calif.)—Social
conditions.   I. Title.   II. Series: Asian American history and culture
series.
F869.M7F68 1994
979.4'93—dc20   93-20562

CONTENTS

Preface   vii

Introduction: A New and Dynamic Community   3

1
Ramona Acres to the Chinese Beverly Hills:
Demographic Change   15

2
Enter the Dragon: Economic Change   35

3
"I Don't Feel at Home Anymore": Social and Cultural Change   55

4
Community Fragmentation and the Slow-Growth Movement   73

5
Controlled Growth and the Official-English Movement   96

6
"City with a Heart"?   118

7
The Politics of Realignment   138

8
Theoretical Perspectives on Monterey Park   157

Conclusion: From Marginal to Mainstream   173

Notes   179

Select Bibliography   203

Index   211

PREFACE

I first heard of Monterey Park on August 1, 1986. At that time I was producing a series of five half-hour radio documentaries for California Tomorrow, a statewide, nonprofit organization that researches and draws public attention to the state's future as a multiracial society. I had just completed interviews for my third documentary when a feature article on the front page of the *San Francisco Chronicle* made me sit up and take notice. "Tense Town" was the bold-print teaser over a photograph of a grim-faced elderly Chinese protester shading his eyes against the hot sun with an American flag. The headline read, "Influx of Asians Stirs Up L.A. Area's 'Little Taipei.'" I read the piece by Evelyn Hsu carefully, and I knew right then that Monterey Park would be the subject of my next documentary project.

By mid-September I had begun in earnest to contact individuals in Monterey Park. During this preproduction period I talked on the phone to older white residents who consistently complained that they felt like strangers in their own town, as if they were living in a foreign country, not in America. It was Chinese-language business signs that seemed to bother them the most: How could anyone know what a store was selling if there were no English signs to tell them? they asked.

I remember thinking at the time, "What's the big deal about a few Chinese-language signs?" Having grown up in Oakland and frequently visited my grandparents in San Francisco's Chinatown, I was used to seeing a heavy concentration of signs that I couldn't read.

I visited Monterey Park for the first time at the end of October 1986. When I picked up my rental car in Los Angeles and the counterperson asked me where I was headed, I told her, "I'm spending a few days in Monterey Park." "Oh," she said as she handed me the car keys, "isn't that where all the Chinese are?" "So I've been told," I responded.

I entered Monterey Park at the southern end of Atlantic Boulevard, the main commercial thoroughfare. It was an unusually hot autumn day, and the combination of dirty smog, glaring sun, and a proliferation of big, bright, colorful Chinese-language business signs on both sides of the street made my eyes squint and my jaw drop. When I reached the city's original downtown area, I turned right and proceeded east. All along Garvey Avenue were Chinese signs, Chinese restaurants, Chinese supermarkets, Chinese book stores, Chinese herb shops, and Chinese banks. These were my first visual impressions of Monterey Park. "It really does feel like a foreign country," I thought to myself.

For months before my arrival the city had been embroiled in a heated controversy over development, land-use issues, and English as the official language. The media—the *Los Angeles Times* in particular—painted the town as a hotbed of racial backlash against immigrant Chinese. A statewide election was to be held the following week, and one of the issues on the November 4 ballot was Proposition 63—a proposal to make English the official language of California. Concern over increased immigration and the changing of our cultural landscape was an issue not only in Monterey Park but throughout California and, indeed, across the nation.

The documentary on Monterey Park, then, was both timely and effective. It was the pilot program when the five-part documentary series aired on public radio stations around the state in early 1987. But I knew I had only scratched the surface of the dynamics that had created the rancor in Monterey Park. A five-day visit and a half-hour documentary could not possibly answer satisfactorily all the questions I had. What brought Chinese immigrants specifically to Monterey Park? How were they able to gain such an economic foothold without assimilating? Was economic competition at the root of the problem? Would residents have reacted as vehemently if the newcomers had been white? How would the city recover from this ugly episode in its history?

This book is my attempt to answer these and other questions. Because it could not have been written without the participation of the people of Monterey Park, I wish to thank especially those who agreed to be formally interviewed, and those who spoke to me informally as well.

I was aided immeasurably by the members of the Monterey Park Historical Society and the Monterey Park Historical Heritage Commission, whose sponsorship of my oral history research helped me get established in the community. I particularly thank Mary Duce, Cledith Gerard, Bob Gerard, Eva Gribble, Rosa Keehn, Pauline Lemire, Bea Rexius, Russ Paine, and Win Paine. I also received support from the offices of the Monterey Park city manager and city clerk, the recreation and parks department, and the city library staff. I am especially grateful to Aimee Arakawa, Lillian Bow, Virginia Nonaca Chavez, Beth Fujishige, Jose Galvan, Dana Lubow, Julie Saldana, Evana Shu, Pat Tomayosu, and Peggy Williams. Help in gathering the photographs was provided by Southern California Community Newspapers photo editor Juan Ocampo and staff writer Marie Vasari. Their patience was invaluable.

My colleagues and professors at the University of California at Berkeley deserve high praise for their intellectual guidance and constant encouragement. Extra thanks go to Professors Ling-chi Wang, Mario Barrera, and Franz Schurmann. Special thanks to Wei-chi Poon, head librarian at the Asian American Studies Library at Berkeley, for her help in tracking down necessary resources. High praise also goes to John Horton and his sociology researchers at the University of California at Los Angeles for their pioneering research at Monterey Park during the mid-1980s. The data they collected and their insightful analysis deserves special acknowledgment. In addition Patricia Sterling, free-lance copyeditor, and Debby Stuart, my production editor at Temple University Press, helped shape this book with their professional advice.

I am particularly indebted to Sucheng Chan, editor of the Temple University Press Asian American History and Culture Series. She saw the potential in my original raw manuscript and challenged me to make it better. Without her exceptional dedication, attention to detail, intellectual rigor, and constructive criticism, this book would never have been published.

Finally, my deepest appreciation goes to my parents, Henry and Elva Fong, my wife, Elena Almanzo, and our supportive family and friends.

THE FIRST SUBURBAN

CHINATOWN

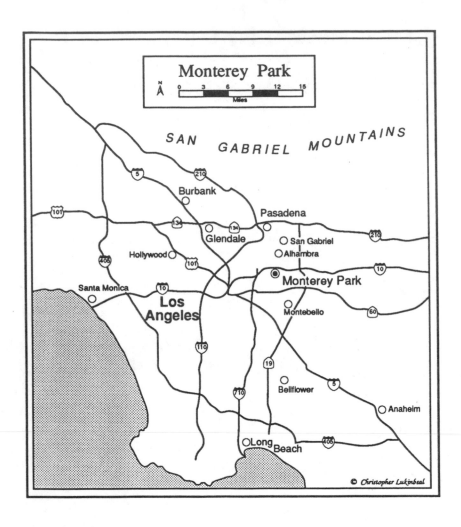

Monterey Park

SAN GABRIEL MOUNTAINS

Burbank

Pasadena

Glendale

San Gabriel

Hollywood

Alhambra

Santa Monica

Los Angeles

Monterey Park

Montebello

Bellflower

Anaheim

Long Beach

© Christopher Lukinbeal

INTRODUCTION

A New and Dynamic Community

On an early morning walk to Barnes Memorial Park, one can see dozens of elderly Chinese performing their daily movement exercises under the guidance of an experienced leader. Other seniors stroll around the perimeter of the park; still others sit on benches watching the activity around them or reading a Chinese-language newspaper.

By now children are making their way to school, their backpacks bulging with books. They talk to each other in both English and Chinese, but mostly English. Many are going to Ynez Elementary, the oldest school in town.

When a nearby coin laundry opens its doors for business, all three television sets are turned on: one is tuned to a Spanish novella, another to a cable channel's Chinese newscast, and the third to Bryant Gumbel and the *Today* show.

Up the street from the park a home with a small stone carved Buddha and several stone pagodas in the well-tended front yard is an attractive sight. The large tree that provides afternoon shade for the house has a yellow ribbon tied around its trunk, a symbol of support for American troops fighting in the Persian Gulf. On the porch an American flag is tied to a crudely constructed flagpole. Next to it, taped to the front door, Chinese characters read "Happiness" and "Long Life" to greet visitors.

These sights and sounds are of interest not because they represent the routine of life in an ethnic neighborhood but because they signal the transformation of an entire city. Monterey Park, California, a rapidly growing, rapidly changing community of 60,000 residents, is located just eight miles east of downtown Los Angeles (see Frontispiece). An influx of immigrants primarily from Taiwan, Hong Kong, and the People's Republic of China has made Monterey Park the only city in the continental United States the majority of whose residents are of Asian background. According to the 1990 census, Asians make up 56 percent of the city's population, followed by Hispanics with 31 percent, and whites with 12 percent.[1]

In the early 1980s Monterey Park was nationally recognized for its liberal attitude toward newcomers. In fact, on June 13, 1983, *Time* magazine featured a photograph of the city council as representative of a successful suburban melting pot. The caption read, "Middle-class Monterey Park's multiethnic city council: two Hispanics, a Filipino, a Chinese, and, in the rear, an Anglo."[2] Another national public relations coup came in 1985 when the National Municipal League and the newspaper *USA Today* named Monterey Park an "All-America City" for its programs to welcome immigrants to the community.[3] Nicknamed "City with a Heart," it took great pride in being a diverse and harmonious community. But despite these accolades, there were signs that the melting pot was about to boil over.

Tensions had begun to simmer with the arrival in the late 1970s of Chinese immigrants, many of whom were affluent and well educated. New ethnic-oriented businesses sprang up to accommodate them: nearly all the business signs on Atlantic Boulevard, the city's main commercial thoroughfare, conspicuously displayed Chinese characters with only token English translations. In 1985, the same year Monterey Park received its "All-America" award, some three thousand residents signed a petition attempting to get an "Official English" initiative on the municipal ballot; a local newspaper printed an article accusing the Chinese of being bad drivers; and cars displayed bumper stickers asking, "Will the Last American to Leave Monterey Park Please Bring the Flag?"[4]

In April 1986 the two Latinos and the Chinese American on the city council were defeated in their bids for reelection. Voted into office were three white candidates, one a proponent of controlled growth, the other two closely identified with the official-English movement in Monterey Park and the state. In June the new council passed Resolution 9004, which, among other things, called for English to be the official language of the United States of America.[5] Though the resolution was purely symbolic and carried no legal weight, it was immediately branded as a deliberate slap at the city's Chinese and Latino population. Undaunted, the council continued to take controversial actions that critics labeled "anti-Chinese," among them adopting a broad moratorium on new construction and firing the city planning commission that had approved many Chinese-financed developments. But it was rejection of the plans proposed by a Taiwanese group to build a senior housing project that prompted a rare display of public protest by the usually apolitical Chinese community. Four hundred people, mostly elderly Chinese, marched to City Hall carrying American flags and signs reading, "Stop Racism," "We Are Americans Too," and "End Monterey Park Apartheid."[6]

These high-profile controversies, lasting throughout the 1980s were not isolated or incidental cases of cultural conflict. Indeed, events in this community have received publicity in local, national, and even international media; recently, scholars too have become interested in Monterey Park, focusing primarily on ethnic politics and race relations.[7] Close study of the community is important for several reasons. To begin with, Monterey Park's Chinese residents reflect the changing pattern of Chinese immigration nationwide. Chinese newcomers to Monterey Park and elsewhere are not analogous to the historically persecuted and oppressed male laborers who came to this country in the mid-nineteenth century; they are men and women generally much better educated and more affluent than either their Chinese predecessors or their white counterparts.[8] Further, similar demographic and economic changes are occurring not just in Monterey Park but throughout southern California's San Gabriel Valley and Orange County, and in the northern California cities of San Francisco, Mountain View, and San Jose. Increasing Chinese influence is felt also in New York City's boroughs of Manhattan and Queens (particularly Flushing), in Houston, Texas, and Orlando, Florida. Outside the United States, recent examples of a rapid influx of Chinese people and capital are found in Sydney, Australia, and in Vancouver and Toronto, Canada.[9]

Next, because demographic change and economic development issues have created a complex controversy in Monterey Park, the intersection of ethnic, racial, and class conflict shows up quite clearly there. One prominent aspect of the social, economic, and political dynamics in Monterey Park is the popular call for controlled growth combined with a narrow nativist, anti-Chinese, anti-immigrant tone in debates that crossed ethnic lines throughout the community. And again, these developments too are relevant nationwide, occurring as they did at a time of increasing concern over immigration: over statistics showing that almost 90 percent of all legal immigrants coming to the United States since 1981 have been from non-European countries,[10] and over the numbers of undocumented immigrants crossing the southern U.S. borders. Documented and undocumented immigrants are rapidly changing the face of many urban centers.

Finally, the conflicts in Monterey Park took place in a period of increased anti-Asian sentiment and violence. Debate occasioned by the large trade deficit between the United States and Japan, suspicion raised by large Asian investments throughout the nation, and envy generated by repeated headlines about Asian superachievers in education all fueled the fires of resentment throughout the 1980s. The 1982 killing of Vincent Chin in Detroit, a widely cited act of anti-Asian violence, prompted a U.S. Commission on Civil Rights investigation.[11]

The commission concluded that the upswing in animosity toward Asians reflected a perception that all Asian Americans, immigrants, and refugees are "foreigners" and as such are responsible for the economic woes of this country.[12]

This study of Monterey Park examines the evolution of conflict in the city and locates the beginnings of its recovery from internal strife and unwanted negative media attention. I argue that what was generally seen by the media and outsiders as a "racial" conflict was in fact a class conflict. At the same time, I demonstrate the highly charged saliency of ethnicity and race in the political arena and show how they were used to obscure class interests and to further political interests.

The Literature on Chinatowns

A brief review of previous studies of Chinatowns reveals that Monterey Park is a new phenomenon. Scholarly research on Chinese American history and community life has focused primarily on the nature and consequences of the hostile treatment the group has received since entering the United States in the mid-nineteenth century. One category of this work—external examination—takes an "outsider's" perspective on the causes of anti-Chinese sentiment. Mary Roberts Coolidge (1909) and Alexander Saxton (1971), among others, have demonstrated that anti-Chinese sentiment in California during the late nineteenth century stemmed from the economic and political battles between business owners and white workers. The threat of "cheap" Chinese workers served as a convenient issue around which the California Democratic Party could rally in its effort to recapture the leadership it had lost during the Civil War. It was also an issue around which the labor movement could organize and gain influence.[13] Stuart Creighton Miller (1969) and Robert McClellen (1971) have gone further to make racial antagonism the centerpiece of their analyses. Miller documents the existence of anti-Chinese sentiment across the nation well before the arrival of large numbers of Chinese in California and stresses that by 1870 Sinophobia had transcended class and party lines. Similarly, McClellen traces the initial negative American stereotypes of the Chinese and followed their evolution in relation to the domestic treatment of the Chinese in America and to American foreign policy in the Far East.[14]

The need for an internal perspective—studies of the reactions of the Chinese and their leaders—became apparent after Gunther Barth (1964) blamed the hostility on the Chinese themselves. According to Barth, they were not real immigrants who wanted to settle in the United States but sojourners who wanted little more than to make money and go back home to China. This rootless status, he argues, created great bitterness among white workers, who saw the Chinese willing to work for low wages in order to secure temporary employment.[15] Since the early 1970s many broad surveys have been published to explain how the Chinese generally confronted, organized, and coped with the oppressive situation they faced.[16] But easily the best examples of the insider's perspective are local histories and community studies. These more specific approaches better capture the Chinese American experience, the kind of work the Chinese did, the conditions under which they lived, and their interactions with other ethnic groups.

Community studies focusing extensively on occupations held by Chinese Americans include Paul C. P. Siu's *Chinese Laundryman: A Study of Social Isolation* (1953), and James W. Loewen's *The Mississippi Chinese: Between Black and White* (1971). Siu concentrates on Chinese laundries in Chicago, which served mostly whites; Loewen focuses on the successful Chinese groceries in the Yazoo-Mississippi delta, which catered to blacks. Both authors recognize the initial Chinese "sojourner" mentality but regard this attitude as having been helpful in creating and maintaining a previously unmet business niche.[17]

Probably the earliest work on Chinese in rural communities is Rose Hum Lee, *The Growth and Decline of Chinese Communities in the Rocky Mountain Region* (1947). Later research includes books by Sandy Lydon (1985), who describes the life of the Chinese in California's Monterey Bay region; Sucheng Chan (1986), who analyzes the social and economic impact of the Chinese on California agriculture; and Sylvia Sun Minnick (1988), who details the experience of Chinese living in California's San Joaquin County.[18] Each of these rural community studies seeks to address three main misconceptions inherent in the external examinations: the notion that the Chinese were passive people who did not, or could not, resist the subordinate status that the dominant society imposed on them; the one-sided description of the Chinese as sojourners who had no intention of settling or assimilating in the United States and thus deserved the scorn they received; and the portrayal of Chinese as mere peasants whose skills were limited to little more than manual labor.

Not surprisingly, the most numerous Chinese American community studies concentrate on San Francisco's and New York's Chinatowns and the inner workings of these segregated urban ghettos. For example, Victor and Brett de Bary Nee's *Longtime Californ': A Documentary Study of an American Chinatown* (1972) uses oral history interviews to describe the history and evolution of San Francisco's Chinatown and the conflicts between its various segments and generations. More detailed research has been conducted in New York's Chinatown by

Chia-ling Kuo (1977) and Bernard Wong (1988). Kuo focuses on the voluntary self-help organizations that have evolved in the community and concludes that they are powerless to bring about fundamental change because they lack the necessary material and human resources. Wong examines the role of the powerful businessmen at the top of Chinatown's social and political hierarchy.[19]

Two books by Peter Kwong, *Chinatown, New York: Labor and Politics, 1930–1950* (1979) and *The New Chinatown* (1987), also focus on the inner workings of New York's Chinatown but look beyond the American context to describe how international events directly affect Chinese in the United States.[20] In his first book Kwong argues that during World War II American society saw the Chinese in New York in a more positive light than previously, because of the wartime alliance between China and the United States, but that this positive reassessment abruptly ended after the 1949 Communist takeover in China. The fervent anti-Communist policies of the U.S. government not only thwarted Chinese integration into the American mainstream but also served to consolidate the power of the Chinatown business and political elite, who were themselves ardent anti-Communists. Kwong's second book continues this theme to show how the power of the traditional elite has been augmented by a recent wave of affluent immigrants with considerable capital to invest. Chinese from Taiwan and Hong Kong began arriving in New York's Chinatown during a time of tremendous political uncertainty throughout East Asia following the 1975 Communist victory in Vietnam. Together, the traditional and new immigrant elite have engaged in property speculation that benefits affluent "uptown" Chinese business leaders at the expense of poor "downtown" Chinese renters and workers. According to Kwong, this increased class conflict with its international dimensions is destroying New York's Chinatown community.

Continuing interest in urban American Chinatowns is reflected in four recent books. Chalsa M. Loo's *Chinatown: Most Time, Hard Time* (1992) uses extensive surveys and interviews conducted in the early 1980s to examine the attitudes and opinions of the residents in San Francisco's Chinatown. Challenging the "model minority" myth of Chinese American success, Loo finds that many of the Chinese living in Chinatown—81 percent of whom are foreign-born—are trapped in low-paying jobs and have little time to learn English, though 95 percent of the residents she interviewed believe they could secure better employment if they could speak English well. Loo also explores attitudes toward housing and mental health. She concludes that the problems in San Francisco's Chinatown have been ignored for too long and that the community is very much in need of assistance.[21]

In *Chinatown* (1992), Min Zhou uses the enclave economy model (discussed in Chapter 8) to explain the continued existence of New York's Chinatown. She argues that the Chinese there are not exploited but are in fact provided with viable employment and business opportunities impossible to find outside of the community. The enclave economy is not, according to Zhou, a "failure" of assimilation. Instead, she believes, the adaptation and integration of second- and third-generation Chinese Americans will be enhanced by the increased economic opportunities the enclave economy provides for the first generation. In short, staying in Chinatown is a better option than leaving. This analysis contradicts the findings of both Kwong and Loo that American Chinatown communities are highly oppressive to immigrant workers.[22]

Journalist Gwen Kinkead's *Chinatown: A Portrait of a Closed Society* (1992) is a descriptive account of the "mystery" and "chaos" of New York's Chinatown. As an outsider, Kinkead states, she found doing research there much like "opening an oyster without a knife"; as a result she devotes much of the book to the seamy side of New York's Chinatown: its poverty, greed, and dirty restaurants; the tentacles of organized crime that infiltrate it. While she admits that there is much to learn from the Chinese—dedication to hard work, reverence for education, respect for elders—in the end she believes that the residents' self-imposed isolation and unwillingness to assimilate make it impossible for the enclave to get any help.[23]

Hsiang-shui Chen, a Taiwanese anthropologist, studied the social and cultural life of post-1965 Taiwanese immigrants in the Flushing and Elmhurst neighborhoods of Queens in New York City. His *Chinatown No More* (1992) downplays the role of ethnicity in keeping the community together and shows that Chinese immigrants are separated by class differences. Rather than a rigid social structure controlled by secret societies, Chen found very little homogeneity or interaction among his respondents in Queens. Though he does not deny the continued salience of ethnicity, especially in political organizing, an explicit class model is the centerpiece of his analysis. But Chen's exclusive reliance on interviews with one hundred immigrant Chinese households representing workers, small business owners, and professionals (he did not interview any large capitalists, as he originally intended), seriously weakens his general conclusions and leaves questions unanswered. First, there is no indication of what role, if any, Chinese capitalists overseas play in this community. Are they simply not a factor? Second, because Chen did not interview any non-Chinese residents, we do not know how they have been affected. The author describes the Flushing-Elmhurst area not as a second Chinatown but as a diverse multiethnic "world town" where people come together to make a formerly depressed area "more prosperous, more beautiful, and more peaceful."[24] Is there, then, no discernible anti-Asian sentiment there? It is difficult to believe that so many immigrant Chinese could move into Queens so smoothly.

My study of Monterey Park departs from the works described above in attempting to combine the external and internal perspectives. I have consciously sought to present a cross section of the voices and experiences of the multi-ethnic residents of Monterey Park and their various reactions to changes in the community. At the same time, I have endeavored to analyze the intra- and inter-ethnic political battles that have taken place.

This study chronicles the growth and evolution of a Chinese population large enough, and affluent enough, to empower itself in America's first suburban Chinatown. Previous works have focused on how the dominant society in the United States has negatively affected the Chinese and on their inability to fight back. But the large numbers of immigrant Chinese who settled in Monterey Park dramatically changed the demographic, economic, social, cultural, and political landscape of this once sleepy suburban bedroom community, and there they *have* fought back. This book places that story within the interplay of the broader social, economic, and political forces at work in the city. In short, this study seeks to combine macro and micro levels of analysis to provide a comprehensive, balanced examination of the vexing conflicts and complexities found in one community. This approach, I believe, can enable a better understanding of the dramatically changing race relations in urban centers throughout the United States where Chinese Americans are now present in significant numbers.

Methodology

I took an interdisciplinary approach in charting the odyssey of Monterey Park. I adopted the stance of an ethnographer to describe demographic, economic, social, and cultural changes and the reactions to them; I utilized the increasingly popular method of oral history to gain acceptance into the community and to give a voice to its residents; and I employed sociologist C. Wright Mills's notion of "sociological imagination" to combine history, biography, and social context in a broad analysis of the city's dramatic transitions.

Ethnography

Ethnography, the process of understanding another people's point of view, has historically been the standard research method used by anthropologists to study cultures or communities in distant lands.[25] More recently, however, the ethnographic approach has been applied to segments of the population within our own society. Michael Agar's (1979) study of the culture of drug addicts and James Spradley and Brenda Mann's (1975) study of cocktail waitresses are two examples. Among ethnographic studies of racial minorities are Elliot Liebow's *Tally's Corner* (1967) and Nee and Nee's *Longtime Californ'* (1972).[26]

A key element of ethnography is participant observation, based on the belief that gaining entrance to the society being studied heightens the investigator's awareness and understanding of it. Short visits were not enough; I knew my research efforts would not be viable unless I lived in the community I was examining. So, in March 1990 my wife and I moved to Monterey Park. Together we lived, shopped, dined, and played there until December 1991. I attended city council meetings, took part in city-sponsored events, and accepted invitations to social functions—being careful to establish relationships with individuals from all political segments and all ethnic groups.

My research also included gathering documentation: city council minutes, materials from the city's historical archives, city-generated reports, city-funded consultants' reports, voting patterns and campaign statements from the city clerk's office, articles from the quarterly publication *Monterey Park Living*, material about the city's service clubs and its chamber of commerce. The local Bruggemeyer Memorial Library, a repository for many past city records and historical documents, also has on microfilm back issues of the city newspaper, *Monterey Park Progress*, a rich source of information about and community attitudes toward local events and developments.

Oral History

Before I moved to Monterey Park I had decided to conduct oral history interviews.[27] Though oral history would merely supplement the large amount already written by and about outspoken advocates of growth, growth control, official English, and racial harmony, I believed it would enable me to learn about the everyday lives of residents and their reactions to recent changes. At the same time, it seemed a nonthreatening way to meet people and integrate myself into the community. But doing oral history was not easy in a town clearly on the defensive. Still recovering from the intense controversies of recent years, residents were highly suspicious both of reporters seeking the sensational story and of academics conducting research.[28] One snapped at me, "We've had enough vultures come into our town." When I told another that I was a graduate student from the University of California, Berkeley, he frowned and said, "Oh, that Communist school."

Fortunately, in August 1989 I had happened upon an article in the *Los Angeles Times* about an oral history project coordinated by Monterey Park's own Historical Heritage Commission.[29] Since 1984 the commission had been recording the recollections of thirteen long-time residents—all older whites—but was also interested in interviewing Latinos and Japanese Americans who had come to town in the 1950s, Chinese Americans who came in the 1960s, and newer immigrant Chinese who have been arriving continually since the late 1970s. Consequently, I called Russ Paine, director of the program, and offered my services. By joining efforts with the Historical Heritage Commission, a well-established and well-respected institution in town, I was able to gain almost immediately an acceptance into the community which under ordinary circumstances could well have taken six months or more.

Between April and December 1990 I interviewed thirty local residents; I had set a deadline of nine months for this aspect of my research and interviewed as many as I could during that time. All these formal interviews were recorded on audio tape and conducted in English. Each interview took from one to twenty hours, and most of the subjects were interviewed several times. All the interviews were transcribed and edited to clarify responses and in some instances to make factual corrections, with the permission of the respondents. I made clear to all of the narrators that I was writing a study of Monterey Park, that I was working with the Historical Heritage Commission, and that the interviews would be taped and transcribed. Each narrator signed a form releasing ownership of the tapes and transcripts to the commission, with the understanding that these would be housed in the Bruggemeyer Memorial Library and made available to the public for historical and educational purposes.

Oral history is not quick history; it requires exhaustive and often tedious effort; for example, every hour of interviewing requires six to eight hours of verbatim transcription. Further, my selected narrators were not always readily available.

I tried to include a cross section of the community: persons born in Monterey Park, persons who had moved to the city—and the country—at different times, persons of varied ethnic backgrounds. I invited 45 individuals (15 white, 15 Asian, and 15 Latino) to be formally interviewed; 15 either chose not to participate or, could not be scheduled in time. The final list comprised 14 white (11 male, 3 female), 8 Chinese American (4 male, 4 female), 2 Japanese American (both male), and 6 Latino (4 male, 2 female) respondents.

I also conducted scores of semiformal interviews with other residents; these were structured and often, but not always, taped. In addition, my fieldwork included spontaneous informal interviews that were untaped but incorporated in my fieldnotes. Quotations from semiformal and informal interviewees, unless they gave me permission to use their names, are presented anonymously in this book, as are comments made off-tape by the oral history narrators. Attributed quotations are taken only from oral history interviews and transcripts, newspapers and magazines, radio and television broadcasts, city council audio and video tapes, and public documents.

Sociological Imagination

Ethnography and oral history are highly descriptive and personal methods of gathering data but are not in themselves sufficient. It is "the sociological imagination" that "enables us to grasp history and biography and the relations between the two within society," writes C. Wright Mills. "No social study that does not come back to the problems of biography, of history and of their intersections within a society has completed its intellectual journey." The sociological task requires us to place ourselves in the historical stream of events, to bring together "the personal troubles of milieu" and "the public issues of social structure."[30] Throughout this book I have used biographical sketches of the residents/actors to illuminate their experiences in the Monterey Park setting; at the same time, I have incorporated descriptions and analyses of social, economic, and political activities and trends external to the city's municipal boundaries, since the controversies in Monterey Park did not evolve in a vacuum.

In an appendix, "On Intellectual Craftsmanship," to *The Sociological Imagination*, Mills criticizes what he calls "socspeak," the style of convoluted sentences and polysyllabic jargon commonly used in the social sciences. "In many academic circles today anyone who tries to write in a widely intelligible way is liable to be condemned as a 'mere literary man' or, worse still, 'a mere journalist,'" he warns. "To overcome the academic prose you have to overcome the academic pose."[31] With this in mind, and having worked as a journalist, I have made a conscious attempt to bridge the rigor of scholarship and the accessibility of journalism. By combining ethnography, oral history, and sociological imagination, I have tried to capture the range and fullness of human experience, the diversity and conflict of ideals, and the complexity of the Monterey Park situation. I know that some people in Monterey Park will be pained by what I have written and shared with the world; I have not pulled any punches in describing the best and the worst of the city they care so much about. But I am sure that the many residents and city staff who took the time to talk with me, introduce me to both friends and adversaries, and provide me with background information would not want it any other way.

Organization

This book traces the evolution of intense conflict in Monterey Park up to the beginnings of recovery. Chapters 1 through 3 detail the unique convergence of demographic, economic, and social-cultural changes that have taken place there in recent years. Chapters 4 through 6 examine the complex political reactions to change following the influx of Chinese immigrants to the community, focusing primarily on the ten-year period from 1978 to 1988. Chapter 7 looks at the more recent political reactions to change from 1988 to 1992 and the community's difficult attempts to recover from internal strife. Chapter 8 provides an overview of various immigrant, ethnic, and race relations theories in the United States, examines the effectiveness of these theories in explaining the Monterey Park situation, and suggests some revisions and new assumptions needed in the new era of race relations of the 1990s. The book concludes with a summary of Monterey Park's dramatic metamorphosis from a small bedroom community to America's first suburban Chinatown.

It should be noted that because the meanings of racial and ethnic terms evolve and change, certain groups are identified here by several terms. For example, Hispanic, Latino, Mexican American, and Spanish American are used interchangeably, as are Anglo, Caucasian, and white; black, negro, and African American; and Indian and Native American. All Asians living in the United States are identified as Asian Americans, regardless of their citizenship status. Likewise, all Chinese in the United States are identified as Chinese Americans. I do, however, use the term Chinese immigrant to describe individuals of Chinese ancestry who have only recently arrived in this country.

CHAPTER 1

Ramona Acres to the Chinese Beverly Hills: Demographic Change

Monterey Park became a city shortly before the First World War and undertook plans for development that would transform the small farming community into an elite suburb. To lay the foundation for this study of Chinese immigration, I have divided the city's demographic history into three periods: its incorporation and push to develop, during which racial segregation policies were common and condoned; its growth from the end of the Second World War to 1970, when diverse groups of newcomers seemed to be united by a spirit of optimism and a sense of opportunity; and the coming of the immigrant Chinese, chiefly in two waves during the 1970s. (Were this a comprehensive discussion of the demographic history of Monterey Park and its surrounding region, I would include the Native Americans, as well as the Spanish and Mexicans who inhabited the area prior to the 1848 signing of the Treaty of Guadalupe Hidalgo, when the United States took governmental control over Alta California. These topics, however, are tangential to this study.)

Origins and Early Days

Before there was Monterey Park, there was Ramona Acres, built on a portion of a Spanish land grant originally awarded to Don Antonio Maria Lugo, one of the first "native sons" of Alta California. By 1838 Lugo claimed 30,000 acres, a property so vast that it was said he could ride from sunrise to sunset without leaving his land.[1] But financial difficulties following the Mexican War forced Lugo's son to sell 5,000 acres of his patrimony in 1866 to an Italian immigrant and entrepreneur, Alessandro Repetto. One of the first settlers in the area, Repetto made an existing dirt road usable for wagons and developed a successful sheep ranch. He became a wealthy man.[2]

Local historians agree that a new era for the region began with the arrival in 1879 of Richard Garvey, a former U.S. Army mail carrier whose route had taken him through Monterey Pass (now Garvey

Avenue). After Garvey sold his prosperous quartz mines in California and Arizona, he purchased 4,000 acres in the San Gabriel Valley along his old mail route. He constructed the first major road through the area, developed its first water system, and built the fifty-four-foot dam that created Garvey Lake in order to irrigate the land.[3]

In 1906 a portion of the Repetto Ranch—lying north of present-day Garvey Avenue and east of Garfield Avenue—was subdivided and developed into Ramona Acres (each lot being no less than one acre).[4] When Garvey, to pay off his development debts, added to its size by selling portions of his property, inexpensive land prices attracted a number of small farmers to the area. With the majestic San Gabriel mountains to the north, the growing city of Los Angeles to the west, and an ideal climate, Ramona Acres was billed as "the most healthful place in America. Where fruit trees and flowers grow abundantly, where one's dreams are met by the fragrance of orange blossoms, where almost perpetual balmy sunshine and gentle breezes serve at nature's behest."[5]

Still, Ramona Acres had few residents and no permanent business establishments before the Janss Investment Company of Los Angeles bought land in the locality and began to develop small plots at modest prices. Not until 1914 did the Gribble General Store, owned by John Henry Gribble, become the first business to locate in Ramona Acres. But the slowly growing, pastoral community stood up for itself when in 1915 the neighboring cities of Alhambra, Pasadena, and South Pasadena threatened to annex the area and turn it into a "sewer farm." Formal annexation proceedings begun on April 17, 1916, were immediately challenged by a Ramona Acres committee; headed by Thomas A. Berkebile, the committee's strategy was to incorporate the community as a city.

On May 16, 1916, the day Monterey Park celebrates as its birthday, residents of Ramona Acres voted overwhelmingly in favor of incorporation. Just two weeks later Berkebile and P. A. Hannigan rushed up to Sacramento to file the necessary papers, beating Alhambra to the punch.[6] At the very first meeting of the new city's board of trustees on June 2, 1916, at the Ynez School auditorium, the city was renamed Monterey Park.[7] One month later, the board passed an ordinance making it unlawful to establish, maintain, or operate a sewage plant in the city of Monterey Park.[8] It took four years in court and even some state legislative battles to settle the matter, and for several decades following its incorporation, Monterey Park had a well-earned reputation in California of being fiercely independent and a strong supporter of the home-rule concept.

By 1919 the population of the city was just approaching 5,000.[9]

Except for a few individuals who owned large parcels of land and the exclusive Midwick Country Club, built in 1914 to serve the wealthy in nearby Pasadena, Monterey Park was made up primarily of one- or two-acre subsistence farms whose owners lived in small houses and grew their own fruits and vegetables for family consumption. According to Kenny Gribble, son of the general store's proprietor, "Nearly every family had a few chickens, and we usually had a garden of some kind at home. People raised rabbits [and] we had goats. . . . I don't remember much in the way of commercial farming . . . but I do remember nearly every family sold eggs." [10]

Monterey Park did have a few Japanese families who leased land and made a living growing fruits, vegetables, and flowers for sale. In fact, it was the Japanese who were credited with smoothing the roadway through Monterey Pass, in order to get their produce to market in Los Angeles. Most of these families, however, lived in an area known as "Yokohama Village," located just south of the city limits.[11] Kenny Gribble remembered one produce market in town, run by "a Japanese family that used to live on the Garvey Ranch. They started a little store in the old building on the northeast corner of Garvey and Garfield where my Dad had his store." Gribble had a Japanese friend in school: "Goro Kuwaki . . . lived with his family, who came here sometime after World War I, entered grammar school, and stayed here until he was out of high school." Gribble also saw Chinese truck farmers traveling through town at night in order to reach the Los Angeles produce market early the next morning: "What was moving on Garvey Avenue was produce and such things from the farms east of us. The next day the driver would go to sleep in the wagon, and the horse would take him home." Gribble could recall only "very few" Mexican Americans during his youth: "There wasn't much work for them to do here. They did graze some of the land and pasture and raise some grain." [12]

The 1920s were a decade of great land speculation and home-building activity. One of the first and most aggressive firms to follow up on the success of the Janss Investment Company was the Loftus Land Company, which in 1922 opened the Garvey Heights Tract and began offering homesites for as little as $157 for a fifty-foot lot.[13] The company's public relations campaign, intended to rouse support for growth in the city, advised local residents to buy property before the tract was offered to the Los Angeles market. "Boost Monterey Park" and "Ten Thousand People in 1925" were popular slogans coined by Loftus. A second Loftus Land Company project was located south of the Midwick Country Club. The Ramona Home Gardens Tract opened in 1923, offering 180 fifty-foot lots at $450 and up. Within a month thirty-five lots had been sold, most to Monterey Park residents anticipating future profits. One Loftus ad read: "A lot we sold for $600 four months ago was resold last week for $900, netting $300 profit." [14]

Home and business construction was also on the rise during the early 1920s. In June 1924 Monterey Park recorded the most active half-year of construction in its short history. City Clerk Arthur Langley reported that total valuation of construction in March was a record $82,725; by August the monthly figure was $94,970. [15] Touting the city's new-found success, the *Monterey Park Progress* printed a special twenty-four-page "Prosperity Edition" of the newspaper. In one article, H. Sands noted Monterey Park's recent growth and anticipated a rosy future, citing its low-cost property, favorable climate, country life-style, and "population estimated at about 6,000, all Caucasians." [16] To sustain the growth trend, real estate agents and civic leaders were determined to make the city a racially restricted community. The Monterey Park Chamber of Commerce held a special meeting on April 25, 1924, to discuss ways to "keep out all negroes, Mexicans and Japanese." It was decided at the meeting that "any real estate people, when approached by any of these nationalities, or in their behalf, should exercise civic pride, forgo their fees and not bring undesirable people into the community." [17]

In 1924 Monterey Park, by then known as "one of the whitest spots in Southern California's white spot," [18] played host to the largest Ku Klux Klan "event" in the San Gabriel Valley. According to a press report, an estimated 25,000 people gathered on Garvey Avenue one Saturday evening to watch the initiation of five hundred new Klan members, many attracted to the spectacle by searchlights that tracked two airplanes circling in the dark evening sky. Some 3,000 Klansmen in white robes formed a square surrounding an electrically lit cross that stood thirty feet high. Alhambra Klan No. 8, a reporter on the scene was told, was 2,500 strong and taking in new members at a rate of about one hundred a month. [19]

By the late 1920s ambitious developers were recognizing Monterey Park as more than a collection of chicken and truck farms. One of the most active players was Peter Snyder, a Greek immigrant and Los Angeles developer who in 1928 invested $2 million in 367 acres of barren land in the Monterey Park hills; his grand plan was to develop expensive homes and an exclusive business district to compete with already established Beverly Hills and Bel Air in attracting southern California's elites. [20] One fundamental feature of Snyder's Midwick View Estates was a rigid racial restriction policy that would "exclude those whose blood is not wholly of the Caucasian race." [21]

Another feature Snyder planned was extensive landscaping that would include several parks planted with exotic trees, rare shrubs, ornamental flowers, and lush lawns. He also wanted to build a 5,000-seat amphitheater in the hills, a smaller version of the Hollywood Bowl. He hoped to attract a community-supported symphonic or theatrical group that would bring culture to the western San Gabriel Valley region. Snyder, who had married into the De la Fuente family, an old-time Californio clan, wanted the Midwick View Estates to have a Spanish-Mediterranean architectural theme. Street names such as "De la Fuente," "El Portal," and "El Mercado" were the first to be proposed.

To begin his visionary project, Snyder had his architects design a man-made waterfall as a centerpiece for his new development. Completed and dedicated with much fanfare in June 1928, the seventy-foot structure gracefully carried water down ceramic tile terraces to a pool on what is now Atlantic Boulevard. From colored lights under the water, beams of blue, red, yellow, and orange played against the falling sheets of water. Across the street Snyder built a two-story Spanish-style structure named "Jardin El Encanto" to house administrative offices for Midwick View Estates. Its lavish interior had a Spanish Revival atmosphere with exposed ceiling beams and a stucco arch. The building and the waterfall attracted their share of tourists, prospective home buyers, and investors to Monterey Park, for many years known as "the City of Cascades." The waterfall still functions today, a reminder of the early city's haughty aspirations.

Hopes and predictions of an impending boom ran high. Newly elected council member I. B. Alkire could barely control his enthusiasm: "When I say that the population of Monterey Park will reach 20,000 within the next two years I am not by any means over-stepping the possibilities," he beamed. "All I can say is, that I wish I had $50,000 at my command right now. I WOULD INVEST EVERY PENNY OF IT IN MONTEREY PARK REAL ESTATE" (original emphasis).[22] His optimism seemed justified as construction continued, and on Sunday, October 6, 1929, Midwick View Estates held its formal grand opening. An overflow audience of interested investors, curious well-wishers, and opportunistic politicians gathered for the gala event, which featured an appearance by movie star Eddie Dowling and entertainment by premier Spanish dancer Senorita Catalina Lagrave and the Jose Arias String Orchestra.

With the collapse of the stock market a few weeks later and the onset of the Depression, however, all building on the Midwick View Estates was halted, and Snyder's dream ended. For the next two decades very little development took place in Monterey Park, and the city reverted to the status of small farm town. Not until World War II did it start to recover from the real estate crash of 1929.

New Growth and Integration

From the beginning of World War II until 1960, Monterey Park experienced remarkable growth. The wartime economy brought new life and new people from across the country to southern California and eventually to Monterey Park; after the war new housing developments emerged to serve veterans armed this time with GI loans. The city's population expanded from 8,500 in 1940 to 20,000 in 1950 and almost 38,000 by 1960.[23] Howard Fry and Eli Isenberg were two of the "new generation" of pioneers who came to Monterey Park during this time.

Fry was born in Pierce County, Nebraska, in 1909 into an old-stock American family that moved several times across the state and into South Dakota. Fry's mother was a schoolteacher and his father a barber, but they eventually settled into farming. One exceptionally good flaxseed harvest in 1928 allowed the family to send young Howard to college; he graduated from the South Dakota School of Mines and Technology in 1933 with a degree in electrical engineering. While at college he met Emma, whom he married in 1934. Because of the Depression, however, Fry found it difficult to find steady work. Hearing that there were job opportunities in California, he visited an uncle there and was immediately hired by the Southern California Gas Company. In April 1941 he moved his wife and young son to Los Angeles.

After three years of renting, Fry decided it was time to own a home. A co-worker at the gas company introduced him to Monterey Park, where lots that had been part of an old chicken ranch were for sale. Like so many newcomers during this time, he was attracted to the small-town feeling of Monterey Park. Because of that, "we were convinced that we were going to be long-term residents here," he recalls."[24] Fry immediately became involved in his new community, volunteering for PTA work, teaching Sunday School at the Methodist Church, and taking a leadership role in the Monterey Park Lions Club. He also participated in local politics, bringing with him his brand of no-nonsense midwestern conservatism. He served on the city council from 1960 to 1966 and became mayor in 1962.

Eli Isenberg was born in Peabody, Massachusetts, in 1913, the son of Russian Jewish immigrants. His father was an educated man who could speak, write, and read Russian, Hebrew, and Polish. Drafted into the Russian army, the elder Isenberg served as a "scribe" for his company, writing and reading letters for the other men. Eli's mother, the youngest child in a family of ten, had emigrated to the United States as a teenager.

Isenberg's parents made a living as mechants in Peabody. They worked long hours in the store to achieve only a modest income, so Eli and his older brother helped out by selling newspapers at a street-corner stand after school. Despite the Depression, Isenberg considers his family lucky: with everyone working, they managed to earn enough money not only to take care of their week-to-week needs but to send both brothers to college. Eli Isenberg entered nearby Boston University in 1931. He really wanted to get away from Massachusetts, but given the family's financial situation, he understood why he could not leave town. He majored in journalism and throughout his college years worked as a stringer for newspapers in the Boston area.

After college, Isenberg went to work for the *Telegram News* in Lynn, Massachusetts. Following World War II he and his wife, Jo, decided to strike out and run their own newspaper business. The young couple came out west because Jo had gone to college in southern California and liked the area. After some searching, they came to Monterey Park in March 1947 as the new owners and publishers of the *Monterey Park Progress*. For Isenberg, the *Progress* was affordable and the city a community ripe for growth: "I knew Monterey Park would grow," he says with confidence. "It offered a lot of opportunity." [25] Isenberg's populist liberal leanings would be reflected in the editorial pages of the newspaper, which offered a strong voice in the community for the next three decades.

Fry and Isenberg typify the people who settled in Monterey Park during and just after World War II, and they reflect the idealism and pioneer spirit of many newcomers to the community. As long-time residents, they were both witnesses to and actors in the dramatic changes that followed.

Throughout the 1950s new housing tracts were developed and the homes bought up primarily by returning veterans. By 1960 Monterey Park was recognized as a friendly and modest middle-class suburb. With its proximity to downtown Los Angeles and its suburban comforts, the city also began to draw Latinos from adjacent East Los Angeles, Japanese Americans from the west side of Los Angeles, and Chinese Americans from nearby Chinatown. No longer committed to keeping residency only for those "whose blood is wholly of the Caucasian race," Monterey Park's population was about 85 percent white, 12 percent Latino (officially designated "Spanish-surname"), and 3 percent Asian and others (see Table 1). [26]

In 1952, four-year-old Alice Ballesteros and her family moved to Monterey Park from East Los Angeles. They were typical of the first Mexican Americans to arrive and, like many who followed, regarded this move as a step toward the American dream. "They all saw Monterey Park as definitely a sign of upward mobility," Ballesteros re-

T A B L E 1
Population by Ethnicity in Monterey Park: 1960–1990

Ethnicity	1960 Number	%	1970 Number	%	1980 Number	%	1990 Number	%
Anglo	32,306	85.4	24,476	50.5	13,552	25.0	7,129	11.7
Hispanic	4,391	11.6	16,477	34.0	21,079	38.8	19,031	31.4
Asian[a]	1,113	2.9	7,441	15.3	19,046	35.0	34,022	56.0
Black	11	< 0.1	111	0.2	661	1.2	330	0.5
Other[b]	–	–	–	–	–	–	226	0.4
Total	37,821	100.0	48,505	100.0	54,338	100.0	60,738	100.0

Source: Monterey Park Community Development Department.
Note: Percentages are rounded.
[a]Includes "Other" in 1960, 1970, and 1980.
[b]Includes Native American in 1990.

calls. Though both of her parents worked in blue-collar occupations, coming to Monterey Park brought them status: "Mom and dad, until my dad retired on disability, were considered to be upper income. I remember we had a new car every couple of years." In the mid-1950s Monterey Park was known to many in East Los Angeles as the "Mexican Beverly Hills." But living the middle-class life in the 1950s also included some costs. Ballesteros was raised in an English-speaking home and regrets the fact that she does not speak Spanish: people who moved out of East Los Angeles "thought that was what was expected of them so that they would blend in. . . . This was especially true for my mom because she was Spanish speaking until she started school. She recalls instances when teachers would rap knuckles with rulers when [students] didn't speak English." Nevertheless, Ballesteros, who works as a bank manager in a Monterey Park branch office, bought the house she grew up in when her parents left it in 1975 and lives there with her husband and three daughters. "I like Monterey Park," she says happily. "As soon as I knew [my parents] were leaving, it was just a natural that we would buy their home. I have no desire to leave it."[27]

In the late 1950s, when Edgar and Daniel Cohen began building new tracts of homes in the Monterey Park hills, a group of Japanese Americans met with the developers. They wanted to buy homes in Monterey Park; however, the delegation said, they would not come if it would cause a racial problem. According to Eli Isenberg, "The Cohens assured the Japanese that they had every right to come and urged them to do so."[28] Kei Higashi was unaware of any such meeting but heard through friends of his wife about "a tract in Monterey Park that was opening up and admitting Japanese." Higashi worked for a furniture manufacturer and found that Monterey Park was the same distance from downtown Los Angeles as the place on the west side where they were living at the time. "That's when we made a deal to buy the place," he says. "The house wasn't even completed when [we] bought it, but it was completed in the fall of 1958."[29]

Higashi, who had been interned in a relocation camp in Poston, Arizona, during World War II, was among the first of many Japanese Americans who found Monterey Park a welcome place. As word spread that it was a community where Japanese Americans could buy homes, more and more Japanese American families relocated to the area. By 1963 Higashi was so pleased with his new location that he started his own furniture manufacturing plant there. As his business flourished, he became an active leader of the Monterey Park Chamber of Commerce, the local Rotary Club, the Nachi Kaatsuura Sister City Association (Monterey Park's sister city in Japan), the California-Japanese American Republicans, and the Boy Scouts of America. Higashi has been honored several times for his business, civic, and charitable involvements in the city.

No outright racial confrontation took place in Monterey Park until February 1962, when members of the Congress of Racial Equality (CORE) charged that a developer had refused to sell a house to Bob and Helen Liley, a black physicist and his wife. A picket line was soon organized outside the office of Montgomery Fisher, developer of the new Monterey Highlands subdivision, and protesters vowed to keep up the demonstration until the matter was settled. The local home-owners' association refused to get involved in the controversy. "The Monterey Highlands Home Owners Assn., Inc. is a non-profit civic league incorporated under the laws of the State of California, devoted to the health and safety, public educational, recreational, cultural and aesthetic betterment of the residents of the Monterey Highlands," read its statement to the press. "In line with the above, the association has not, does not, and will not take a stand on social issues such as integration or segregation which are primarily matters of individual conscience."[30]

A few Monterey Highlands residents took a harder line. Raymond Erhart sent out letters to his neighbors stating: "My attitudes have always been pro-segregation on matters of housing and social functions. . . . As much as the minority groups feel they have a right to live in any area they want, I feel I have the same right. If I choose to live apart from them, for any reason, be it social or a case of economics, and the laws of this land say I am not allowed to live apart from them, then, either I have been denied my rights under this democratic order, or a democratic order does not exist."[31] But in a symbolic gesture of support for the Liley family, Al Song, a newly elected Korean American city council member, and Howard Fry jointly introduced a resolution endorsing existing state statutes prohibiting discrimination and the segregation of races. The resolution passed unanimously. "I, partly because of my background of having lived on an Indian reservation in South Dakota for years, felt this was not the time for us to stand in the way of what ultimately changed our values as far as ethnicity is concerned," says Fry.[32]

Bob and Helen Liley and their infant daughter seemed the ideal suburban family. A twenty-nine-year-old Ph.D. candidate at the University of California, Los Angeles (UCLA) who made it very clear that he was not a crusader, Bob Liley saw himself just as a man who wanted to own a home in a small community: "What we like is something we can call our own, and we're especially looking forward to being able to work in the garden."[33] Helen Liley had a degree in home economics and was planning to make her own curtains and bedspreads for the family's new home.

For more than a month the picketing continued. During this period, letters of support for the Lileys were published in the *Progress*, and both the South San Gabriel Ministerial Association and the Monterey Park Chamber of Commerce offered to mediate the dispute. Finally, after Liley filed a $50,000 lawsuit, Earl Snyder, owner of the housing tract, said he would personally sell a home to the family. "Kenbo Corp. policy," Snyder told the press, "is to sell homes to any person meeting our financial requirements."[34] Earl L. Walter, chairman of CORE in Los Angeles, diplomatically commended Snyder "for his prompt response to dictates of good citizenship" and praised the community for showing "an enlightened attitude toward the issue of racial injustice."[35] Liley himself expressed his awareness of support from residents: "We're happier over the response of the community than anything else."[36] In his weekly editorial Eli Isenberg wrote: "I am sure that the overwhelming number of residents will accept the Lileys in the same spirit that they deal with any new move-ins. And that's the way the Lileys want it. No city in the Southland, no large group of people have dealt with a problem as potentially explosive as the Liley case as well as Monterey Park has."[37]

Following the Liley incident, Monterey Park took great pride in considering itself a model integrated, liberal community. Not long thereafter the first wave of Chinese Americans started to take an interest in the city, among them aeronautics engineer Howard Jong, who came in 1964 at the urging of two Chinese American friends. "Actually, I heard that Monterey Park was just for Caucasians only," Jong recalls, "but Bill and Ernie had already purchased homes here at the time. I followed them." Like most of these first Chinese who settled in Monterey Park in the mid-1960s, Jong was born in the United States; his parents were immigrants from southern China. "Most of the progressive and enterprising people came from the south part of China," he is quick to interject. Born in Los Angeles in 1917, Jong proudly states that he and his siblings are all "true native Californians."[38] Though he grew up not in Chinatown but near the Los Angeles produce market at 10th and San Pedro Streets, Jong's first language as a child was Cantonese. Today, however, he speaks English without the hint of an accent.

Jong's father had a small produce business in the market district and worked there his whole adult life. But young Howard had no interest in the family business; he decided at an early age to be an aeronautical engineer. After finishing high school he attended the Curtis Wright Institute, a school of aeronautics in Glendale, California, specializing in engineering and mechanics. When he graduated in 1936, businesses were not hiring Chinese, so Jong had to find his first job with Luscomb Airplane Company in Trenton, New Jersey. "It was strange . . . an entirely different world," he recalls. "I had to learn how to use a knife and fork." He also vividly remembers watching Nazi sympathizers in New York on parade for Adolf Hitler: "I could see trouble," he says. After two years in New Jersey, Jong got a job with Douglas Aircraft Northrop Division (later McDonnell-Douglas) in El Segundo, California, building war planes for the Allies in the European theater. But he is particularly boastful about his work on fighter planes that were used by Americans during World War II and he lights up just talking about them: "After the war [with Japan] started, we devoted all our time to Navy airplanes. . . . In fact, we designed the SBD dive-bomber, which I think is the one that won the war in the Pacific."[39]

The first wave of Chinese Americans who moved to Monterey Park were commonly young professionals eager to move out of the Los Angeles Chinatown and assimilate into an integrated suburban life. Jong, like many others, found Monterey Park's proximity to major freeways an important attraction. "My dad and sister bought houses in South Pasadena, but I'd rather be here," he said. "McDonnell-Douglas moved to Long Beach, so it was more convenient. . . . It is a straight shot to work down the 710 freeway."[40]

After he retired, Jong became a volunteer police officer, using his aeronautical expertise to help maintain the city's ultralight surveillance airplane. (The air surveillance program is now defunct, but because it operated in one of a handful of such programs across the country, the plane was donated in 1988 to the Smithsonian Institution

T A B L E 2
Asian Ethnicity in Monterey Park: 1970–1990

	1970		1980		1990	
Ethnicity	Number	%	Number	%	Number	%
Japanese	4,627	56.9	7,533	39.6	6,081	17.4
Chinese	2,202	27.1	8,082	42.4	21,971	63.0
Filipino	481	5.9	735	3.9	1,067	3.1
Korean	118	1.5	1,011	5.3	1,220	3.5
Vietnamese[a]	–	–	731	3.8	2,736	7.8
Other/unidentified[b]	700	8.6	954	5.0	1,823	5.2
Total	8,128	100.0	19,046	100.0	34,898	100.0

Source: Monterey Park Community Development Department; and 1990 U.S. Census.
[a]Included under Other/unidentified in 1970.
[b]Includes Asian Indian, Cambodian, Hmong, Laotian, Thai, Hawaiian, Samoan, Guamanian, Tongan, and, for 1970 only, Native American and Vietnamese.

in Washington, D.C., for public display.) In addition, Jong served as a police block captain, organizing residents to participate in a Neighborhood Watch program. Obviously proud of having established himself in his career and in the Monterey Park community, Jong strongly believes that America is a land of opportunity and meritocracy. Though he has faced racial discrimination in his life, he feels he has overcome it—no small accomplishment for Chinese Americans of his generation. "The truth is, we proved ourselves. Despite hardship, we got in and we produced. That was the main thing, and they respected us."[41]

The period of integration saw greater ethnic diversity in Monterey and newcomers who were generally educated, middle-class, and assimilated. Moreover, they all believed in the American dream of upward mobility and bought into a suburban life-style. By 1970 the population had grown to almost 49,000. Whites were still a majority but just barely. Numerically, Latinos were the fastest-growing group, by then representing 34 percent of the community. Japanese Americans outnumbered Chinese Americans 4,627 to 2,202 (see Table 2), but together Asians made up 15 percent of the city's residents. The number of African Americans had increased from 11 in 1960 to 111 in 1970.[42]

The Immigrant Chinese Period

Beginning in the early 1970s, immigrant Chinese became the predominant newcomers in Monterey Park, though both the city's population and its ethnic diversity continued to grow. The 1980 census recorded for the first time that Monterey Park was a "majority minority" city: Latinos were 39 percent of some 54,000 residents; the Asian population had mushroomed to 35 percent (with Chinese outnumbering Japanese 8,082 to 7,533); whites now represented just 25 percent; African Americans, 1 percent.[43]

Three factors contributed to the influx of immigrant Chinese to Monterey Park: changes in federal immigration policy; changes in international politics; and the work of a man named Frederic Hsieh.

Chinese immigration to the United States can be easily divided into four distinct periods. The first, from 1849 to 1882, saw massive migration of mostly male Chinese laborers from southern China, who came to this country to escape poverty at home and to seek their fortunes after the 1848 discovery of gold in California. Later, Chinese were imported to help build the transcontinental railroad (1865–69) and to provide a cheap source of menial labor in other sectors of the economy. The steadily rising number of Chinese immigrants during this first period peaked between 1871 and 1880, when more than 120,000 arrived (see Table 3).

In response to this influx of Chinese, the second period, 1882–1943) is marked by the Chinese Exclusion Act of 1882, which barred

T A B L E 3
Chinese Immigration to the United States: Fiscal Years 1841–1989

	China[a]	Hong Kong[b]
1841–1850	35	–
1851–1860	41,397	–
1861–1870	64,301	–
1871–1880	123,201	–
1881–1890	61,711	–
1891–1900	14,799	–
1901–1910	20,605	–
1911–1920	21,278	–
1921–1930	29,907	–
1931–1940	4,928	–
1941–1950	16,709	–
1951–1960	9,657[a]	15,541
1961–1970	34,764[a]	75,007
1971–1980	124,326[a]	113,467
1981–1989	306,108[a]	83,848

Source: Immigration and Naturalization Service, 1989 Statistical Yearbook (Washington, D.C.: Government Printing Office, 1990), pp. 2–4.
[a]Beginning in 1957, China includes Taiwan.
[b]Data not reported separately until 1952.

the entrance of Chinese workers for ten years; only diplomats, merchants, students, temporary visitors, and children of Chinese holding American citizenship could legally come into this country. The exclusion legislation was extended for another ten years in 1892 and indefinitely in 1902. When the Chinese exclusion law was finally repealed in 1943, after the start of World War II, a quota was set specifying that only 105 persons of Chinese ancestry could enter the United States a year.[44]

During the third period, from 1943 to 1965, many more Chinese entered than the established quota, thanks to the passage of special provisions for Chinese war brides, refugees escaping Communism after 1949, and scientists and other trained professionals. Between 1951 and 1960, more than 25,000 entered the United States from China and Hong Kong (see Table 3).

The fourth period, which continues to the present, began when President Lyndon Johnson signed the landmark 1965 Immigration Act, which revised the quota system for non-European applicants. The new law, basing admission policy on needed skills and family reunification, allowed as many as 20,000 quota immigrants per sending country per year; in addition, the spouses, unmarried minor children, and parents of U.S. citizens could enter as nonquota immigrants. Between 1961 and 1970 the number of immigrants from China (including Taiwan and Hong Kong) approached 110,000; it more than doubled between 1971 and 1980, and from 1981 to 1989 it jumped to almost 390,000 (Table 3).

These increases were at least partly due to changes in international politics—United Nations recognition of the People's Republic of China and ouster of Taiwan in 1971; talks between the British and the PRC on the return of Hong Kong to China by 1997—which drove many Chinese from their homelands.

When the Communists came to power in China in 1949, the flight of Chiang Kai-shek's Nationalist government to Taiwan brought turmoil to the island, which—after decades of Japanese domination—had been put under Chinese rule following World War II. The native Taiwanese are ethnic Chinese, descendants of those who migrated during the seventeenth and eighteenth centuries, but they regard themselves as culturally distinct. Moreover, the Nationalists considered their stay on Taiwan a "temporary retreat"—yet though they were only 15 percent of the island's population, they dominated the government, the economy, and the military. The martial law they imposed in 1947, following a native rebellion for independence, was not removed until 1988; they shut the Taiwanese out of government affairs; their children made up a disproportionately large number of the university students. Political repression of Taiwanese opposition groups was enforced and censorship of the media asserted.

After President Richard Nixon announced plans to visit the People's Republic of China, a pall of uncertainty fell over the small island nation. Some feared that the country's rapid economic development would suddenly take a nosedive, or that foreign businesses would no longer invest in Taiwan. If the country lost international status, could the Nationalists hold power against twelve million Taiwanese clamoring for self-government without again resorting to brutality (as they had in executing 10,000 dissidents in 1947)?[45] In 1979 President Jimmy Carter formally established U.S. diplomatic relations with Beijing, and the United States severed official ties and terminated a mutual security treaty with Taiwan, bringing fear of a PRC takeover.

These uncertainties were very evident to Monterey Park architect David Tsai, who moved to the community in 1971; in his view, Chinese were leaving their countries for the United States "because of the political situation over there. They think it is not going to be very stable—especially when the U.S. and [the People's Republic of] China establish relations."

Tsai, born in China in 1945, knew firsthand about the fear of Communism. His father was a government official who fled with his family after the Communist victory. Tsai grew up in Taiwan before coming to the United States to earn a graduate degree in architecture at the University of California, Berkeley, in 1969. He moved to Monterey Park to join his brother two years later. According to Tsai, most Chinese in Taiwan and Hong Kong feared the PRC government. Those who emigrated were "looking out for the future and also for their children," not wanting them "to be brought up in war."[46]

Changes in U.S. immigration policy and international politics, then, help explain the overall increase of Chinese immigrants to the United States. But one individual accounts in large measure for the influx of Chinese specifically to Monterey Park. In 1977 Frederic Hsieh, then a young realtor, boldly announced to a gathering of the city's Chamber of Commerce the reason he was buying so much property in Monterey Park: the city, he said, was going to be a "modern-day mecca" for the new Chinese who, because of political insecurity in Asia, were looking for a place in the United States to invest their money and their future.[47] For several years Hsieh had not only been buying property but, in Chinese-language newspapers throughout Hong Kong and Taiwan, aggressively promoting Monterey Park as the "Chinese Beverly Hills."[48] Though some established local business owners took his comments to the Chamber of Commerce as a threat of a Chinese takeover of the town, Hsieh claims he was only stating the truth.

"It was not a takeover, but what was going to happen, nobody could prevent it," he explains. "I came here in 1972. The movement of Chinese immigrants has been taking place ever since then. So by the [late 1970s] the tide, or the trend, [had] already formed. But the [Monterey Park] business leaders were not aware of it. They were not as sensitive."[49]

Hsieh's prophetic "sensitivity" was very much a product of his personal background. He is a man of tireless drive, and the story of how he reached his conclusion about Monterey Park is instructive. Hsieh was born in Guilin, China, in 1945 and lived in Shanghai until he was twelve years old. His father was an architect who escaped to Hong Kong just before the Communists took over in 1949. His mother repeatedly applied for permission to join her husband in Hong Kong, but permission was not granted until 1957.

After finishing high school in Hong Kong in 1963, the eighteen-year-old Hsieh came to the United States as a foreign student. At first he worked in a Los Angeles fast food restaurant, frying chicken for $1.00 an hour. He then enrolled at Hartnell College in Salinas, California, where he paid $15 a month to live with several other students in an apartment over a Chinese laundry. Two years later he transferred to Oregon State University, where he earned a bachelor's degree in civil engineering and then a master's degree in water resources engineering. As he was finishing his graduate degree in April 1969, he was recruited by the City of Los Angeles to work as a city engineer.

Separating temporarily from his pregnant wife, who was also a graduate student at Oregon State, Hsieh came back to southern California to start his new job. He lived in a one-room bachelor apartment in Chinatown to save money until his wife finished her degree in June. In the meantime, he searched for an apartment but found it difficult to locate one willing to accept children, not to mention the dog, cat, rat, tropical fish, and several birds he counted as part of his family. Finally he decided to buy a home, and by the time his wife arrived, he had saved $1,000 and borrowed another $1,000 from his credit union. This money served as a down payment on a $32,000 five-unit apartment building in Silverlake, a suburb of Los Angeles. But even before he closed the deal, a friend showed him another apartment building. Borrowing again, Hsieh managed to place a down payment on that four-unit complex as well. The rental income from the two buildings more than paid for the mortgages, and Hsieh became convinced that there was a great deal of money to be made in real estate.

Working by day as an engineer, Hsieh went to school at night to earn a real estate sales license, and with the permission of the City of Los Angeles, he began selling property part time. That was how he was first introduced to Monterey Park: "The person I showed the property to did not take it," Hsieh remembers. "I thought it was a good property, so I put my money where my mouth was and bought it myself."[50] It was a house with three rental units and sold for $66,000 in 1972. Income from the rentals allowed Hsieh and his family to live free in the house; he later sold the property for $180,000. The rest, as they say, is history.

Many of the first wave of Chinese immigrants to come to Monterey Park arrived in the United States with education, professional skills, strong political and class ideologies, and, in some cases, capital to help them on their way into the economic mainstream. From personal experience, Hsieh knew that the crowded and unattractive Los Angeles Chinatown would not suit these affluent newcomers: "There's no place to live. By word of mouth they came to Monterey Park. We did some promotion, such as advertisement in the magazines [and] in the newspapers over there in Hong Kong and Taiwan to encourage people to come and invest and patronize our company. Pretty soon everybody knows San Francisco's Chinatown, Monterey Park, and New York's Chinatown. We became famous."[51] Hsieh often compares the rapid influx of Chinese immigrants to Monterey Park to a missile; he takes no responsibility for setting it off, but he does feel that he had a hand in determining where it would land.

Throughout the 1980s Monterey Park and adjacent cities continued to be popular destinations for immigrant Chinese, according to statistics produced by the Immigration and Naturalization Service. Since 1983, applicants have been required to state the zip code of the area in which they plan to reside. Between 1983 and 1990 Monterey Park ranked third among the top ten communities where Asians chose to live (see Table 4). Only parts of New York's Chinatown and Flushing, Queens, proved to be more popular. More specifically, however, Monterey Park ranks second among the choices of those coming from Hong Kong, the People's Republic of China, and Taiwan (see Table 5). Two adjacent cities, Alhambra and Rosemead, rank eighteenth and twenty-fifth, respectively, among Asian immigrants overall, but fourth and sixth for Chinese newcomers.

The 1990 census counted more than 60,000 residents living in Monterey Park, with Asians in the majority at 56 percent of the population. Among them, Chinese far outnumber Japanese by 21,971 to 6,081, and make up 63 percent of the 34,898 Asians counted. Hispanics number 19,031, or 31 percent of the total population; the 7,129 whites make up 12 percent; African Americans and others were less than 1 percent (see Tables 1 and 2). In cities throughout the San Gabriel Valley, Asians showed impressive population gains since 1980:

TABLE 4
Asian Immigration to Selected U.S. Zip Codes: Fiscal Years 1983–1990

		Largest Group	
Zip Code	**Total Asians**	**Country of Birth**	**Number**
10002 New York, N.Y.	17,935	People's Republic of China	13,943
11373 Flushing, N.Y.	12,369	People's Republic of China	2,786
91754 Monterey Park, Calif.	10,501	People's Republic of China	2,479
60625 Chicago, Ill.	9,232	India	1,838
11355 Flushing, N.Y.	9,056	Korea	2,304
90701 Artesia/Cerritos (Los Angeles County), Calif.	7,937	Korea	2,410
96819 Honolulu, Hawaii	6,789	Philippines	5,940
60640 Chicago, Ill.	6,762	Vietnam	1,770
94015 Daly City, Calif.	6,733	Philippines	4,036
94112 San Francisco, Calif.	6,668	Philippines	4,548
91801 (18th) Alhambra, Calif.	6,129	Vietnam	1,558
91770 (25th) Rosemead, Calif.	5,159	Vietnam	2,130

Source: Immigration and Naturalization Service.

TABLE 5
Chinese Immigration to Selected U.S. Zip Codes: Fiscal Years 1983–1990

Zip Code	**People's Republic of China**	**Taiwan**	**Hong Kong**	**Total**
10002 New York, N.Y.	13,943	437	2,248	16,628
91754 Monterey Park, Calif.	2,479	2,328	768	5,575
11373 Flushing, N.Y.	2,786	1,116	551	4,453
91801 Alhambra, Calif.	1,426	1,301	464	3,191
11355 Flushing, N.Y.	1,550	1,245	322	3,117
91770 Rosemead, Calif.	1,014	486	288	1,788
90701 Artesia/Cerritos, Calif.	529	1,077	83	1,689
94112 San Francisco, Calif.	1,118	77	276	1,471
94015 Daly City, Calif.	678	171	400	1,249
60640 Chicago, Ill.	362	56	58	476

Source: Immigration and Naturalization Service.
Note: Two qualifiers should be kept in mind. First, the country persons emigrate from may not be their place of birth: e.g., someone born in China may have moved to Taiwan and emigrated from that country. Second, place of birth does not necessarily equate with ancestry. A person born in Hong Kong may be East Indian; conversely, a person born in Vietnam may be ethnic Chinese but is not included in the Chinese immigration totals. This table, then, is a general rather than specific view of immigrant Chinese residential patterns.

T A B L E   6

Increase in Asian Population in the San Gabriel Valley: 1980–1990

	1990			
City	Total Population	Asian Population	Asian % of Total	% Change from 1980
Alhambra	82,106	30,715	37.4	289
Arcadia	48,290	11,175	23.1	543
Diamond Bar	53,672	13,065	24.3	684
Hacienda Heights	52,354	13,824	26.4	219
Monterey Park	60,738	34,022	56.0	104
Rosemead	51,638	17,316	33.5	371
South Pasadena	23,936	5,002	20.9	98
South San Gabriel	7,700	2,496	32.4	250
Walnut	29,105	10,572	36.3	732
West Covina	96,086	15,675	16.3	182

Source: 1990 U.S. Census.

289 percent growth in Alhambra; 371 percent in Rosemead. And even these gains are modest compared to those in some of the more affluent outlying areas of the valley: Asians increased 732 percent in the city of Walnut, 684 percent in Diamond Bar, and 543 percent in Arcadia (see Table 6).[52] Today, roughly one-third of San Marino's population is of Asian ancestry.[53]

Many of the Chinese who have lived in Monterey Park for a number of years are now beginning to move to other areas, often to more affluent communities away from the first suburban Chinatown. Even the less affluent Chinese who replace them see Monterey Park as a way station. Chiling Tong fits this pattern. Tong came to the United States from Taiwan in 1984 and was a student at California State University, Long Beach. "Monterey Park is a good place for new immigrants," she says. "Chinese stores and restaurants make this place so convenient for Chinese people. . . . It's just like their own home." But Tong, who works for the California Employment Development Department, wants eventually to move to one of the outlying cities. "They used to call Monterey Park, 'the Chinese Beverly Hills,' but right now I think it's probably Arcadia [that deserves that name]. A lot of people are also moving to San Marino. They stop in Monterey Park or in Alhambra, but moving out is their ultimate goal after they establish themselves."[54]

For herself, Tong is looking toward the city of Hacienda Heights and adds, "The cities east of Monterey Park are the places for young couples."[55] Hacienda Heights boasts the largest Buddhist monastery in the Western Hemisphere, and Rowland Heights recently opened one of the largest Asian grocery stores in the nation.[56] Walnut, and Diamond Bar are also becoming new residential hubs for the Chinese. Tong knows, though, that older Chinese prefer to stay in Monterey Park. "They feel very comfortable. . . . You don't have to speak English to live here. I think that is the main reason." When she eventually has children, Tong hopes they will be comfortably bilingual and bicultural; they will be Americans, "but I hope they still consider themselves Chinese Americans and adopt both countries."[57]

The movement of Chinese immigrants throughout the San Gabriel Valley is no surprise to realtor Frederic Hsieh, whose prophetic statements in 1977 seem to be coming to fruition. He recognized that the Chinese newcomers would spread out residentially but that Monterey Park would continue to be their social, cultural, and economic "mecca." In 1989 he told the *Los Angeles Times*: "Monterey Park will always be the center, but living-wise, people are moving further away. For anyone who can drive, there's no reason to stay anymore."[58]

Many of the Chinese newcomers to Monterey Park are distinctly different from the Chinese immigrants who came before them. The dominant influence—economic, social, and cultural—of these new immigrant Chinese is the subject of the next two chapters.

CHAPTER 2

Enter the Dragon: Economic Change

Before the influx of Chinese immigrants, Monterey Park was a quiet, comfortable, and spacious bedroom community of tree-lined streets and modest single-family homes with expansive yards. It was seen as a safe and ideal integrated community in which to raise a family.

The early 1970s, however, brought dramatic changes as the relative wealth of the new immigrant Chinese became apparent. Many of the newcomers purchased houses in the best neighborhoods. A few years later, the development of multiple-unit condominiums offered a popular housing option for many of the less wealthy Chinese as they began to spread throughout the community and were no longer concentrated in just a few affluent hillside areas.

The city's original commercial district too had an old-town, Norman Rockwell flavor that was appealing to residents but economically inadequate for a changing and mobile suburban region. By the late 1970s, with political unrest in Asia, overseas Chinese investment interest in the community grew, and property values skyrocketed at an uncontrollable rate. During this time, with Chinese-owned and -operated businesses springing up rapidly in town, there was hope that Chinese investors would save the city's ailing economy. But though some individuals became rich, the community as a whole suffered greatly from runaway land speculation and never fully received the benefits of the increased development.

This chapter examines the residential and commercial development in Monterey Park from the end of World War II to the mid-1980s and the animosity—much of it with strong ethnic and class connotations—brought on by rapid change.

Residential Development

Before the stock market crash of 1929, Monterey Park was sparsely populated, and homes stood on one-acre or even larger lots. Residents were concentrated in the flatlands located in the northern and southern portions of the city. The surrounding hills, too steep for farms and used primarily to graze cattle and sheep, were regarded as natural barriers to further development. The end of World War II saw a revived growth trend, however, and as explosive population gains began to take place, many new housing tracts reached into the previously undeveloped hills.

Home Ownership

During the 1950s, according to the Monterey Park Building Department, 6,136 housing units were built in the city. Of those units, 4,695 (76.5 percent) were single-family homes. This trend continued, though at a slower pace, throughout the 1960s: of the 2,303 housing units constructed during this decade, 1,552 (67.4 percent) were single-family homes (see Table 7).

Since 1970, the highest percentage of home ownership has been among Asians; according to the 1970 census, 74 percent owned their homes. This figure dropped to about 66 percent in 1980, but Asians still had a higher rate of home ownership than any other group in town (see Table 8). Throughout the period of the Chinese influx, the median value of owner-occupied homes showed a dramatic increase: from 1970 to 1980 it soared from $26,600 to $96,400 and by 1990 to $238,800.[1]

In 1970 the median family income in Monterey Park was $12,381, an increase of 61.8 percent from 1960, whereas the figure for Los Angeles County was $10,970, a 55.7 percent increase over the same period. A 1973 report, *Monterey Park, California, Population and Housing Profile*, lists figures by group—"Negro," $11,332; "Spanish American," $11,270—but does not include Asians.[2] By 1980 the city's median family income had risen to $22,568, as compared with the Los Angeles County figure of $17,563. The group breakdown shows wider disparities: for whites (non-Hispanic), $28,242; for blacks, $16,364; for Hispanics, $21,595; for Asians, $30,119.[3]

From the 1960s on, Monterey Park was generally considered a well-integrated community. But looking at 1970 census data, Charles Choy Wong discovered that 70 percent of all Asians (mostly Japanese Americans at that time) were then clustered in just three of the city's ten census tracts and represented 30 percent of the population in these tracts, located in the city's newer and more affluent hillside housing developments on the western and eastern ends of town.[4] By 1980 the increasing Asian population accounted for slightly over 50 percent of the residents in the three census tracts, but Asians living there accounted for just under 50 percent of the total Asian population in town. At the same time, the median value of homes in the

T A B L E 7
Residential Building Permits Issued in Monterey Park: 1950–1990

| Year | Number of Units | | | Total Value[a] |
	Single Family	Multiple Family	Total	
1990	9	43	52	$9,628,668
1989	29	64	93	11,651,109
1988	28	55	83	7,452,459
1987	7	7	14	835,315
1986	16	52	68	5,011,367
1985	9	141	150	12,154,766
1984	4	69	73	7,735,973
1983	13	24	37	2,455,189
1982	48	325	373	32,376,219
1981	9	193	202	15,764,214
1980	11	351	362	25,893,547
1979	40	405	445	24,088,229
1978	114	294	408	22,374,010
1977	150	605	755	29,158,538
1976	106	321	427	15,276,515
1975	16	91	107	3,302,612
1974	9	89	98	2,493,614
1973	5	331	336	7,501,111
1972	24	88	112	2,162,151
1971	8	86	94	1,618,612
1970	61	49	110	2,616,667
1969	41	4	45	2,126,048
1968	87	14	101	3,400,811
1967	24	30	54	1,082,866
1966	101	144	245	4,779,172
1965	34	14	48	2,506,622
1964	223	52	275	5,248,420
1963	78	365	443	4,819,523
1962	102	50	152	7,187,390
1961	543	36	579	10,680,925
1960	319	42	361	7,630,100
1959	374	338	712	7,250,720
1958	648	411	1,059	11,391,174
1957	440	170	610	4,152,060
1956	513	66	579	5,928,300
1955	149	97	246	1,959,380
1954	552	103	655	6,396,265
1953	624	80	704	7,008,337
1952	431	110	541	4,537,805
1951	413	36	449	3,436,150
1950	551	30	581	4,418,750

Source: City of Monterey Park Building Department.
[a]Residential values only.

TABLE 8
Residential Occupancy Status by Ethnicity: 1970–1980

Ethnicity	1970		1980	
	Own	**Rent**	**Own**	**Rent**
Anglo/Hispanic	58.5%	41.5%	52.8%	47.2%
Black	36.8%	63.2%	14.5%	85.5%
Asians/Others	74.0%	26.0%	65.8%	34.2%

Source: City of Monterey Park Community Development Department.

three tracts rose dramatically. From 1970 to 1980 the median value for a home in tract 4820.01 increased from $38,301 to $136,300; in 4820.02, from $34,030 to $132,500; and in 4826, from $29,317 to $109,300 (see map).[5]

In 1970 Chinese made up only 34.7 percent of all the Asians living in the three tracts, while Japanese were 58.7 percent. In 1980 Chinese made up 43.9 percent of the Asians living in these tracts, compared with 45.9 percent Japanese (see Table 9). These statistics show that many newer Chinese residents were relatively affluent and able to move directly into prime housing areas. They also show that less affluent new immigrants were beginning to spread themselves geographically throughout the city and into less expensive residential areas. But established residents in town saw all newcomer Chinese as rich. As the Chinese immigrants began arriving in Monterey Park in earnest, stories circulated of their buying homes sight unseen, at inflated prices, and for cash. Most residents are still familiar with these accounts; rarely are they based on direct personal experience, however. "I heard stories repeated by a man who lived in the area," relates forty-four-year Monterey Park resident Howard Fry. "He talked about an elderly Chinese gentleman riding his bicycle down the street with a satchel slung on one of the handlebars, and if he saw anybody in the front yard, he would approach them and ask: 'Would you like to sell your house? I've got the money.' It's never happened to me, but I've heard from fellows who say it definitely happened."[6]

Condominium and Apartment Development

During the immigrant Chinese period a fundamental shift in residential construction was taking place. By the 1970s Monterey Park was moving from a community predominantly made up of single-family homes to a community of multiple-family housing units. As early as 1967 a consultant reported to the Monterey Park Planning

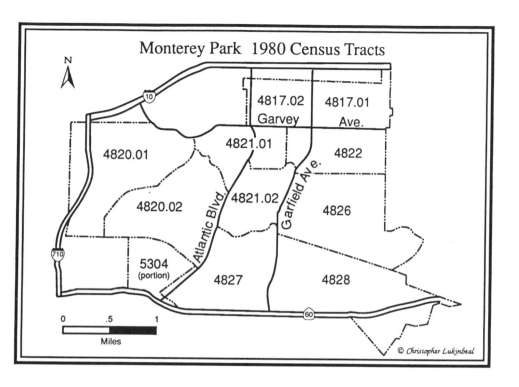

Monterey Park 1980 Census Tracts

TABLE 9
Asian Population by Selected Census Tract in Monterey Park: 1970–1980

Census Tract[a]	Total Pop.	Japanese	Chinese	Korean	Filipino	Other[b]	Total
				1970			
4820.01	3,490	532	648	42	94	2	1,318
4820.02	7,155	1,657	1,020	31	103	2	2,813
4826	6,610	854	135	14	48	6	1,057
				1980			
4820.01	4,078	790	1,072	151	53	37	2,103
4820.02	6,873	1,924	1,860	180	35	75	4,074
4826	2,932	1,473	1,075	155	160	69	2,932

Sources: Charles Choy Wong, "Ethnicity, Work, and Community: The Case of Chinese in Los Angeles" (Ph.D. dissertation, University of California, Los Angeles) p. 289; Monterey Park Community Development Department, *Housing and Population Profile,* November 1984, Table C, Appendix A.
[a]See map for location of census tracts.
[b]Includes Asian Indians, Vietnamese, Hawaiian, Guamanian, and Samoan.

Commission: "Today, all land is either developed or committed to non-residential uses. Therefore, population growth will result from new multiple family units."[7] Most of the new multiple units would be constructed primarily in the oldest residential sections in town because they were on flat ground and the homes there were on large lots. Of 2,847 new housing units built in Monterey Park during the 1970s, 2,214 (81.3 percent) were multiple-unit developments (see Table 7). The 1950s and 1960s showed owner occupancy to be 65.4 percent and 64.9 percent, respectively. But thereafter the rate of owner occupancy began to decline steadily, to 59.2 percent in 1970 and 53.9 percent in 1980 (though it did increase slightly, to 54.9 percent, in 1990).[8]

Multi-unit development reached its peak in the late 1970s. "Building Boom's Outta Sight!" screamed a January 1978 headline in the *Monterey Park Progress*. The article reported that in 1977 the city's building department had issued permits for 755 units of housing—the highest number in sixteen years—whose total value exceeded $38.9 million, three times that of the last major development boom in 1961 and more than the combined totals of any two years in the city's sixty-one-year history. Of 581 permits for multiple-dwelling units, 106 were issued to Kowin Development Company, owned by Winston Ko, a young Chinese architect responsible for much of the recent development in town. Kowin also received permits to build eighteen single family homes in Monterey Park.[9]

Before 1980 the census did not provide multiple-unit data. But in 1980, 5.1 percent of the city housing stock was shown to be condominiums and apartments. Of these, 76.9 percent were occupied, 68.9 percent by owners and 31.1 percent by renters. In a range from $88,012 to $250,000, the median value of a condominium unit was $96,800, slightly more than the median price of a standard single-family house in Monterey Park.[10]

The complexes built during the late 1970s were typically twin shoe-box-shaped, two-story buildings of ten to twenty units each, often with a driveway between that gave the complex the look of a bowling alley. There was very little landscaping beyond perhaps a token strip of lawn, and no such amenities as a pool or children's play area. According to a former city manager, Lloyd de Llamas, the earlier condominiums built in Monterey Park, when land values were still $2.00 to $3.00 a square foot, were attractive because amenities were added to each project to make them more marketable. But as demand increased and residential land values went up to $20 to $30 a square foot, "developers would . . . jam as many units into a lot as they possibly could. . . . the units would sell even if the development was cramped and ugly. They were meeting the standards, but the standards had originally been established to provide some design flexibility. . . . No one had anticipated this explosion of international demand for units that didn't offer the amenities that the market had previously demanded." [11] As a result, there are blocks in the northeast sector in which identical-looking complexes are lined up one after the other; many of these are occupied by the less affluent Chinese families who have recently come to Monterey Park.

Cuong Huynh and his family are among those who took up residence in one such condominium. Huynh is an ethnic Chinese-Vietnamese born in Saigon in 1972, the youngest of ten children. His father and grandfather were successful dentists, but three years after the 1975 overthrow of the U.S.-backed South Vietnam government, the entire family, including the grandparents, decided to escape the new Communist regime. Pulling together all their resources, they paid their way on a boat headed for the coast of Malaysia. For several weeks the family survived stormy weather, and even a life-threatening robbery by pirates on the open sea. Once in Malaysia they were immediately placed in a temporary refugee camp. Their ten-month stay left them with bitter memories of illness, hunger, and unsanitary conditions. Eventually, informed that they would be allowed to come to the United States, they were transferred to another camp with slightly better conditions—one with shower facilities—and remained there for another six months before coming to the United States. But the family had been split up: the three oldest sisters were sent to Canada to live with other relatives or in-laws, and the grandparents were resettled in Australia.

A relative managed to help the rest of the family find a one-bedroom motel apartment in Los Angeles, which became home for the next two years. Huynh's parents slept in the bedroom, and the siblings shared the living room, the sister had the couch to herself, and the brothers rotated between a double bed and the floor. Though Huynh's father was a dentist and his mother a dental technician, neither could practice in this country; moreover, in their mid-fifties, they had great difficulty learning English. As a result, the three oldest sons worked full time to keep the family fed, clothed, and sheltered—one as a mechanic, another as an electronic technician, and the third as a waiter in a Chinese restaurant.

In 1981 the same relative told the Huynhs about a brand new four-bedroom condominium in Monterey Park. The family again pulled together and borrowed just enough money from relatives to make a down payment. Only nine years old at the time, Chuong Huynh remembers feeling awed by his new and spacious home: "We didn't have that much to move, a few clothes, some pots and pans, and a suitcase.

We went to the condominium in Monterey Park and it was a big adjustment. I thought, 'Wow, this is nice! Is it going to get any better?'"[12] He and his family have lived in Monterey Park ever since.

A Proposed Moratorium

On July 10, 1978, the Monterey Park Planning Commission recommended that the city council pass a moratorium on construction of multiple-dwelling units, engendering the most controversial public fight to that date over the changing landscape of the community. Planning Commissioner Harold Fiebelkorn told the council that a moratorium would give the city staff a chance to study the impact of multiple-unit construction on population trends and their long-range effects on city services. "I think it's time we took a little vacation to see where Monterey Park wants to go," he said politely.[13]

Eight speakers, mostly developers and local businessmen, argued against the moratorium. Realtor Frederic Hsieh, told the council that such a move would be discriminatory: since it was mostly Chinese immigrants building in and moving to Monterey Park, they would be the ones disproportionately hurt. Seven other citizens expressed their right for community control and their concern over the changing character of the city. But Mayor G. Monty Manibog, echoing the general sentiments of the council, said that the building boom had been going on the last two or three years and asked, "Why the urgency at this particular time?" With that, council member Matthew Martinez made a motion to reject the moratorium but to order the city staff to go ahead with a study of the city's multi-unit developments. "I would say we can study where we're going without a moratorium," he told the audience. Referring to Manibog's question, Martinez also suggested that the proposal might have been racially motivated "in reaction to not how many more people are coming into Monterey Park but what kind of people are coming to Monterey Park." The city council then unanimously rejected the planning commission's recommendation.[14]

Henry Terashita, director of the planning department for over thirteen years, angrily denounced Martinez's claim and denied that the moratorium was racist. "Being Japanese and an Oriental," he said firmly, "I would be the first one to blow the whistle on [any] racial consideration." Just one week before the council meeting, Terashita had spoken to the Monterey Park Rotary Club and warned that city services such as water supplies, sewage facilities, and police and fire personnel could be severely strained if growth continued at its current pace.[15] A week after the council meeting, a furious Fiebelkorn demanded an apology from Martinez for raising the racial specter. As a regular columnist for the *Monterey Park Progress*, Fiebelkorn had not written about planning commission issues, avoiding a possible conflict of interest. Now, however, he felt that "extraordinary circumstances" compelled him to set aside his customary homey wit and comment seriously. "We have seen a great many injustices visited upon minorities over the years," he wrote. "It is more than happenstance that many of the minorities have settled in Monterey Park because the citizens of our city have displayed a warmth and tolerance that is not found in most communities. . . . However, Monterey Park is facing a danger of implied bigotry that can become serious if our leaders fail to exercise a little more judgment than was displayed by a city councilman last week."[16]

In the late 1970s many established residents began resenting the infringement and redefinition of space brought about by high-density apartments, condominiums, and additions to existing houses. In 1984 the Monterey Park Community Development Department reported that overcrowding—defined as more than one person per room within a housing unit—had increased 132 percent from 1970 to 1980. Records show that 3,185 housing units, or 17.2 percent of all occupied units in the city, were considered overcrowded. (By contrast, another figure shows that the average number of persons per dwelling had reached its lowest level since 1960; however, city officials point out this latter figure takes into account all dwellings, including single-family and vacant units.) Residential development, particularly multiple-unit construction, became the target of much of the growth-control sentiment in the city, but it was commercial development that generated most of the media attention and fanned the flames of resentment.

Commercial Development

Monterey Park for years had a very inactive commercial district; the historical downtown area around the intersection of Garvey and Garfield Avenues is fondly remembered by many long-time residents for its friendly, small-town atmosphere. Today, primarily because of Chinese immigration and investment the city's downtown features an international finance and heavily service-oriented economy.

Included within Monterey Park's 7.7-square-mile city limits are three Chinese language newspapers with international distribution; some sixty Chinese restaurants and more than fifty realtors; numerous Chinese supermarkets, herb shops, and bakeries; medical, dental, accounting, and legal offices; nightclubs, and dozens of "mini-malls" housing hundreds of small specialty services and curio shops. According to city officials, in 1978–79 there were 2,700 business licenses issued in Monterey Park. By 1985–86, there were 4,300. Today there are approximately 5,000 businesses of various sizes. In the early 1970s just a handful of Chinese-owned businesses were operating in the city, but today, Chinese are estimated to own between two-thirds and three-fourths of all business enterprises.

Downtown Monterey Park: From Romance to Reality

For many years the largest and most famous business in Monterey Park was the factory owned by Laura Scudder, southern California's potato chip pioneer. After settling in town in 1920, Laura Scudder and her husband, Charles, operated a small gas station on the corner of Atlantic and Garvey. They also owned an abandoned brick building next to the gas station, and on November 26, 1926, Mrs. Scudder made her first batch of potato chips there. "I didn't start the business in my kitchen, as some people believe," Scudder said in a 1957 interview. "Instead, before I did anything else, I built the plant. My idea was to make the best potato chips possible." At first the Scudder family ran the production alone, but after just a few months neighborhood women were hired to keep up with the increasing demand. Scudder was also a pioneer in advertising. She started with billboards but later successfully used newspapers, radio, and the new medium of television to sell her products. Laura Scudder herself appeared on television in 1957 and was one of the first sponsors of the Lawrence Welk show. At the peak of its success in the 1950s, Scudder Food Products produced not only potato chips but also mayonnaise and peanut butter. With factories in Monterey Park, Oakland, and Fresno, business sales exceeded $15 million a year.[17]

Another notable business enterprise got its start in the 1920s as the Edwards Theater on Garfield Avenue and eventually grew to be one of the largest movie theater chains in southern California. A rundown building on the site, known as the "New Mission Theatre," had originally showed silent films. After it closed down, a young man named Jimmie Edwards, who had already made a fortune in the parking lot business, canvassed the area to see whether it would be feasible to reopen the theater. Despite warnings, Edwards successfully began showing first-run motion pictures in Monterey Park before expanding to other areas.[18]

Most other businesses, however successful, were much more modest. Probably the most notable in the hearts and minds of long-time Monterey Park residents was the Garvey Hardware Store, started by Aaron Rodman and Bill Le Kachman in 1923. It was noted for its friendly owners, exceptional service, and 10 percent discounts to any customer who presented the store's ad from the *Monterey Park Progress*. "Garvey Hardware did not have the capital to carry everything that was required," remembers Ed Rodman, nephew of one founder and an employee of the store for several years starting in 1950. "But Bill Le Kachman and Aaron Rodman had the philosophy that if they didn't have it, they would get it. They would make a special trip to the warehouse and pick up whatever they needed for their customers. They gave real old-town service." Men would often drop by the store in the evenings, sit on nail kegs, and talk about life. "You've seen comics talk about the small-town store where everyone congregated to talk and so forth?" asks Rodman. "In essence, that's what Garvey Hardware was." [19]

Another small-town enterprise was Ed Kretz Motorcycle, located on Garvey Avenue just east of Garfield. Owner Ed "Iron Man" Kretz was a nationally recognized motorcycle racer and the winner of the first Daytona 200 in 1937. In 1938 and again in 1949 he was voted most popular rider in a poll taken by the American Motorcyclist Association.[20] Kretz started his business in 1944, while he was still a competitive racer, and ran it (later joined by his son) for forty-four years. The elder Kretz was well known in town and was active in business and civic affairs.

Two other much-loved establishments that began in the 1950s were Paris' Restaurant and the Midtown Pharmacy, both on Garvey Avenue. When Paris Tripodes, a Greek immigrant, opened a popular roadside stop on what was then the main route from Los Angeles to the resorts in Palm Springs, Hollywood stars were frequently seen there. "We used to get a lot of movie actors like Debbie Reynolds and others I didn't know myself," says Louis Tripodes, younger brother of Paris and later owner of the restaurant.[21] Paris' also became the hangout for Monterey Park's legendary "Kaffee Klatch," the daily morning gathering of local merchants and old-time residents who got together to argue about local, national, and international events. Sam Pearlman started the Midtown Pharmacy in 1959, an era when "we used to keep the condoms under the counter and sanitary napkins were wrapped in plain brown paper," he remembers.[22] Over the years, Pearlman established himself as the friendly family pharmacist who knew his customers by their first names, gave free helpful advice, and home-delivered prescriptions.

The early image of the Garvey-Garfield area is still vivid in the memories of many old-time Monterey Park residents. But it had already begun its decline in the late 1950s when Atlantic Square, a 14.7-acre regional shopping center, opened for business in the southern portion of town next to the Pomona Freeway. Within a few years, the Prado Shopping Center opened across the street. The new restaurants, brand-name stores, specialty shops, services, banks, and commercial offices made the two shopping centers together the new commercial anchor for Monterey Park and a primary retail destination for shoppers from the surrounding area.

According to Ed Rodman, some merchants in the Garvey-Garfield district welcomed the new shopping centers, anticipating a spillover of new business in their part of town; but others bitterly opposed the centers, convinced that the competition would ruin their business. The actual results were mixed. Rodman noted that some stores held onto their customers: "Garvey Hardware continued to give service and continued to keep customers, but there weren't enough stores that gave that kind of service." [23]

By 1965 the evidence of a new era was apparent. A consulting firm hired by the city to analyze Monterey Park's economic status reported in 1966: "The Garvey-Garfield area has traditionally been the center of business and government in Monterey Park, but over the last 15 years its growth has not kept pace with city population increases. . . . While retail sales in the Garvey-Garfield area have not decreased in volume, they have not increased in proportion to increases in city sales. . . . [This] clearly indicates that [the area's] importance as a retail center is declining." By way of example, the consultants provided statistics showing that between 1963 and 1965 retail sales increased 17.1 percent for Monterey Park as a whole but only 0.2 percent for the Garvey-Garfield area. At the same time, even though Atlantic Square appeared to be doing well, the city as a whole was not. The consultants figured that Monterey Park's actual retail sales of about $47 million in 1965 was some $28 million short of their expectations for the area, indicating that many residents were shopping elsewhere. [24]

Per capita, Monterey Park generated only $1,068 a year in retail sales, a poor showing compared with $1,596 in Los Angeles County, $1,615 in Montebello, $1,536 in South San Gabriel, and $1,933 in Alhambra. Food and drug stores accounted for over 48 percent of the total retail sales in Monterey Park—an extremely high percentage reflecting the very low sales of other types of goods. [25] For major purchases, Ed Rodman admits, people simply had to go out of town: "If I wanted to buy a suit, I went out of Monterey Park. If I wanted to buy any object that costs a great deal of money, I went out of Monterey Park." [26] Vacant stores signaled the decline of the central business district.

Foreseeing serious financial trouble for Monterey Park, consultants Wilsey and Han recommended a series of options for redeveloping the Garvey-Garfield area, but it was nearly a decade before any official action was taken. "I didn't realize how bad it was until I got to Monterey Park," recalls Lloyd de Llamas, who was hired as city manager in late 1976 specifically to straighten out the city's finances. "They only had a contingency reserve of $14,000 [and] had been deferring maintenance on their equipment and infrastructure for almost five years."[27] A seventh-generation Californian whose ancestors were among the first Spanish settlers, de Llamas had successfully managed two smaller towns in southern California before being asked to run Monterey Park. The job would prove challenging.

Enter the Dragon: New Chinese Investors

Before de Llamas's arrival, however, private-sector redevelopment had begun—led by Chinese investors. "I remember both around Atlantic and Garfield Avenue, there were many pieces of vacant land full of overgrown grass and so on," recalls Frederic Hsieh.[28] Local businesses were steadily leaving the community, and neither city officials' discussions with merchants about upgrading Garvey-Garfield nor the options recommended by the 1966 consultants' report resulted in any action. But Hsieh, now settled in Monterey Park and an active member of the chamber of commerce, did act. He started buying inexpensive abandoned properties whose owners wanted to get out of town, and quickly resold them at handsome profits to Chinese investors.

"In real estate, there is such a thing as 'social canvassing,' which means you get to know people intimately," Hsieh explains. People from the chamber of commerce whom he had worked with and known as friends "contacted me first when they wanted to sell. . . . they felt I was qualified to buy, that I would follow through. . . . Consequently, I had the first opportunity to buy many properties." In 1975, for example, "I handled Houston Barry's mobile home park on the southeast corner of Atlantic and Garvey. I put it together and sold it to friends of mine for $7.50 a square foot. At that time it was an unheard of price— $7.50! Usually, at that time, it was between $3.00 and $5.00. . . . So I knew firsthand [that] things [were] going on, and I knew pretty soon it was going to be more."[29]

It was just over a year later that Hsieh startled the Monterey Park Chamber of Commerce with his prediction that their city was about to become "the mecca for Chinese business. Not only [for] Monterey Park, but for the surrounding communities," he remembers saying. "Residential areas will spill over to San Marino, Diamond Bar, Rosemead, Arcadia, and many places. But, the commercial and entertainment center . . . will be Monterey Park."[30]

"Everyone in the room thought the guy was blowing smoke,"

recalls Harold Fiebelkorn.[31] Undaunted, Hsieh and others continued to deal in real estate.

The Chinese immigrants who had moved into Monterey Park in the early 1970s, though affluent, did not cause much stir because they were mostly young engineers and other professionals. They lived in the best neighborhoods and were high achievers who adjusted quietly to the community. In the mid-1970s, however, Taiwan and Hong Kong businessmen started to arrive. "First it was the real estate people, and then trading companies, heavy investors, people that come with hundreds of thousands of dollars in cash," explained Wesley Ru, a Monterey Park businessman and an unsuccessful candidate for city council in 1984. Some of these newer immigrants brought not only considerable wealth but a certain ostentation that aroused a generalized animosity in the community. Residents spoke with disdain of the sudden increase of luxury cars in town, of $100 bills flashed in restaurants, of business people wearing tailor-made suits and sporting expensive jewelry. "Their first stop would be the Mercedes dealer, and the second stop would be the real estate broker. This group of businessmen—entrepreneurs—were bolder, more boisterous, more demanding and sometimes even cunning," Ru later told a reporter.[32]

These newcomers could afford to pay for homes and commercial property in cash, engage in land speculation, and sometimes even establish businesses or subsidiaries to serve as a base for bringing money out of their home countries into the United States. "Let's say I'm a manufacturer in Taiwan who exports one million dollars of merchandise," hypothesized Monterey Park realtor Gregory Tse in a candid interview with *Forbes*. "I should get one million dollars back to Taiwan, but instead I say: 'I'm the manager here [U.S. branch]. I'd like to pay myself a salary of $100,000 here, my wife $50,000 and my oldest son, he's got a business degree, $50,000.' So I send $800,000 back to Taiwan. There's nothing illegal."[33]

In fact, large profits were not the primary concern; the overriding objective was to gain long-term stability over short-term profits. Some investors were even willing to take a loss for several years in order to secure a place in the United States. Opening a business here allowed the individual and his or her immediate family to obtain visas to reside in the United States. After a while, the business owner could apply for permanent residence. And the automatic American citizenship of a child born here gave the family a firm foothold in the United States.

Historically, the pattern of Chinese immigration was for the men to come alone to work and earn money, while the wife and family stayed behind. But in the late 1970s it was not uncommon to see wives and children living in Monterey Park while the husbands commuted

T A B L E 10
Deposits in Monterey Park Financial Institutions: 1981–1989 ($\times$ 1,000)

Fiscal Year	Bank Deposits	Savings and Loan Deposits	Credit Union Deposits	Total Deposits
1981	$302,247	$156,257	$592	$459,096
1982	414,051	171,316	474	585,841
1983	604,965	197,019	506	802,490
1984	709,570	264,504	532	974,606
1985	868,879	333,317	2,828	1,205,024
1986	945,409	420,412	5,191	1,371,012
1987	958,878	506,700	1,465	1,467,043
1988	1,101,500	549,257	1,612	1,652,369
1989	1,371,429	548,444	1,522	1,921,395

Source: Monterey Park Management Services Department, *Comprehensive Annual Financial Report,* June 30, 1990, p. 77.

across the Pacific. Sometimes both parents stayed in Asia and the children were sent over as students; they were set up with a home and sometimes a car, if they were old enough. Once the children were established as permanent residents, they could help the parents immigrate. This pattern, though not the case for the majority of Chinese immigrants to Monterey Park, does continue to this day.

That Monterey Park has become a focal point for Pacific Rim investment is also manifested by the rapidity with which new banks open in the city. Former shoe stores, tire stores, veterinary hospitals, and even doughnut shops have been converted into banks. A 1990 report shows that by 1989 the combined deposits in Monterey Park's twenty-six financial institutions, most of which are Chinese-owned and -operated, had swelled to over $1.9 billion (see Table 10)—roughly $30,000 for every man, woman, and child in town.[34]

The arrival of entrepreneurs and their new money worked to reinvigorate a previously inactive business area in Monterey Park, create construction and retail job opportunities, and provide the push for the city to economically recreate itself in a fashion not seen since the mid-1920s. But unlike the residents excited by Peter Snyder and his futuristic plans for Monterey Park in the 1920s, few townspeople in the late 1970s were pleased by what they saw.

By 1978 several regional shopping malls had opened for business throughout the western San Gabriel Valley, and a new study reported that Monterey Park was not keeping up with the competition: "On a per capita basis, retail sales increased by an annual average of 11.9 percent between 1974 and 1978. Allowing for an annual inflation rate of approximately 10.1 percent during this period, retail sales' real growth occurred at an annual rate of only 1.8 percent compared to 16.3 percent for Los Angeles County."[35] Chamber of commerce manager Dave Johnson told the *Monterey Park Progress* in 1978: "We are losing the clothing stores and the kind of shops that make a balanced community. We're buying more outside the city than the city is selling." But beyond just getting Monterey Park residents to shop in Monterey Park, Johnson argued that it was imperative for the city to reach out to other communities. "For us to sell more than we spend we have to bring in people from surrounding cities. And you've got to have some kind of an attraction to do that."[36]

Just before that interview was published, Johnson had proposed such an attraction to the business and industrial development committee of the chamber of commerce. Pointing out that 30 percent of the city's business licenses were registered under Asian names; that every new chamber member since he had been hired was Asian—most often, Chinese; that nearly every developable lot was owned by Asians (some living in Hong Kong and Taiwan); and that there were approximately 100,000 Asian residents throughout the San Gabriel Valley at the time, he proposed the adoption of a theme for a program of events to give Monterey Park some much-needed publicity. Unfortunately, he made the mistake of calling it a "Chinatown" theme—and met a courteous but swift rejection. The thirty local merchants who had gathered at the Szechwan Restaurant on Garvey Avenue to enjoy a nine-course feast hosted by Winston Ko, president of Kowin Development, found the suggestion no more palatable than Frederic Hsieh's earlier prediction. Most objected to focusing on one ethnic group, and though they agreed that they needed to do a better job of reaching Asian customers, they did not want their business district to be called a Chinatown. No action was taken, and as Johnson feared, an opportunity for communitywide economic gains was lost.

Certainly fortunes were being made in Monterey Park. Aside from Frederic Hsieh, whose property holdings were estimated to be worth several million dollars, and Winston Ko, who is said to have become "a millionaire before he was 30 years old," several others benefited from the city's demographic and economic changes.

Gregory Tse, owner of Wing On Realty, is one of these. Having lived in Monterey Park since 1968, Tse established himself in the community; he ran, unsuccessfully, for city council in 1984 and became president of the chamber of commerce in 1986. He had studied law in Hong Kong, but when he first arrived to this country, he taught English to other immigrants for the Los Angeles Unified School District. Tse says he became interested in real estate after a feasibility study commissioned by his father showed that the best economic opportunities would be in the Los Angeles area, and when he saw how cheap land prices were in Monterey Park. In crowded Hong Kong, where property is a prime commodity, the cost of real estate was thousands of dollars per square foot, whereas commercial land in Monterey Park was just a few dollars a square foot. Highly confident and articulate, Tse has been quoted many times in the local and national press. "From where I came from, Monterey Park is still way underdeveloped," he told *Forbes* in 1985. "We don't have highrises here. Look at Westwood! Look at Century City!" [37]

When Alan Co, an ethnic-Chinese refugee from Vietnam, came to the United States in 1975, he shunned welfare or refugee assistance and worked three jobs—as inventory clerk, property manager, and janitor—to support his family. Although he had not succeeded at selling life insurance, in the late 1970s he tried selling real estate and claims he made "big bucks" from sales commissions and putting together deals that gave him a share in the property in lieu of a standard percentage of the price. Modest about his own abilities but blunt about the results, Co says: "People say I work hard, but I think it was luck because anybody during that period, 1976–79, could buy anything—you could buy garbage—and make money." [38]

Nor were Chinese immigrants the only ones who did well in Monterey Park. Several former residents who do not want to be identified chuckle with embarrassment when they admit that they bought homes on one-acre lots before World War II for $5,000 and recently sold them for $200,000 or more. And though many white merchants spent the better part of the 1970s and early 1980s trying to deny and fight off the new Chinese presence in town, some capitalized on it. In 1980 Kelly Sands, then in his twenties, took over his family's electrical contracting firm, Bezaire Electronics, and turned the sputtering business into a success story by hiring Chinese-speaking managers and aggressively seeking out the new market. Sands estimates that nearly 80 percent of his customers are Chinese. "Either you adjust your mindset to reality or you'd better get out of the way," he says. [39]

A similar philosophy guides John Weidner, an immigrant from the Netherlands who has been internationally honored for helping lead 1,000 Jews and downed Allied pilots out of his Nazi-occupied country during World War II. When Weidner's Nutrition Center, opened in 1971, started losing business in the late 1970s, the owner hired and trained Chinese- and Spanish-speaking sales help; he also translated product brochures and started stocking many Chinese herbal and health food products. Since that time Weidner's sales have increased, and in front of his new, larger location he posts a sign on which Chinese and English are equally prominent. [40]

Despite these successes, the new-found interest in Monterey Park, and the increase in construction, however, city officials reported that taxable income remained flat, rising less than 2 percent between 1977 and 1985 (after adjusting for inflation). During the same period, taxable sales rose 10 percent in the western San Gabriel Valley area overall, and 23 percent statewide.[41] The uncontrollable land speculation, which topped out around $80 a square foot in the mid-1980s, produced two distinct and unanticipated consequences that together have undermined the city's economy: the proliferation of small, low-profit businesses run by immigrant families; and the inability to draw high-volume retail stores to the community.

Because of the inflated cost of the property, owners had to charge high rents that most individual proprietors could not afford. For example, the Midtown Pharmacy went out of business because the rent shot up from $3,100 a month to $6,000. When a single business could not survive such increases, the owner's only option was to carve up the property into smaller storefronts and charge high enough rent for each lease to realize a return on the investment. The partitioning of Garvey Hardware and Ed Kretz's motorcycle shop following their sale are examples of this phenomenon in action. Many of these cubicle businesses were low-volume, family-run immigrant enterprises that survived on minimal profits. Often these marginal immigrant entrepreneurs spoke little or no English and had little opportunity for work outside of Monterey Park in the mainstream economy. So intense was the competition for these mini-stores that owners could demand "key money"—an illegal but openly acknowledged fee assessed to every tenant who moved in or renewed a lease. According to Shant Agajanian, a consultant hired in 1987 to look into the city's economy, since a family-run business had no labor costs, the only major expenses were rent and inventory: if an owner "can make $6,000 the first year, he's happy as hell." The key to improving Monterey Park's retail sales tax problems, Agajanian insisted, was to get away from the many "12-seat restaurants and 500-square-foot boutiques that sell $3.96 blouses and $4.95 dresses."[42]

Lloyd de Llamas, now a partner in a successful consulting firm, agreed that low-profit businesses—a by-product of out-of-control land values—took away the city's ability to attract the large-volume retailers it needed to generate adequate sales tax revenue. Retail operations such as department stores, large wholesale outlets, and car dealerships—important to the economic vitality of a community—require a great deal of inexpensive space. "The speculators really hurt us," de Llamas explains. "To build a tax base you need to bring in large-volume retails that will generate large amounts of sales tax. But when

T A B L E 11
Valuation of Construction in Monterey Park: 1950–1990

Year	Commercial	Residential	Total
1990	$24,500,183	$9,628,668	$34,128,851
1989	23,934,447	11,651,109	35,129,183
1988	23,389,425	7,452,459	30,841,884
1987	12,712,935	835,315	13,548,250
1986	34,748,691	5,011,367	39,760,058
1985	56,877,194	12,154,766	69,031,960
1984	21,554,735	5,735,973	27,290,708
1983	26,682,474	2,455,189	29,137,663
1982	10,027,673	32,376,219	42,403,892
1981	16,169,585	15,764,214	31,933,799
1980	17,562,690	25,893,547	43,456,237
1979	30,146,033	24,088,229	54,234,262
1978	13,088,368	22,374,010	35,462,378
1977	9,749,129	29,158,538	38,907,667
1976	9,998,407	15,276,515	25,274,922
1975	3,888,666	3,302,612	7,191,278
1974	3,580,867	2,493,614	6,074,481
1973	3,844,035	7,501,111	11,345,146
1972	3,067,313	2,162,151	5,229,464
1971	4,962,701	1,618,612	6,580,863
1970	5,590,027	2,616,667	8,206,694
1969	2,682,673	2,126,048	4,808,721
1968	3,639,837	3,400,811	7,040,648
1967	3,535,560	1,082,866	4,618,426
1966	2,740,221	4,779,172	7,519,393
1965	4,948,521	2,506,622	7,445,143
1964	5,303,526	5,248,420	10,551,946
1963	3,533,593	4,819,523	8,353,116
1962	2,197,949	7,187,390	9,385,339
1961	2,205,774	10,680,925	12,886,699
1960	2,988,983	7,630,100	10,619,087
1959	3,332,578	7,250,720	10,583,298
1958	1,665,743	11,391,174	13,056,917
1957	1,877,552	4,152,060	6,029,612
1956	1,384,959	5,928,300	7,313,259
1955	1,825,310	1,959,380	3,784,690
1954	1,435,535	6,396,265	7,831,800
1953	1,771,064	7,008,337	8,779,401
1952	617,771	4,537,805	5,155,576
1951	778,207	3,436,150	4,214,357
1950	582,241	4,418,750	5,000,991

Source: Monterey Park Building Department.

you have people coming in and paying $40 or $50 a square foot for property, and large-scale retailers can only pay $8 or $9 a square foot, then the opportunities for balancing the tax base are actually reduced."[43] De Llamas often cites Superior Pontiac, a car dealership that alone generated 10 percent of the city's sales tax but left Monterey Park in 1987 after the land it had leased for twenty years was sold to a Chinese developer.

Though no one would deny that outrageous land speculation created many problems, some would argue that the anemic sales tax base was a direct result of the controlled-growth movement that emerged in the city in the early 1980s. A major commercial development plan scrapped by the voters in 1984 was, in de Llamas's mind, Monterey Park's last best hope to take advantage of investment interest in the community and guide it toward a balanced economy. But "every time we came up with a workable plan," he says, "by the time we got through satisfying the opposition, speculators would come in and raise the property value another $20 a square foot so that the economics of the plan would be obsolete by the time it got adopted. We were never able to get on top of it."[44]

Clearly, both residential and commercial development engendered widespread acrimony that only worsened when construction in Monterey Park reached an all time high in 1979. With building projects whose permits had been issued in the mid-1970s then either being completed or getting under way, the valuation for commercial construction alone reached $30 million, and the total valuation for all construction soared to over $54 million, far surpassing the record of $39 million set just two years earlier (see Table 11). But into the early 1980s, runaway land speculation and construction offering no short- or long-term community benefit created inflated property values, rising rents, and a shortage of productive businesses.[45] With Monterey Park's economy obviously heading in the wrong direction, class and economic conflicts severely destabilized the community. Unfortunately, ethnic and cultural conflicts incited even greater calamity and divisiveness.

CHAPTER **3**

"I Don't Feel at Home Anymore": Social and Cultural Change

From the 1940s through the 1960s, Monterey Park was a community whose activities revolved around active service clubs, friendly churches, and a collegial chamber of commerce. Two hotly competing weekly newspapers (the *Progress* and the *Californian*) together thoroughly informed residents about what was going on in town. Since the early 1970s, however, the city's social and cultural landscape has been reshaped. This chapter describes the changing environment in Monterey Park from the 1940s through the conflicts of the 1970s and 1980s, when ambivalence toward the new immigrant Chinese, antagonism toward bilingual education, and hostility toward the proliferation of ethnic-oriented businesses escalated into a clearly anti-Chinese backlash.

A Homogeneous Community

For more than thirty years Nell Bruggemeyer was a columnist for the *Monterey Park Progress*, writing exclusively on the social scene during "the good old days" of the city. Until her illness in 1963, Bruggemeyer's regular feature "Bird on Nellie's Hat," attracted a loyal readership that particularly enjoyed her detailed depictions of an ideal small town where everyone knew everyone else. She often wrote about how people would get together for parties to celebrate not only every holiday but even the construction of a new room in a house. Communal activities from square dances at Ynez Elementary School, large picnics in the park, and block parties to building floats for the Pasadena Rose Parade on New Year's Day figured prominently in her columns and in the residents' image of their city.

Social Institutions

The people who settled in Monterey Park between 1916 and the end of World War II were primarily white Anglo-Saxon Protestants who had a strong faith in themselves and a strong pioneering spirit. They also had a strong faith in God, whom they considered their partner in building a city reflective of American virtues, values, and ideals. Although Catholic Saint Stephens is the oldest church in town, the Methodist Church was easily the most influential.

Methodists played an active role in Monterey Park's major secular institution, the Lions Club. Chartered in 1937, the Lions Club was the center of civic and social activities for many years. Notably, it participated in war-related services, constructed several public facilities in Barnes Park, and was instrumental in starting the city's first large senior housing project—the six-story, 126-unit Lions Manor. The Lions Club was also the motivating force behind "Play Days," a yearly festival that started with the city's golden anniversary in 1966 and is still celebrated every May with a parade down Garvey Avenue and a carnival at Barnes Park.

The Monterey Park Lions Club initiated projects to help blind and vision-impaired people, such as testing the eyesight of young children in local schools every year, paying for eyeglasses for needy students, and selling small "white cane" pins to raise money for these activities. "White Cane Days," now a national Lions Club operation, actually began in Monterey Park in 1952, when member Walter Koetz came up with the idea of making pins from white pipe cleaners to resemble canes carried by the blind.[1] Several years later members Johnny Johns and Kenny Gribble built a machine capable of turning out millions of white cane pins; since that time the Monterey Park Lions have been responsible for manufacturing and distributing the pins to Lions Clubs all over the country.

From the 1940s to the late 1970s the organization was also a major political force, having had several members elected to the city council. "The Lions Club itself was not political," explains Joseph Graves, a Monterey Park native born in 1916 and the 1956 president of the Lions Club, "but it provided personnel who were well known and had friends who would provide a good political team. That's how it worked."[2] Moreover, Lions Club and Methodist Church members formed the core of the group of merchants and long-time residents who gathered every morning at Paris' Restaurant for coffee and conversation. The long-running Kaffee Klatch, as it was known, had a consistent turnout of fifteen to twenty, plus perhaps a dozen others who came intermittently, among them several top city staff members. Regulars included Harold Fiebelkorn, Howard Fry, Johnny Johns, Ed Kretz, Kenny Gribble, and *Monterey Park Progress* publisher Eli Isenberg (though he was neither a Lions Club nor Methodist Church member).

Newspapers

Aside from the Lions Club, probably the most influential voice in the community was the *Monterey Park Progress*. Competition for circulation and advertising dollars between the local *Progress* and the regional *Monterey Park Californian* actually benefited members of the community and kept them better informed. According to Isenberg, the *Californian* was not exceptional editorially but, as part of a small chain of newspapers, offered merchants the opportunity to advertise in several communities.

Because of this competition, the *Progress* placed a strong emphasis on local news and editorials. Besides Bruggemeyer's "Bird on Nellie's Hat," regular columns included Fiebelkorn's "Kaffee Klatch," Ruth Diesing's "The Church Mouse" about church events, and Isenberg's own "It Seems to Me," a weekly opinion piece. In addition, the *Progress* hired stringers to cover various neighborhood events, ran a feature called "Neighbor of the Week" that profiled a Monterey Park family, and regularly printed births, deaths, marriages, school honor rolls, Boy Scout awards, and club news. "We reported when a kid was born," says Isenberg, "we marked his history as a Little Leaguer, scout, playing in the band, and acceptance in college."[3]

Editorials in the *Progress* were also highly influential. "I think we were well read for a community newspaper," said Norman Lieberman, who was just twenty-five when he joined the staff in 1953. "We felt our role in the city was not necessarily to persuade people to any point of view but to encourage them to discuss important issues and to develop their own point of view. Nevertheless, we did make endorsements during city council elections, and an astonishing number of our recommendations were approved by the voters."[4]

The *Progress* also prided itself on being an activist newspaper. In 1957 the County of Los Angeles wanted to take over a large piece of the land in the northern highlands of Monterey Park for a county dump. When the city council balked at the plan, the county said it was going to do it anyway. Because of this blatant disregard for the wishes of the city, the *Progress* led the fight against the dump by organizing residents and community leaders. They soon started lobbying the California legislature and the governor to approve a "home rule" bill that would prohibit larger governmental bodies from placing dump sites without the local jurisdiction's permission. The effort succeeded when Governor Goodwin Knight signed the bill into law. That year, the *Progress* gained statewide recognition and was cited for "exceptional community service" by the California Newspaper Publishers Association.

The *Californian* folded in the late 1960s. The *Progress* remained dominant until Isenberg sold the paper and retired in 1979. For several years thereafter the new owner tried to maintain its stature by keeping on former editors and columnists, including Isenberg. In the mid-1980s the *Progress* was challenged briefly by upstart community newspapers such as the *News Digest* and the *Independent*, both of which folded after short runs. By the late 1980s, however, the *Progress* itself had been eclipsed by the *Los Angeles Times*, the *San Gabriel Valley Tribune*, and Chinese-language newspapers.

Effects of Chinese Immigration

As the influx of Chinese to Monterey Park began, most community leaders and residents compared the newcomers with the American-born Japanese *nisei* who had moved to the community twenty years earlier and quickly assimilated. Together they welcomed the Chinese as yet another group of hardworking people who would naturally be more than happy to settle into the established wholesome life of the community. But because these Chinese were new immigrants, expectations for their immediate assimilation proved unrealistic, and several areas of friction developed—involving business and social organizations, schools, and even supermarkets.

Divided Organizations

When it became obvious that no one could stop the influx of Chinese immigrants to the community, Eli Isenberg wrote a conciliatory column in December 1977 titled, "A Call for Open Arms," which was later translated into Chinese and republished in the *Progress*:

> Twenty years ago, Monterey Park became a prestige community for Japanese. At first they settled in Monterey Hills. Today they live throughout and are active in the community. They were invited and accepted invitations to become involved. Today George Ige is our mayor, Keiji Higashi, a past president of chamber of commerce, is president-elect of Rotary. Fifty other Japanese men and women serve on advisory boards and in other leadership roles.
>
> Today we must offer the same hand of friendship to our new Chinese neighbors. They should be invited to join service clubs, serve on advisory boards, become involved in little theater and PTA. . . . To become and stay a good community, there must be a structured effort to assimilate all those who want to become

a part of Monterey Park. The city itself should coordinate this effort through the community relations commission and call on all organizations in Monterey Park to play their part in offering a hand of friendship to our new neighbors.[5]

Isenberg may have written partly in response to the formation of an independent Monterey Park Chinese Chamber of Commerce in September 1977—much to the chagrin of the original chamber. A great deal of animosity and criticism were leveled at this separate group for their reluctance to cooperate with established merchants. Shortly after Isenberg's column appeared, a series of meetings between the two groups resulted in the admission of the Chinese organization to the regular city Chamber of Commerce and the formation of a new Chinese American committee. "Helping keep the doors open was Fred Hsieh," recalls Isenberg. "Fred played an important role in maintaining an integrated Monterey Park Chamber of Commerce."[6]

After the proposed "Chinatown theme" was rejected in 1978, however, some dissatisfied Chinese business people resurrected the idea of a separate Chinese business organization and grumbled about other aspects of their chamber membership. For one thing, few of the Chinese businessmen spoke much English and could understand little of what was being said during meetings. Chinese merchants also resented having to seek chamber approval for business decisions; they wanted more autonomy. Furthermore, unlike Frederic Hsieh, most of the Chinese saw little to be gained by interacting with established merchants who, they felt, were antagonistic. Though they remained in the chamber, the tension was not resolved, and flare-ups periodically occurred.

The Lions Club was even less successful at amalgamating with the newcomers. In the early 1980s an ad hoc group of Chinese asked Lions Club International to charter the Little Taipei Lions Club in Monterey Park. Given the historical prestige of the Lions Club in Monterey Park, its aging and dwindling membership was embarrassed by the formation of a separate club. Although they formally voted to sponsor the Chinese Lions organization in 1985, there was a great deal of reluctance. "The effort to recreate Little Taipei in Southern California," says Joseph Graves, was "unfortunate": "We would infinitely rather they had joined the existing, strong, long-time club with traditions." Graves spoke with pride of the original club's accomplishments, such as "screening all the children's eyes in Monterey Park. . . . [And] it looks like about 50 percent to 60 percent are Oriental."[7]

The projects of the Little Taipei Lions Club have been admirable, as well. Twice a year, during Chinese New Year's Day and on Thanksgiving, it sponsors a free lunch for senior citizens in Monterey Park's Langley Center, and it has raised considerable money for various non-profit organizations in the community—for example, making major donations to the city's public library to purchase Chinese-language books. But Graves objects that the Little Taipei Lions Club just gives out money rather than organizing work projects: "The Lions Club believed in the idea of going down and pouring cement to build a Memorial Bowl, or hammering nails to the roof of the pavilion at the park," he insists. "As older members, we look down our noses at any organization that doesn't get their hands dirty."[8]

In the mid-1980s the Monterey Park Kiwanis Club refused to sponsor a separate Chinese chapter, but one was formed anyway. To persistent rumors that a Chinese Rotary Club would soon be organized as well, long-time Rotary member Eli Isenberg responded in 1985: "Apartheid, whether in South Africa or in service clubs in Monterey Park, is a giant step back." In a tone quite different from that of his 1977 "Call for Open Arms," he continued: "Asians do not have a Con-stitutional right to form service clubs where they will be comfortable with members of their kind. All service clubs, from their international, should ban this happening. Provided, of course, that the Anglo clubs are willing to accept Asians as is the case in Monterey Park."[9]

Little Taipei Lions Club members interviewed during their Thanksgiving day luncheon in 1990, however, denied that they are separatist. While passing out plates of turkey and trimmings to senior citizens, many said they meant no disrespect toward the established Lions Club and had no intention of competing with it in service to the community. As a master of ceremonies in the background called out winning door prize numbers in both English and Chinese, one mem-ber asserted that there was plenty of room for both clubs. Another member found nothing surprising about preferring to be with people his own age who spoke his language: "What is wrong with a service club that happens to be sensitive and in touch with the Chinese com-munity?" Angered by any perception that the Little Taipei Lions Club serves only the Chinese, he added: "Look around you. There are lots of different people here. We happily serve them [all]. . . . But we do things for the Chinese in this city that no one else would."[10]

Bilingual Education

The impact of the newcomers on the local schools also generated a great deal of tension. Brightwood Elementary School is located in the heart of one of the most heavily concentrated Asian sections in Mon-terey Park (census tract 4820.02), and surrounded by well maintained middle-class homes built in the 1950s. In early 1978 a Chinese bilingual education plan initiated at Brightwood School opened what the PTA president called "a bucket of worms."[11]

On January 21, 1974, the United States Supreme Court had ruled in the landmark *Lau v. Nichols* case that the San Francisco Unified School District had failed to provide necessary assistance to nearly 2,000 Chinese American students who did not speak English. The district was ordered to implement "appropriate relief," subject to approval by the court. This precedent-setting case established bilingual education in public schools for students who speak limited or no English.[12]

In 1976 the school district of which Brightwood was a part was cited by the Department of Health, Education and Welfare's Office of Civil Rights for having an inadequate English-as-a-second language (ESL) program. The department ruled that affirmative steps should be taken to correct the language deficiency of many minority children, in order to give them equal educational opportunity. The district complied the following year with a Spanish bilingual program in elementary and secondary schools and planned to phase in a Chinese bilingual program in 1978.

The proposal divided the Brightwood School—which was 70 percent Asian at the time—along English- and non-English-speaking lines. The plan called for all students from kindergarten to third grade to be taught in Chinese *and* English. Opposition to the program was led by American-born parents of Japanese and Chinese ancestry who were fearful that implementation would impede their children's educational progress in the future. Some threatened to take their children out of Brightwood and place them in private schools, or move them out of the district entirely. Supporters of the plan, mostly immigrant parents, welcomed bilingual education because they believed it would help their children maintain their native language and provide them with emotional and psychological support and the acceptance they needed within a new environment. A small third group of more moderate parents supported bilingual education but wanted the district to consider a "transitional" program that would instruct children in their native language but at the same time teach them enough English to allow their eventual transfer to a regular classroom.

During meetings to discuss the plan, the debate became intense. "Let them talk English," cried out one angry mother. "Why don't they leave the whole damn school as it is?"[13] Eventually, even supporters of the program asked the school board to delay implementation until the district could provide parents with more information and options. The delay was granted, and the bilingual program at Brightwood School did not start until early the following year. The result of months of meetings by the Brightwood Bilingual Committee turned out to be a much weaker variation of the original plan. Only one second grade class offered Chinese bilingual instruction; other Chinese students were taught English by "traveling teachers" at the parents' request.

Asian Markets

The prominence of Chinese-owned and -operated businesses in town became an even greater source of resentment. Non-Asians in Monterey Park commonly complain that Chinese merchants quickly replaced many established businesses and catered almost exclusively to an Asian and Chinese-speaking clientele. The best examples are food stores and eateries. Chinese have taken over all but two of the town's major chain supermarkets. Bok choy is more common than lettuce in produce departments, and dim sum and tea more readily available than a hamburger and coffee in the restaurants.

The first Asian grocery in Monterey Park was opened in 1978 by Wu Jin Shen, a former stockbroker from Taiwan. Wu's Diho Market proved to be an immediate success because the owner hired workers who spoke both Cantonese and Mandarin, and sold such popular items as preserved eggs and Taiwan's leading brand of cigarettes. Wu built the Diho Market into a chain of stores with 400 employees and $30 million in sales.[14] Likewise, the Hong Kong Supermarket and the Ai Hoa, started in Monterey Park, were so successful that today they operate satellite stores throughout the San Gabriel Valley.

In Monterey Park there are now half a dozen large Asian supermarkets and about a dozen medium-sized stores. Their proprietors also lease out small spaces to immigrant entrepreneurs who offer videos, newspapers, baked goods, tea, ginseng, and herbs. Together, these enterprises attract Chinese and other Asian residents in large numbers to shop for the kinds of groceries unavailable or overpriced in "American" chain stores: fifty-pound sacks of rice, "exotic" fruits and vegetables, pig parts (arranged in piles of ears, snouts, feet, tails, and innards, as well as buckets of fresh pork blood), live fish, black-skinned pigeon, and imported canned products used in Chinese, Vietnamese, Indonesian, Thai, Philippine, and Japanese menus. In these markets, Chinese is the dominant language of commerce, and much of the merchandise is unfamiliar to non-Asian shoppers.

Growth and Resentment

For many residents, the redevelopment and replacement of businesses in the Garvey-Garfield district, along Atlantic Boulevard, and throughout other areas in the city seemed sudden and dramatic. In January 1979, under the headline "Monterey Park Is Due for Big Facelift," the *Monterey Park Progress* reported that a northern portion of Atlantic Boulevard was set to "be transformed so it's unrecognizable." Construction there was to include the completion of a shopping center, office, and theater complex developed by the Kowin Development Company; groundbreaking for a new office building at the northeast corner of Atlantic and Newmark Avenue; and a hillside condominium project on the west side of Atlantic Boulevard. The article went on to state with great anticipation that "a large international concern" planned to "locate its international service center in Monterey Park," that substantial construction in anticipation of new tenants was to be done at McCaslin Industrial Park in the eastern section of town, and that several street and park improvement projects were in the works. In addition, a major city-sponsored Community Redevelopment Agency (CRA) project would erect a new civic center complex and make necessary improvements on a senior center, a school cafetorium, a community center, and the municipal library.[15]

Between the influx of new Chinese immigrants, the infusion of large amounts of capital, the rapid introduction of Chinese-owned and -operated businesses, and the disruptions caused by construction crews tearing up the city and starting new projects, rumblings of discontent among long-time established residents became quite audible.

"I Don't Feel at Home Anymore!"

At first the new Chinese-owned businesses seemed novel, innocuous, even humorous. "The gag was that if it wasn't a bank, it was going to be a real estate office, or another Chinese restaurant," says Lloyd de Llamas.[16] But as these and other Chinese businesses proliferated rapidly from 1978 on—taking over previously established merchants, displaying large Chinese-language signs, and seeming to cater only to a Chinese-speaking clientele—residents became increasingly hostile.

The famous Laura Scudder potato chip factory, converted into a Safeway store in the 1960s, became a bustling Chinese supermarket. Frederic Hsieh bought the Edwards Theater and began showing Chinese-language movies; when people complained he added such English-language films as *Gone with the Wind*, *Doctor Zhivago*, and *Ryan's Daughter* to the afternoon repertoire. Even the locally revered Garvey Hardware Store was sold to new Chinese owners who divided the premises into mini-shops, relegating the much-reduced hardware department to the back of the building. Kretz Motorcycle, Paris' Restaurant, and the Midtown Pharmacy were similarly redeveloped, engendering resentment among many residents, particularly older whites.

For "old-timers" the loss of a familiar business could be akin to the loss of an old friend. "Just a few years before they sold Paris' Restaurant I walked in there for lunch alone," remembers Ed Rodman, "and . . . there wasn't a single person in there that I knew by name! That describes the changes in Monterey Park." [17]

Such losses were compounded when many long-time residents felt they were not welcomed by new businesses because they were not Chinese. Avanelle Fiebelkorn, wife of Harold Fiebelkorn, told the *Los Angeles Times*: "I go to the market and over 65 percent of the people there are Chinese. I feel like I'm in another country. I don't feel at home anymore." Emma Fry, wife of Howard Fry, agreed: "I feel like a stranger in my own town. You can't talk to the newcomers because many of them don't speak English, and their experiences and viewpoints are so different. I don't feel like I belong anymore. I feel like I'm sort of intruding." [18]

Joseph Graves particularly remembers an incident that occurred in the late 1970s when he was a member of the Monterey Park Chamber of Commerce. A group of visiting dignitaries from Taiwan asked the chamber whether a statue of Confucius could be built in one of the parks to remind young Chinese to respect and honor his teachings. Graves had no objection but told them that "the people coming over here ought to be building Statues of Liberty all over town." Graves, who was born in Monterey Park the year the city was incorporated, continues to live there and says he harbors no resentment toward the Chinese. "I ride my bike everywhere and I see all these Chinese people out there taking their walks. They are so warm and friendly. How can you end up with anger? And yet, [if] I look at something they're doing that forces me to change, then I can be temporarily angry. I reserve the right to be temporarily angry as long as I don't nurse grievances." [19]

Others, however, *have* nursed grievances, and white flight has been the most obvious reaction to the changes in the community. While the Asian population in Monterey Park has grown and the Latino population has remained relatively stable, the white population has plummeted. In 1960 the 32,306 white residents made up 85 percent of the population; by 1990 the number of whites had dropped to 16,245, or just 12 percent. When former Monterey Park resident Frank Rizzo moved out, he cited the large condominium complexes on either side of his house and the people in them as reasons he could no longer stay. Prior to the influx of Chinese, Rizzo said, his neighborhood had been a quiet and friendly block of mostly single-family homes with expansive yards. But his new neighbors lived in large extended families in cramped quarters, spoke little English, and seemed unwilling to give up their traditions and settle into an American way of life. Rizzo, who sold his home to a Chinese developer, was emphatic about leaving Monterey Park: "What I might do is hang a little American flag on my truck and drive through town on my way out and wave goodbye to all my old friends. . . . I'm moving far away from here."[20]

Latinos in Monterey Park too were concerned that they were losing the integrated community they thought they'd moved into. David Barron has lived in the city since 1964 and raised his family there. Previously, he attended nearby East Los Angeles Community College and California State University, Los Angeles. He still remembers when Monterey Park was referred to as the "Mexican Beverly Hills." Fluent in Spanish and proud of his heritage, Barron thought he had found the ideal integrated community. He is still involved in many of the city's social and civic activities and has no immediate plans to move, but he misses the diversity he initially found in the town. "I would like to see a balance maintained," he explains. "I cannot live in a mono-ethnic community. I wouldn't want to live in an all-Hispanic . . . or all-Chinese . . . or all-white community. I want to live in a mixed community."[21]

Similar sentiments were expressed by Fernando Zabala, a hair stylist who grew up in East Los Angeles and also found Monterey Park a stepping-stone out of the barrio. "It was very important that my children grow up in a racially diverse community," Zambala said. "When we moved to Monterey Park, we had a little bit of everybody: whites, blacks, Latinos, and some Chinese and Japanese. But we lost that mix. In my neighborhood alone, it went from twenty-five Latino families to three."[22] Unlike Barron, Zabala sold his house and moved out.

One woman, who asked not to be identified, said that she was one of the first Mexican Americans to move into a new hillside housing tract in Monterey Park in the late 1950s and that she had worked very hard to integrate into the community. Like many whites, she expressed anxiety about the rapid change in the commercial areas in town: "It wasn't like one business changing at a time, it was like two or three at a time. When they put in the Diho [supermarket], that right away changed the appearance of Atlantic Boulevard." She recalled with particular sadness a Mexican restaurant she and her mother used to frequent. This small restaurant, greatly appreciated for its home-style cooking and family atmosphere, was forced to close when new owners bought the property. "The owner was very upset, and she put [up] a big sign . . . 'I'm not leaving my friends because I want to, but the mall has been bought and my rent has been raised and I cannot afford it.' Things like that you would get upset about."[23]

Like the Latinos who had settled in Monterey Park, long-time Asian American residents had lived their entire lives believing in the "American Dream" that proclaimed just rewards for hard work and initiative. It was an affront to their sensibilities to see so many newcomers acquire the fruits of a material society seemingly without having to struggle. The newcomer Chinese were simply not playing by the rules of assimilation: they bought property, started businesses and banks, and built shopping malls as soon as they arrived—and many of them didn't even speak English! John Yee—whose great-great-grandfather had come to California during the gold rush, whose great-grandfather died building the transcontinental railroad, and whose grandfather and father owned a Chinese laundry business that served steel factory workers in Midland, Pennsylvania—is particularly articulate in this regard. "When I first came to L.A., I lived in China-town, went into the service, came out, worked in a lot of jobs, and step by step I moved to Monterey Park. It took how many years? Thirty, forty years? It seems like these immigrants . . . want to live in Mon-terey Park as soon as they get off the boat. Not the boat, now they come by airplane. Give them another forty years, they'll be in Beverly Hills. I won't ever get to that point. . . . Maybe I'm jealous like every-body else."[24]

The resentment of the older Latinos and Asian Americans who had experienced racial segregation and witnessed the civil rights struggles of the 1960s also stemmed from a feeling that Monterey Park's new Chinese immigrants were taking for granted the equality won by the struggles of others. Yee says: "I don't mind the people too much, don't get me wrong; I am of Chinese descent. But the thing is, you get these people with this attitude. . . . they think [everything] was like this all the time. It wasn't. I hear people say, 'China got strong and now the United States and the rest of the world has more respect for us.' Maybe so, but . . . if it wasn't for some of these guys [people of color born in the United States] who squawked about it, went into the service, these changes wouldn't happen. You got the blacks and Mexicans, they all helped change the government. . . . That attitude [among new Chinese immigrants] just burns me up."[25]

Particularly for Asian Americans born in the United States, the ap-pearance of Chinese immigrants raised questions about their assumed assimilation and acceptance into American society. "When there were just Japanese people in Monterey Park, it was no problem because we were just like them [whites]," explains long-time resident Kei Higashi. "But now all of a sudden [with the arrival of the new immigrant Chi-nese] when we walk into a place and start talking perfect English, they [non-Asians] look at us like we're some foreign creature," he laughs. "That's what happened in Monterey Park."[26]

In the middle of all this are many of the Chinese immigrant profes-sionals, who found themselves lumped together with the development-

and business-oriented newcomers. Many express appreciation for the large Chinese population that makes them feel welcome, but at the same time, they say, had they wanted to live in a crowded, exclusively Chinese environment, they never would have left home. This is the case for Dr. Frances Wu, who moved to Monterey Park in 1971, after she was accepted in the doctoral program at the University of Southern California. Born and educated in China, Wu lived in Taiwan for four years following the Communist takeover; in 1953 she went to Canada to earn a master's degree from McGill University, then spent fifteen years in New York working in the Child Welfare Department.

When Wu came to southern California, she changed her social work specialty to gerontology, and shortly after earning her Ph.D. she started the Golden Age Village, a retirement center located in Monterey Park. Although the project is open to all elderly people who qualify, Wu told the *Monterey Park Progress*, "My motivation was to develop a social program for elderly Chinese and we selected Monterey Park because of its growing Chinese population," as well as its uncongested, small-town atmosphere.[27] The overall design of the Golden Age Village is obviously Asian, with its curved roofs and a courtyard that features a babbling brook surrounded by a decorative Oriental-style garden. The majority of residents are retired Chinese, many of whom speak little or no English, and the communal food garden grows bok choy and Chinese parsley among other vegetables. But the serene environment that Wu found in Monterey Park and recreated at the Golden Age Village is threatened by what she considers too much growth too fast. "I would rather keep this community a bedroom community," she says. "For retired people, we like a quiet environment. . . . People describe Monterey Park as 'Little Taipei,' but Taipei is horrible. I don't want Monterey Park to be like that."[28]

The Specter of Gangs

As immigration continued and urban problems related to increased congestion began to emerge in Monterey Park, the fear that Chinese gangs and organized crime were infiltrating the city made for dramatic headlines. In July 1980 the Monterey Park Police Department reported that criminal activities had increased 21 percent during the first six months of that year. Especially alarming was the sharp rise in major offenses: burglary, robbery, grand theft, assault. The number of reported residential burglaries, typically the most common urban crime, jumped from 348 in the equivalent period of 1979 to 445 in 1980—a 28 percent increase. Robberies were also up to 51 from 40 the previous year, and grand theft (involving amounts over $200) to 129 from 95. The incidence of assault took the biggest jump, a 58 percent increase from 60 to 95 cases.[29]

Trying to downplay the figures, Police Chief Jon Elder noted that crime statistics for the first half of the year are often misleading because they include the traditionally high crime activity that occurs during the Christmas season: "It's my educated guess that when the year is over, we won't show a 21 percent crime increase." Elder also cited the nation's sluggish economy and rising unemployment rate as prime reasons for the increase. "Crime is up in the county, the state, and across the nation and I still feel Monterey Park has a good overall atmosphere," he asserted confidently. "We're not experiencing any great crime wave, and there's really nothing to get alarmed about."[30]

Despite his reassurances, three months later the Monterey Park Police Department reactivated its Asian Detail, which the *Progress* reported in a lead paragraph as "an effort to halt burgeoning Chinese gang activity in the community." The police said that the Wah Ching and the Joe Fong Boys were the two gangs "preying" on the city, "focusing primarily on extortion, but also engaging in robbery, fraud and drive-by shootings."[31] Although there were no reports of extortion leading to violence, one Monterey Park restaurant employee was seriously wounded during a June 1980 robbery attempt allegedly staged by gangs. Police expressed fears of a repeat of the "San Francisco Massacre"—when three masked gunmen entered the Golden Dragon Restaurant and killed five innocent people during a gang-related shootout in 1977—as a major reason for their renewed vigilance.

Detective Jones Moy and Officer Tony Jiron headed the Asian Detail; along with four overtime police officers, they patrolled the streets each evening. Jiron said that gangs were "testing the waters" in Monterey Park and waiting to see how the police responded to their presence. "The potential for a big problem certainly exist[s] but gangs do not have a foothold in this area and as long as we keep on top of them they won't gain any foothold."[32]

On November 5, 1980, a *Progress* headline read, "Chinese Gang Activities: MP Police Claim Success." The story reported that crime was down in Monterey Park and that the Asian Detail was working to educate the Chinese merchants to report any incidents of gang activity. One Chinese resident wrote a letter to the editor complaining that the newspaper sensationalized the presence of Chinese gangs and spread undue fear throughout the entire community. "Ethnic emphasis or discrimination in a multiple racial community like ours would usually increase friction and hostility between people of different ethnic backgrounds and could even incite misinformation," wrote Helen Wu. "I feel sure all peace-loving people, regardless of ethnic differences, would agree with me that the name-calling headline, 'Chinese gang activities,' on the front page of the . . . *Monterey Park Progress* was offensively misleading and uncalled for."[33]

The specter of gang activity in previously peaceful and quiet Monterey Park was nevertheless disconcerting and—coupled with allegations of money-laundering through Monterey Park banks—did cast a shadow on the reputation of all immigrant Chinese in the community.

Backlash

More than anything else, it seemed, the change that long-time Monterey Park residents resented most was the unsettling presence of an unfamiliar language. Today, anyone who walks through the city's two main commercial streets, Atlantic Boulevard and Garvey Avenue, will find the Chinese language everywhere. Business signs display Chinese characters, Chinese is spoken in the streets, and Chinese music is piped through public address systems in many businesses. Manifestations of the animosity aroused by such prominent display of Chinese language and culture can be traced back to the early 1980s.

Vandalism and Harassment

The hostility over language in Monterey Park was easily the most volatile and divisive issue the rapidly changing community had to face. Intense feelings exploded shortly after the *Monterey Park Progress*, under its new ownership, announced in September 1980 that it was about to begin printing Chinese-language pages as a regular feature. Vandals splattered paint on the marquee and smashed windows in Frederic Hsieh's movie theater and other Chinese-language theaters in the area. The *Progress* and its sister newspaper, the *Alhambra Post-Advocate*, were also victims of vandalism and hate mail. One letter, flourishing unproven statistics, derogatory language, and outright threats, was signed by the Alhambra Ku Klux Klan:

> American freedom is being violated. We can't even see American movies in our own city. The problem originates from the boat people. All those damn chinks. . . . Three-fourths of Monterey Park population aren't even American citizens and are here on visas. To top that off, Monterey Park has the second highest Oriental population in America. . . . It is unjust to print an American paper in chink language. . . . There will be trouble with your paper if you continue to kiss their asses. . . . KKK Alhambra aims to kick the ass not kiss ass. So if you continue [to] roll out the

Chinese RED carpet, do so at your own risk. The worst is yet
to come.[34]

Early the following year, a fire gutted the offices of the *Monterey Park
Progress* and destroyed the press used to print the Chinese-language
section of both papers. Though the police later determined that the
fire was started accidentally by some teenagers playing with matches
behind the building, a chill swept through the Chinese community at
what they perceived to be an anti-Chinese backlash.

Chinese immigrant children entering the schools in Monterey
Park and surrounding areas quickly became targets of harassment
and playground pranks. "I remember my daughter sharing with me
all the plights she went through," says Loretta Huang. "White boys
were tripping her on the school bus, they were hitting her with throw-
away paper, pouring chocolate milk over her hair." Huang, a former
English instructor and university administrator in Taiwan, arrived in
this country in 1979 with two young children and no job. Her husband,
a history professor, stayed in Taiwan and visits his transplanted family
about four times a year. Wanting the best possible opportunities for
their children, the Huangs had jointly decided that emigrating to the
United States would be the best thing for them. As a working single
parent, however, Loretta Huang has found life very difficult. "It is not
true that all Asians come to the United States with suitcases . . . full
of cash. I came here with very limited resources. Many of us were in
education and public service; I was not in business." She adds emphatically: "We had to re-establish ourselves. I remember we did not have
furniture for at least five years. It was not easy." Incidents of vandalism
added to the Huangs' difficulties. "I remember our car was vandal-
ized by kids," Huang said. "The hubcaps were taken and damaged
and bent." And one winter some children threw a rock through the
family's front window during a rainstorm. They didn't have the money
to fix the damage right away, so they just lived with it for two weeks.[35]

As an ESL teacher and a counselor in the Alhambra School District (one of four districts involving Monterey Park schools), Huang
also saw firsthand the hostility toward other Asian immigrants. In fact,
problems there became so great that in 1981 a group of citizens decided to confront the issue head on. Mancha Kurilich, a school board
member and Monterey Park resident, and Bill Gay, juvenile division
officer for the police department, created the Human Services Task
Force, whose first action was to sponsor a "Youth Values Day Workshop" for a group of sixty Latino, Asian, and white sixth and seventh
graders from the Alhambra and Garvey school districts. "I feel there
are problems all over the community," Kurilich told the *Monterey Park*

Progress in August 1981. "There's an undercurrent of hostility toward ethnic groups. I think it's all underground, and nobody really likes to talk about it."[36] The purpose of the workshop was to get young students to identify with their own cultural backgrounds and values, and then help them relate to those with different cultural backgrounds.

The "Chinese Driver" Stereotype

As soon as they arrived, the Chinese became the butt of jokes about their allegedly erratic driving behavior. Most people attributed this recklessness to ignorance of U.S. rules of the road and to the overly aggressive driving assumed customary in their home countries. But for some in Monterey Park, unskilled driving quickly became generalized as a Chinese cultural deficiency.

"The Chinese people gave us gunpowder, the modern calendar and noodles, giving evidence of their genius as a people," began a July 29, 1981, letter to editor of the *Progress* from resident Steve E. Yusi. "So why can't they drive a car?" Claiming that his observations had reinforced what he first thought a joke, and playing upon local animosity toward rich Chinese immigrants, Yusi continued: "I've seen Mercedes 450 SL's make U-turns on Atlantic Boulevard at 5:30 P.M., Rolls Royces drive up Crest Vista on the wrong side of the street, and Porsches turn left on red lights from the right lane."[37]

The following week the *Progress* ran several responses to Yusi's letter. "How do they get their driver's license in the first place?" asked one. "My life is worth more than all the money they can make." But Norman Lieberman, a former editor of the *Progress* who later went to law school and then became Monterey Park's city attorney, saw Yusi's "somewhat humorous complaint" as "a contribution toward racial bigotry." A young Chinese student too accused Yusi of racial stereotyping and pointed out that "crazy drivers" were not exclusively Chinese.[38] Dissenters apparently were in the minority, however, as denigrating catchphrases became widespread. In addition to "the Chinese Beverly Hills," "the First Suburban Chinatown," and "Little Taipei," Monterey Park became known as "the Traffic Collision Capital of the World," and Atlantic Boulevard was dubbed "Suicide Boulevard." Bumper stickers appeared reading "I Survived the Drive through Monterey Park," and the joke circulated that it should be against the law to be caught "D.W.C." (Driving While Chinese).

In fact, neither the California Department of Motor Vehicles nor the Monterey Park Police Department keeps any records on the ethnicity of drivers involved in traffic accidents, so in the absence of supporting or opposing data, the image persisted.[39] A more likely reason for the proliferation of accidents is Monterey Park's location in what has been called the "Golden Corridor," with easy access to three major freeways: the Santa Monica–San Bernardino (10), the Los Angeles–Pomona (60), and the Long Beach (710). During rush hours, many commuters began to leave the freeways and drive through Monterey Park to beat stalled traffic; weekend traffic in the city, with Asian shoppers arriving from out of town, was soon equally congested. As increased congestion caused an increase in accidents, the increasing numbers of new Chinese immigrants became easy targets for blame. In response to residents' complaints, city officials established traffic safety programs to help newcomers and seniors improve their driving skills. Because few residents saw themselves in need of remediation, however, attendance was so low that the classes were eventually discontinued.

If contention over driving ability seems trivial, its persistence nevertheless reflects broader social and cultural dislocations. It is difficult for an outsider to appreciate the whirlwind of emotions experienced by Monterey Park residents who saw so many changes in their community in just the six years from 1976 to 1982. Long-established residents, even those who recognized that the coherence of a homogeneous small town could not be restored, were resentful when their past and their plans for the future were pushed aside in the dramatic restructuring taking place in the city. The result was controversy and political conflict extending into the present.

CHAPTER 4

Community Fragmentation and the Slow-Growth Movement

B y the 1970s the population of Monterey Park was increasing so rapidly that its traditional tight-knit economic, social, cultural, and political structure could no longer be maintained. The dilution of the core community actually started several years before the influx of Chinese immigrants reached its peak. For many years community life had focused on the older northern residential and central Garvey-Garfield business sections of town, slighting or ignoring areas on the outskirts. Alice Ballesteros, who grew up and still lives in the southernmost, largely Latino section, notes that, "for a long time, the south end did not have the strong identity that the north end or middle section did. . . . I've tried real hard to keep people focused and not let them forget the south end. South end people tend to be seen as stepchildren."[1]

By 1980 the impact of the Chinese influx was clear, and before long a slow-growth movement emerged in Monterey Park. Antagonism toward Chinese immigrants played a part, but a genuine concern over the tremendous sudden development throughout the city and a sweeping anti-establishment attitude also fueled the movement.

This chapter describes the crumbling of community cohesion that occurred throughout the 1970s, traces the emergence of one organized growth-control group, and examines the bitter 1982 city council election that proved to be a key battle between slow-growth and pro-growth interests.

First Signs of Fragmentation

Community breakdown became apparent during three controversial citywide elections in the 1970s: the voters' failure to pass a school unification measure in 1974, to the surprise of many established leaders in town; the 1976 city council election in which, for the first time, two nonestablishment candidates were voted into office; and the 1978 city council election, dominated by a strong anti-government sentiment.

The School Unification Vote of 1974

In 1974 Monterey Park had, and still has, parts of four separate school districts within its city limits—Alhambra, Montebello, Garvey, and Los Angeles—each of which includes schools in other cities. For over twenty years community leaders had been trying to unify the city's schools and establish Monterey Park's own high school. Many argued that the separation of Monterey Park schoolchildren was hurting the community as a whole. "If we were to achieve a high level of community identity, it was essential that we have our own unified school district," explains proponent Eli Isenberg, "so kids who started out [together] in kindergarten and elementary would wind up together in junior high and high school." [2]

Winning the election would be difficult because the surrounding communities affected would have to vote on the issue as well. If passed, the measure would have established three new unified school districts in Monterey Park, Alhambra, and San Gabriel; Montebello would have lost its Monterey Park schools, the Garvey School District would have ceased to exist. But advocates for unification were confident that overwhelming support among residents throughout Monterey Park would cancel out any opposition elsewhere.

As the campaign progressed, however, it became apparent that unity could not be taken for granted. Residents from the southern portion of Monterey Park, where students attended schools in the Montebello district, created the most dissension. A group calling itself "the Committee on Economy in Education" forcefully challenged the proposal in a pamphlet opposing unification: "Don't clown around with unification. Don't let unification make education a three ring circus. Don't let unification make you and your child a clown." [3] Specifically, the committee attacked the assertions of the plan's proponents and the *Monterey Park Progress* that unification would not increase taxes to residents, and might even wind up costing them less: "Mark Keppel [the high school located at the northern end of Monterey Park] is undergoing renovation at a cost of $900,000 for phase one and approximately $300,000 for phase two, which will rest upon Monterey Park residents to pay for if unification passes. . . . The only way I know of this project not costing additional monies to residents is if the *Progress* would pay for it." [4]

Proponents promised that unification would ensure that the money spent per child in the new Monterey Park School District would be roughly equivalent to what was already being spent by the other districts. But a member of the Committee on Economy in Education Irv Gilman, cited figures presented by Richard Wales of the County Committee on School Organization: "Under unification, the San Gabriel District's revenue limit per child will be $1,008.63. Alhambra's will be $996.39 and the new Monterey Park School District's will be $956.88." He added that the new Monterey Park district would spend $102 less per child than Montebello, where his two children attended school, was then spending: "I, for one, do not like a mixture of fact and fiction, especially in an 'unbiased' newspaper. I feel I can make up my own mind on any issue, but it does require truth."[5] Gilman later took to campaigning in a clown suit while carrying a sign reading "Don't Clown Around With Our Kids' Education."

Eli Isenberg defended unification and denounced the opposition as bureaucratic school district chiefs who would lose part of their territory should the measure pass. "The question before voters is who shall run our schools: citizens of Bell Gardens or Alhambra, or men and women of Monterey Park? As for 'economy in education,' who do you trust to get you 100 cents out of your tax dollar: Alhambra, Garvey, Bell Gardens?"[6]

In angry response, Gilman shot back a letter titled "The Clowns' Rebuttal."

> All the miracles and benefits for Monterey Park through unification are merely what you see in your dreams. Your dream may very well become my nightmare! . . . What if it takes 3 to 5 years to establish a good school district rather than overnight as you assume? How will my children's education be enhanced during the transition period? . . . [If] education in Monterey Park [becomes] a three-ring circus of disorganization, disharmony, and disunity with overcrowded, under-staffed, ill-equipped facilities . . . then we and our children will indeed become clowns—sad-faced clowns.[7]

On November 5, 1974, school unification went down to defeat: Proposition G lost by 23,780 votes to 19,101. As expected, cities outside of Monterey Park voted against the measure, but to the surprise of its advocates Proposition G also lost in Monterey Park, 5,771 to 5,696. City voters whose children attended Montebello schools opposed it by 812 votes, residents in Monterey Highlands and Monterey Hills by 347 votes. Affluent residents in the hills did not want to take their children out of Alhambra High School, one of the best in the area. It was particularly disturbing that of the 14,675 residents who cast ballots in the statewide election also held that day, only 11,467 voted on Proposition G: that is, 3,208 Monterey Park voters apparently didn't care one way or the other.[8]

According to Kenny Gribble, chair of the Monterey Park Unification Committee, the dispute over how unification would affect taxes was a key issue. "We couldn't combat the misleading statements about taxes," he told the *Progress*. "Maybe we should have lied about it like the opposition did." Gribble went on to allege that the opponents who made taxes the focus of their campaign had no interest in running their own schools and were opposed to anything that had the possibility of a tax increase.[9]

The *Monterey Park Progress*, which had strongly supported unification, bemoaned the loss. In a subsequent editorial the paper quoted what Adlai Stevenson said after he lost his presidential bid against Dwight Eisenhower: "It hurts to smile and I am too big to cry." Maintaining a stiff upper lip, the *Progress* vowed to continue the fight for school unification: "We have lost a battle. It remains to be seen whether we lost the war."[10]

The City Election of 1976

The fate of Proposition G was the first dramatic indicator that the social fabric of Monterey Park was beginning to unravel. Even greater disintegration became visible during a hotly contested council election two years later. On March 9, 1976, two council seats were up for grabs as well as the positions of city treasurer and city clerk. In addition, two fiercely debated propositions were on the ballot: Proposition A called for restoring the city-run ambulance service; Proposition B called for making the offices of city treasurer and city clerk appointive rather than elective.

Elected to the city council for the first time in decades were two candidates not supported by the establishment. Louise Davis was only the second woman council member, and G. Monty Manibog was a Filipino American attorney who had made two previous unsuccessful attempts. The big loser was Harold Fiebelkorn, long-time merchant in Monterey Park, former president of the Lions Club and the chamber of commerce, former planning commissioner, and well-known writer of the weekly "Kaffee Klatch" column in the *Monterey Park Progress*. He had been a clear favorite to win a council seat because he was very much a part of the establishment that had elected city council members for the previous twenty years.

The established leaders in the community had even encouraged Judy Winchell, former president of the chamber of commerce and wife of a prominent physician in town, to run a last-minute campaign for city council. Few believed that Winchell had a chance of winning but hoped that by dividing the women's vote her candidacy would ensure the defeat of Louise Davis. Davis was considered an agitator because she was running a strong grassroots campaign calling for broader representation and community involvement in city government. She contended that the city council had been run by an arrogant "ruling elite" that for many years had handpicked council candidates and worked for their election. This group, Davis argued, "hurt the community" by trying to maintain its hold on power.[11]

A resident since 1956, Davis was a housewife with seven children and an active community volunteer. Beginning with the PTA, she had become involved with the Monterey Park Welcome Wagon and the March of Dimes; she had served as a Community Relations commissioner, two-term president of the Sister City Association, and chair of the city's Bicentennial Celebration. In 1974 she was Monterey Park's Woman of the Year, and in 1975 she was chosen Citizen of the Year by the local Rotary Club. Tough, opinionated, hardworking, and independent, the then fifty-one-year-old Davis was a firm supporter of the city-run ambulance service that the city council had recently dropped in favor of a private ambulance service. She also strongly supported keeping the city treasurer's and city clerk's positions elective offices, much to the displeasure of the current council members who wanted to make the positions appointed posts. Though Davis was not part of the establishment and held some views antithetical to those of the *Monterey Park Progress*, her unselfish commitment to the community earned her the newspaper's endorsement. The *Progress* also endorsed Fiebelkorn.

During the course of the campaign, dissension within the establishment caused their election plans to go awry. The central disagreement dated back to the debate about the Atlantic Square development in the 1950s: should Monterey Park retain its small-town flavor, or should it develop and grow to meet the needs of an expanding population? There were also elements in the establishment that resented Fiebelkorn's personal popularity and his independent thinking. Despite his later call (in 1978) for a moratorium on multiple-unit housing developments, as the owner of a furniture store he was very much in favor of expansion and modernization in the city's business district—a position that put him at odds with many long-time residents. According to Eli Isenberg's after-election analysis, Fiebelkorn was "victimized by old 'friends.' . . . The establishment split its forces with one group working to elect Judy Winchell. If everybody who worked on Judy's and Fiebelkorn's campaign had worked only for Harold—and Judy was not a candidate—Fiebelkorn would have won by 10 lengths."[12]

As it was, he lost to two untested candidates. Monty Manibog garnered the highest total with 2,789 votes, followed by Davis with 2,471 and Fiebelkorn with 2,227; Winchell finished fifth with only 1,711 votes.[13] Interestingly, Proposition A, which would have restored the city ambulance service with trained fire department paramedics and was supported by both Manibog and Davis, lost by a wide margin. But Proposition B, which called for the city treasurer and city clerk to be appointed positions and was supported by the city council, also lost overwhelmingly.

After the election Manibog, with his pro-development philosophy, was admitted to the city council fraternity, but Davis—a constant critic—remained an outsider and was outvoted four to one on a variety of issues. "I was really out of my element up there with four men who didn't particularly like me," Davis remembers. "In the beginning some people thought it was kind of funny. It was a joke."[14] That she was not considered a colleague by the other council members can be seen in the fact she did not become mayor during her first term in office. At that time the council selected the mayor from its members, and as a matter of courtesy each member usually served a nine-month mayoral term sometime during his or her four-year council tenure, but not until the beginning of her second term, in 1981, was Davis selected—and then only because Matthew Martinez voted in her favor for the first time just before he left city office to become a state assemblyman. Despite her antagonistic relationship with other council members, Davis did gradually earn the respect of the city staff. Lloyd de Llamas, then city manager, told her she was the toughest person he had ever worked for—a comment Davis accepts as a compliment.

Soon after the contentious 1976 election, Monterey Park underwent tremendous change. Most dramatic, of course, was the demographic, economic, social, and cultural impact of the rapid influx of Chinese immigrants. Further, recognizing the desperate need for increased sales tax revenue, the council and City Manager de Llamas moved boldly forward on several ambitious development projects intended to get the city out of its deep financial crisis. The fact that Chinese investment in Monterey Park took place at the same time as the city's plans to proceed with major redevelopment projects appears to have been more coincidental than planned, at least initially. Indeed, the rejection of the Chinatown theme in early 1978 reveals the competition over who would do the most commercial development, who would do it first, and who would profit from it most. It also shows the ongoing struggle among merchants over whether Monterey Park should maintain its old-town flavor or change with the times. All that most individuals saw, however, was their city being torn apart and haphazardly built up.

Mistrust in Government

The first citywide political reaction took place when the seemingly ordinary March 7, 1978, city council election set off a chain reaction that would shortly catapult Monterey Park to national and international attention. Harry Couch, then a relatively unknown thirty-five-year-old electrical contractor, ran a seemingly impossible campaign against three strong pro-development incumbents: Matthew Martinez, George Ige, and George Westphaln. Couch's candidacy was considered a long shot. For one thing, having moved to the city from Arizona in 1971, he was still considered a newcomer. For another, Couch was an active Republican in a predominantly Democratic community. He had run for Congress in 1976 as Republican challenger to the incumbent Democrat, George Danielson—and lost badly.

In his 1978 city council campaign, Couch's main rallying cry was that the city's pro-growth policies forced extra tax burdens on homeowners and were inconsistent with the wishes of the residents. The primary controversy at the time was the council's decision to build a new civic center and proceed with major improvement projects for local parks, schools, and a senior citizens' center. Planning for a population between 65,000 and 80,000 over the next twenty years, city officials said that the City Hall built in the 1940s was too old and too small to meet the needs of a growing community, and other facilities were in desperate need of renovation. To fund these projects, the city created a Community Redevelopment Agency (CRA) in 1977 and sold $14 million in bonds. A portion of the money went immediately toward city improvement, and another portion was allocated for a complicated CRA land purchasing plan: the process would freeze the assessed valuation of undeveloped land; revenue for the CRA would derive from the difference between the lower and the higher valuations once the properties were developed. Officials insisted that any increased tax burden would fall on new residents attracted to the city and not on established residents.[15]

Couch openly opposed the CRA plan, citing city figures that projected a loss in tax revenue of $106,000 in the 1978–79 fiscal year, $232,000 in 1979–80, and $284,000 in 1980–81; the shortfall would have to be paid by all residents, he said. Couch also believed that the expense of the civic center—$7.5 million for construction, furnishing, and equipment upgrading—should not have been approved without a vote of the people.[16] He called for a reduction in the city tax rate of at least five cents a year for a minimum of four years. As treasurer of the Monterey Park Taxpayers Association, a local group advocating the passage of Proposition 13—a sweeping California initiative calling for a two-thirds reduction in property taxes—Couch found himself a niche in these popular issues.

A strong supporter of Harry Couch during this time was Irv Gilman, president of the Monterey Park Taxpayers Association. Gilman's stinging letters to the *Progress*, attacking government and politicians while promoting Proposition 13, became regular fare for readers. One letter poked fun at the city's alleged need to purchase an electronic tally board for registering the five council members' votes, to install "two elevators in a two-story building," and to provide a "200-seat council chamber . . . to accommodate all those people who never come to meetings anyway." Gilman could find "no thought on a local or any other level of government to spend less. However, we, the people, have one option. It's called Prop. 13, the Jarvis-Gann tax initiative. . . . Even though City Manager Lloyd de Llamas, Supervisor Ed Edelman, Assembly Speaker Leo McCarthy, Gov. Jerry Brown, Jr., and a host of others tell us that the sky will fall if it passes, I just don't believe them anymore." [17]

The linkage between growth, unresponsive government, and high taxes proved a successful issue for Couch and his supporters. Though he was not endorsed by the *Progress*, Couch squeaked into office, winning the last of three available seats on the Monterey Park City Council by a mere sixteen votes over two-term incumbent George Ige, a Japanese American who openly supported the civic center project and opposed Proposition 13.[18] Ige, who was not endorsed by the *Progress* because of the newspaper's philosophy that council members should serve no more than two terms, admitted that having expected an easy reelection, he had run a lackluster campaign.

Shortly after the election, Ige appeared before the city council to denounce Proposition 13 and ask the council to oppose it unanimously. Mayor Monty Manibog said that if Proposition 13 passed, $5 billion in tax relief would go to major corporate property owners and "won't benefit the people who really need relief the most—home owners and renters." Even Louise Davis agreed that the initiative would not help renters, because landlords would not lower rents. Only Harry Couch spoke in favor: "The Jarvis Amendment does help the home owner," he contradicted his colleagues. "It tells the home owner he is going to have his taxes cut. I don't think we should cut our own throats just because the big companies are going to benefit, too." Couch's plea went unheard, and the council voted four to one to oppose Proposition 13.[19]

But on June 6, 1978, Proposition 13 passed in the state of California by a two to one margin, and 61 percent of Monterey Park voters supported the measure, despite city officials' warnings of large cutbacks in services. Couch's surprise election victory and the over-whelming success of Proposition 13 fed into the ground swell of resi-dents' mistrust of government and gave community activists a sense of power and control over municipal events that became the impetus for organizing activities in years to come.

The Slow-Growth Movement

Population growth and building construction continued in a seem-ingly unabated fashion in 1979 and 1980. Plans submitted a few years earlier were coming into fruition, and groundbreaking ceremonies—particularly for multi-family housing and commercial properties—were common throughout in the city. It was within this environment that controlled-growth forces emerged.

Proposition A

At a raucous meeting on November 10, 1980, the Monterey Park City Council—despite the planning commission's recommendation to deny the request—voted to rezone a thirty-acre parcel of land on the slopes west of Atlantic Boulevard. The area had been approved as a site of eighty-four single-family homes, but with rezoning it became available for the construction of a 150-unit condominium project.

An overflow crowd filled the meeting room during this council session, and the testimony of fifty-three people continued into the wee hours of the morning. Proponents pointed out that the plan called for approximately 70 percent landscaped open space—far more than conventional single-family homes would permit; that 150 units at $150,000 to $200,000 would provide housing suitable for young adults with moderate incomes; and that the condominium project would work to reinforce the slopes against the mud slides and soil spillage that for years had plagued the unkept hillside area. Opponents ob-jected that the rezoning was a developer's scam and that the additional people brought to the city by the project would only put further stress on municipal services. Bruce Peppin, superintendent of the Alhambra Unified School District, added that the project would greatly burden the already crowded schools in the area.[20]

Recalling the events of that evening, Louise Davis is still amazed at the furor that one decision elicited. "The three of them [Matthew Martinez, George Westphaln, and Monty Manibog] voted for it, Harry Couch abstained, and I voted against it," she says. "Harry couldn't vote against it because he was involved in litigation with these people, so I was the only one to vote against. . . . And that's what started the revolution."[21] In Davis's mind, this event marked the beginning of an organized growth-control movement in Monterey Park.

Outraged residents living near the proposed development incorporated the Sequoia Park Homeowners Association to fight the plan. One of the leaders was Harry Couch's mother, Evelyn Diederich, who was already a defendant in a long-standing lawsuit filed by CVJ, the developers, over another housing project next to her home. "Now they made a pretty serious mistake because those same developers soon were going to try to put 150 condos on the other side of the hill right in the middle of single-family homes," says Diederich, a feisty grandmother and a retired schoolteacher who had moved to Monterey Park in 1971. "All of us [living] in this area complained, but the council didn't care what we had to say. So we got together . . . to fight the rezoning."[22] By gathering over 4,400 signatures citywide, the association forced the city council to put the development to a special municipal vote. This was Proposition A.

The referendum was immediately challenged in court by CVJ. But its lawsuit against the City of Monterey Park and the Sequoia Homeowners Association was thrown out in February 1981, when Los Angeles Superior Court Judge Robert Weil ruled that property zoning changes were subject to referendum. The decision allowed the special election to take place in April 1981. Mark Jabin, attorney for CVJ, told the *Progress* that should voters defeat Proposition A, he would file a court appeal.[23]

Among the strong opponents of Proposition A was Irv Gilman, the tax watchdog and crusader who had made a name for himself with his work in favor of Proposition 13 in 1978 and his opposition to the school unification initiative in 1974. Gilman had been an unsuccessful candidate for city council in April 1980 but was eyeing the seat soon to be vacated by Matthew Martinez, who had been elected to the California State Assembly in November 1980. Though he did not live in the same area, he became a member of and identified with the Sequoia Park Homeowners Association. On its behalf he spoke to the city council and wrote letters to the *Progress* which sometimes took the tone of a campaign speech:

> On Jan. 12 I spoke to the Monterey Park City Council regarding the CVJ hillside condominium project. The gist of my remarks was that 4,422 people cared enough and took the time to sign our referendum petition, making it almost a certainty to be valid. I also asked the city council to avoid the expense of a special election by repealing [the rezoning] Ordinance 1536. . . . At the

Jan. 26 city council meeting, a misguided developer said that I was a big spender, having forced the city to spend $7,000 on an election. That is garbage!

My position as an opponent of big government and big spending is absolutely clear and a matter of public record.[24]

Frank Venti, principal partner in CVJ, wrote a blistering response; he called Gilman "an unknowledgeable gadfly," claimed that some signers of the petition regretted their support, and asserted that most residents upheld the council's decision.[25] At the same time, CVJ attorneys filed another lawsuit in Los Angeles Superior Court charging that ballot statements submitted by opponents of Proposition A were "false and misleading." All those who had signed the ballot argument against the proposition were named in the suit, including Mayor Louise Davis, Planning Commissioner Sonya Gerlach, Irv Gilman and Patricia Chin of the Sequoia Park Homeowners Association, and accountant James Haydon.

Contending that the suit had no merit and was only intended to intimidate opponents, Davis retorted: "I think the people really resent the fact that any time they disagree with your position [you] hit people with a lawsuit. [The developers] happen to know that the Sequoia Park Homeowners Association doesn't have a lot of money and they're trying to drain every nickel out of them. . . . But I'm sure that the voters can see through the facade and comprehend what's best."[26]

As election day approached, the lines became firmly drawn. Proposition A was supported by a majority of council members, the chamber of commerce, and the *Monterey Park Progress*. In addition, according to public documents submitted by the pro-proposition Monterey Park Citizens for Representative Government, $52,740 was raised by the two firms that had a direct interest in seeing the condominium project completed: CVJ Construction and Monterey Views Development Company.[27] With the money, the Citizens for Representative Government published a professional-looking four-page "newspaper," the *Monterey Park Press*, which used comments by city notables to portray Proposition A as a well-planned project that would generate much-needed revenue for the city in the wake of Proposition 13 cutbacks. We think that this proposed project will provide the best use for a problem piece of land," wrote Harold Fiebelkorn. "It provides planned development that will have acres of cultivated open space, a security system, and, above all, will be forever under the strict supervision of the city to prevent land erosion, mud slides and blight."[28]

Former council member George Ige also supported Proposition A. "Your 'Yes' vote will bring $300,000 a year in revenue to the City and

Monterey Park's Community Redevelopment Agency," he wrote in the *Press*. "Governor Brown has cut much of the funds available to local governments. In fact Monterey Park will lose over $600,000 in Prop. 13 bailout funds this year alone."[29] And Mancha Kurilich, a member of the Alhambra School Board and a forty-two-year Monterey Park resident, contradicted Superintendent Bruce Peppin, denying any overcrowding problems in local schools. "Our schools could be a very big winner if Prop. A passes," she claimed. "An estimated 45 students will come from the Monterey Views homes and those students would go to Repetto Elementary, which at this time has enough room for all of those students. . . . Another big bonus from Prop. A is the fact that the builders of the Monterey Views home will pay $135,000 in fees into our school district."[30]

Opponents of the proposition produced only a simple one-page flyer that members handed out door to door because they couldn't afford the mailing costs. "We had very little money and did well to print a brochure," remembers Evelyn Diederich. "So, we divided the town into ten areas. Ten of us took an area and it was up to each of the ten to see that every household got a brochure. . . . I never walked so much."[31] The centerpiece of the "No on A" argument was that the condominium project was a boondoggle for developers. The flyer stated: "We are a multi-racial, multi-ethnic group of Monterey Park residents from every walk of life. We do not oppose single-family homes. DON'T BE FOOLED by the twisting of the facts in the expensive literature written by a high-priced Public Relations firm hired by the developers. The Developers make the added profit and we pay the price."[32] Opponents also argued that the number of new people brought in by the condominiums would increase traffic congestion, overcrowd the schools, and force residents to pay some $90,000 a year for additional police, fire, sewer, and other municipal services or accept the consequences of reduced services.

Despite superior financial backing and the support of the city's establishment, Proposition A was overwhelmingly rejected 6,410 to 1,037—an 86 to 14 percent margin—on April 14, 1981.[33] CVJ general partner Frank Venti, immediately charged that racism was the determining factor: "They voted to keep the Chinese out, and they voted to keep condominiums out of Monterey Park," he told reporters. "I didn't realize that there were so many bigots in Monterey Park."[34]

The issue became even more controversial when it was revealed that James Haydon, a leading opponent of Proposition A, had distributed an unauthorized circular claiming that residents of the proposed 150-unit project would be "primarily Oriental, mostly Chinese." Haydon admitted that he had been criticized by other "No on A" members for injecting race into the campaign but offered no apologies: "What I put out was not a slur," he said. A *Progress* editorial, however, blamed the "No on A" committee for not repudiating Haydon's actions: "Mayor Louise Davis . . . was correct when she said she considered the ballot measure 'a rezoning issue and nothing else.' But she missed the boat, as did other leading Prop. A opponents, such as city council candidate Irv Gilman . . . by failing to completely disassociate themselves from the racially oriented circular. . . . Quite frankly, the *Progress* doesn't know if they have it in them to do it."[35]

The following week, during a forum held for candidates vying for the council seat vacated by Matthew Martinez, the issue of racism was again raised. Irv Gilman, the fiery front runner whose campaign depended on the defeat of Proposition A, dismissed accusations of racism as "horse-feathers." Calling Haydon's survey "strictly statistical reporting," he asked the audience: "Who has been making all the statements? It's the developers." Another candidate, Los Angeles County Administrator Lily Lee Chen—also a Proposition A opponent—maintained that many Chinese residents had cast their vote against the proposition to protest rezoning. "I hope June 2 [the date for the special council election] the vote will show that the citizens of Monterey Park are not bigots and not against the Chinese," she said.[36]

Another Call for a Moratorium

Shortly after the forum, council candidate Irv Gilman, Mayor Louise Davis, Councilman Harry Couch, and Planning Commissioner Sonya Gerlach all began calling for an emergency four-month moratorium on construction in R-2 (medium-density) and R-3 (high-density) zones in the city. Three years earlier the city council (including Davis and Couch) had rejected the planning commission's proposal for such a moratorium, as had Gilman, then a private citizen. In the wake of Proposition A, however, the political climate in Monterey Park was ripe for a growth-control measure.

But Planning Commission Chair Harold Fiebelkorn, who had proposed the moratorium in 1978, now denied that a moratorium was justified. Because the city's density requirements had been reduced by 20 to 30 percent in R-2 zones and by 33 to 40 percent in R-3 zones since 1978, he argued that the building explosion in Monterey Park had already taken place and that concerns over municipal services were now unwarranted. Commissioner Katherine Cuttrell, another moratorium supporter in 1978, wanted more information: "I don't want to jump on this bandwagon just because Louise Davis and Gerlach are all for it. . . . I'm still waiting to see the sewer report that will tell us what our sewer capacity is." Community Development Director Henry Tera-shita, who had also supported a moratorium in 1978, was reluctant to devote his staff's limited time and resources to a moratorium study, but Gerlach countered that a moratorium period would give city staff the necessary time to examine the effects of continued construction in high-density zones.[37]

Responses to City Hall rumblings of a moratorium were mixed. Some people clearly favored the idea: "As a resident of Monterey Park for more than twenty-five years and now a member of the minority [Caucasian] group of local citizens, I feel that what the city really needs is not another 'Winston Ko' type of shopping center," wrote resident E. D. Wright to the *Progress*. "We have enough of these ethnic-type shopping centers that cater only to ethnic groups. . . . Living here are people of many ethnic groups, and rightly so. But we do not want to be known as 'The Chinese Beverly Hills.' "[38]

Others, particularly Chinese residents, were outraged and felt betrayed. As Sim Quan wrote to the *Progress*: "Before April 14, I was told that Prop. A dealt only with one project on a single site. Look what's happening now! I own one R-2 property. . . . why should I not be able to build on it? I am sick of these people who act like mad dogs biting everybody. I don't blame CVJ developer Frank Venti for calling some of us bigots." Quan ended with a terse warning to voters to "think clearly on June 2 as to who should be elected to run our city; otherwise our properties may some day . . . be allowed for the raising of chickens only."[39]

The Election of Gilman

The June 2, 1981, special city council election turned out to be a much closer contest than many local observers ever expected: Irv Gilman defeated Lily Lee Chen by just twenty-eight votes, 2,154 to 2,126.[40] Long identified as the president of the Monterey Taxpayers Association and a close ally of Harry Couch, Gilman rode high on the wave of the April 14 defeat of Proposition A. Lily Lee Chen, though a relatively unknown candidate at the time, was strongly supported by popular Louise Davis and outspent Gilman $28,112 to $3,426 in her losing bid.[41] She accepted defeat gracefully, however, and vowed to run for office again the following year.

In that same election the community also voted on citywide Proposition B, which asked residents to approve a temporary tax that would raise $1.1 million dollars for additional police protection. The measure was favored by 5,125 votes to 2,879, a 63 to 27 percent margin, but lost because it fell short of the two-thirds required for tax increases under guidelines established by Proposition 13 in 1978.[42] Irv Gilman and Harry Couch worked against Proposition B; though both said they supported additional police protection, they thought the city should dip into its reserve funds before passing on any new assessments to residents. Unhappy Police Chief Jon Elder directly blamed Gilman and Couch for the defeat. "I'm really irritated by this 'I'm for the police department, but—' attitude," he said and challenged Gilman as council member–elect to "keep his word" that he would fund extra police protection through the budget process.[43]

When Gilman was sworn into office on June 15, 1981, he had finally fulfilled a three-year dream. He would have to run again the following year to get a full four-year term, but being an incumbent was an important advantage, and he savored the moment. "I have been an activist for nearly five years and I have spoken out on issues and engaged in battles with this same council," he told an audience of well-wishers. "I'm sure I was thought of as the thorn in their side, but many of us felt it was indeed healthy to be watching and listening to our city government." He assured his supporters that he would retain the critical perspective "gained from many long hours of sitting where you are sitting tonight."[44]

An excellent speaker and writer, Gilman was considered by his backers an articulate populist and a "voice of the people." To his detractors he was a dangerous opportunist and demagogue who whipped up sentiment by playing on people's emotions. Gilman's history shows that his fervor for politics began more by accident than by design. An only child born to Jewish immigrant parents from Eastern Europe, he spent his first thirty years in Chicago. He entered the College of Pharmacy at the University of Illinois but left after just one term and went to work in a department store, where he found he was good at business and management. When he was transferred to California in 1964, he did not want to leave his parents but felt he could not pass up the career opportunity. Buying a house in Monterey Park in 1966 helped him adjust to the West: "Here you got to know your neighbors and it [was] very small-townish. The first thing I remember was one of the neighbors was having a party because they refurnished their house."[45]

During Gilman's involvement in the 1974 school unification controversy, he was quite conscious that he was challenging the town's power center. "We were aware of who we were taking on," he says, "but we felt we were doing the right thing for our kids," not just "starting a fight in order to buck the establishment." It was not until he worked with the Monterey Park Taxpayers Association for the passage of Proposition 13 that Gilman realized his passion for politics. The Monterey Taxpayers Association included disgruntled members of the old establishment as well as newer residents who had settled in the community in the late 1950s and 1960s. The members were unified against the pro-growth, high-tax direction the new city council was taking; they wanted to keep Monterey Park a small town. After several organizational meetings, they elected Gilman president: "They just flattered me so that I couldn't refuse." He remembers how terrified he was when he gave his first speech: "I had never done public speaking in my life, yet here I was addressing an audience of three or four hundred angry people. . . . I was so frightened that my voice trembled, and I felt I was just awful. But afterwards, people came up to me and congratulated me. . . . They mistook my fear for sincerity."[46] From that day on, Gilman was a notable political fixture in Monterey Park.

Deepening Division

Buoyed by election successes, a small but dedicated group of slow-growth activists began to organize themselves into a political action committee. "After Proposition A, people said, 'You only did that for your area. Why don't you do it for the rest of the town?'" remembers Evelyn Diederich. "That's when RAMP started."[47]

The Rise of "RAMP"

The Residents Association of Monterey Park boldly proclaimed its presence on July 15, 1981, in a letter to the *Progress* from interim president Sonya Gerlach and interim secretary Pauline Lemire:

> When our forefathers developed the general plan for Monterey Park in 1967, did they envision what life in Monterey Park would be like in 1981? In their haste "to make Monterey Park a better place to live," did they foresee that the increased densities in the northern part of our city would bring . . . congestion, overcrowding, heavy traffic, double sessions and busing in our local schools, as well as sewer deficiencies and an inadequate tax base to support the need for increased police, fire, parks, recreation, water supply, capital improvements? . . .
>
> The goals of R.A.M.P. are to promote the quality of life for all the citizens of Monterey Park and to create a more responsive climate at city hall to the needs and concerns of the community. Through surveys, questionnaires, and meetings we hope to become aware of the pulse of the city and to make it known to all.[48]

After the letter's publication, RAMP grew rapidly. Its members were overwhelmingly white and mostly in their fifties; many had been residents of the community for over twenty years and had had some unhappy experience with developers or a development project near their homes. Politically, they ranged from liberal Democrat Sonya Gerlach to Reagan conservative Evelyn Diederich, yet they stood together in their desire to control growth and development in Monterey Park. One of their first actions, inspired by growth-control measures passed in nearby Thousand Oaks and Villa Park, was to gather signatures from residents to place two of their own growth-control initiatives on the city ballot in 1982. Proposition K called for a construction limit of no more than 100 residential units per year; Proposition L called for a required vote of the residents for any zone changes affecting more than one acre.[49]

RAMP also pushed for the appointment of member Patricia Chin to the planning commission to replace Harold Fiebelkorn, whose term had expired. With three members of the city council supporting her, Chin was soon sworn in and, along with Commissioner Gerlach, added a strong voice in favor of growth limitation.[50] Next, RAMP supported a slate of candidates for the upcoming April 1982 city council election: in addition to incumbents Couch and Gilman, the association endorsed the candidacy of Sonya Gerlach.[51]

In response to RAMP's high-profile activity, Fiebelkorn attacked the group in his January 27 "Kaffee Klatch" column:

> In a valiant effort to preserve our fair city from self-destruction, RAMP proposes to bring progress to a grinding halt. . . .
>
> This group has come up with instant self-made experts in city planning, landslide control, traffic safety, development, zoning and all those other areas normally assigned to an experienced staff. . . .
>
> By circulating referendums every time our elected officials make a decision, RAMP is striking at the very heart of representative government. "Let the people decide" is pure balderdash because the "people" don't give a damn. . . . Hell, there are easily 8,000 people in this town who would sign anything.[52]

In his column the following week Eli Isenberg also denounced what he saw as the group's shortsightedness: "RAMP, an acronym for Residents Assn. of Monterey Park, also stands for 'Residents Against More People.' . . . RAMP has proposed in its initiative that any planned business or residential development involving more than an acre would require a vote of the people. Approval of that initiative would kill 'planned' development of North Atlantic Boulevard [under which] City Manager Lloyd de Llamas estimates the city would get $2.1 million in increased revenues. Without increased revenues from that and

other developments the City of Monterey Park will not be able to provide the quality of services, including police and fire protection, as it
has in the past."[53]

Unmoved by the criticism, RAMP quickly collected enough signatures to place its twin growth-control measures on the June ballot. The
two initiatives were filed at the city clerk's office by a confident Sonya
Gerlach. "I don't think there will be any problems with it," she told
reporters. "Prop. A. showed us that people want control over growth
and a guaranteed quality of life with an assurance that city services
can be provided."[54]

Propositions K and L were immediately opposed by the same
people who had supported Proposition A, on the grounds that both
propositions would restrict their abilities to develop property throughout the city, but opponents too believed that the measures would pass.
"It makes me sick but I know the general public is going to go along
and buy it," admitted pessimistic developer Frank Venti. "No one will
intelligently analyze the issues. . . . I'm sure as hell offended by anyone
who says, 'no more people.'"[55]

In an attempt to avoid the kind of racial controversy that had
erupted during the Proposition A campaign, RAMP member Joseph
Rubin served notice that Propositions K and L were not anti-Chinese.
"The charge of racism is particularly noxious and divisive in our community. As a matter of fact, petitions were circulated by RAMP members of Chinese background and many signatures are from voters of
Chinese background. . . . It is insulting to our Asian community—indeed, it is racist—to suggest that citizens of Asian background care less
about overcrowded schools, traffic congestion, adequate water supply
and the other problems our city faces than do the rest of us. RAMP
seeks to draw our community together to accomplish common goals.
The charge of racism is empty. Worse than that, the charge engenders
racism, and we have had enough of that in the world."[56]

The 1982 Council Campaign

Though many believed that victory for Propositions K and L was a
foregone conclusion, the city council race in April 1982 took a surprising turn. Four candidates emerged who strongly opposed the RAMP-
backed slate for city council and Propositions K and L. The leading
challenger was Lily Lee Chen, who had lost by just twenty-eight votes
to Irv Gilman in 1981. She argued that the initiatives were unnecessary and had been created by ambitious city council candidates. "I
feel that it's important to stop overcrowding and traffic congestion,
but this is something that the city council should be responsible for,"

she said pointedly. The RAMP effort "is simply a good ploy and a political one."[57]

Candidate David Almada agreed that decisions should not be taken away from the council: "I do understand the problems, but I feel that the city council has the authority to act." Almada was a member of the Monterey Park Recreation and Parks Commission and the Lions Club; he had been a strong supporter of Proposition A in 1981. Art and Culture Commissioner Rudy Peralta, a close ally of council member Monty Manibog, expressed similar but weaker opposition: "It's rather early right now, but at this point I would have to say 'no'" to the two initiatives.[58]

Only candidate Bill Feliz, a television repairman and president of the Monterey Park Democratic Club, directly charged that the two propositions were a reaction to the influx of Chinese immigrants and that the slow-growth movement was creating racial divisiveness. "I've been in the community talking and listening to people, and wherever I go, the Chinese question and comments on the new immigrants keeps coming up," Feliz said. "RAMP's initiatives are just a reflex coming out of frustration. But the issue here should be whether we will have an integrated, happy community or instead have different factions fighting and getting mad."[59]

Given its political victories and successful organizing efforts, RAMP was optimistic about sweeping the city council elections, as well as passing Propositions K and L. Though RAMP's issues were solid, however, its candidates did have some exploitable cracks in their armor. First, in November 1981, Harry Couch had asked the Monterey Park Police Department to investigate the possibility of operating poker parlors in the city to offset financial cutbacks created by the passage of Proposition 13. The idea was widely lampooned by the local press, harshly criticized by residents, and quickly dropped.[60] One resident who made a major issue of the proposal at the time was Lily Lee Chen, who appeared before the council on December 8 to say she was disturbed that the council was even discussing the subject of poker parlors as an alternative source of revenue for the city. Later that month Chen wrote in a letter to the *Progress*: "It is ironic that two members of the city council, Mayor Harry Couch and Irv Gilman, while supporting limited growth of our city, should find gambling compatible with their concept. Those of us who want a balanced community will find that gambling discourages good, solid, revenue-producing businesses."[61]

Second, Couch and Gilman had campaigned hard in June 1981 against Proposition B, the call for a municipal tax to support increased police protection which 64 percent of Monterey Park voters had supported but failed to pass by the required two-thirds majority. This stand came back to haunt both men, especially after they took a tough position in new salary negotiations with the police and fire departments. When talks broke down, fire fighters and police officers staged "red and blue flu" sick-outs in protest.[62] These public safety employees were particularly incensed by the city's refusal to grant retroactive pay increases covering the negotiation period, believing that the decision was a means of "punishing" them for not quickly coming to terms.[63] The Police Officers Association even went so far as to spend $2,500 a month for billboard space on Atlantic Boulevard; the sign read, "CAUTION: Fewer police and overpaid management make this a city where crime pays!"[64]

Third, while all other RAMP candidates kept to development and public safety issues, Sonya Gerlach began to direct specific remarks at the Chinese, comments reminiscent of the last-minute injection of race into the Proposition A campaign. "The money is coming in from outside the community and the businesses are being bought by the Chinese," she said. "We should protect the interests of people who have been here and see that our businesses remain reflective of the residential community. What's happening in the commercial areas is that we have one people representing one racial and ethnic group. It doesn't represent what the people need." At the same candidates' forum, by contrast, David Almada praised Monterey Park as an exemplary city and said that its ethnic diversity made it a role model for other communities. "I want to live in an integrated community with the diversity that Monterey Park has."[65]

These three issues combined to tarnish the glow of the RAMP-supported council candidates. But by far the most controversial action during this campaign came with the distribution the weekend before the election of a political mailer attacking Couch, Gilman, and Gerlach. Disguised as a newspaper similar to the one published in support of Proposition A the year before, the *Monterey Park Chronicle* played up the issue of gambling and crime in the city. Under the headline "Start Drive to Elect New City Council, Defeat Pro-Poker Slate," the paper unabashedly endorsed Lily Lee Chen, David Almada, and Rudy Peralta for city council.[66] Public records show that the mailer was paid for by the Monterey Park Citizens against Crime, a group that pumped in $27,365 for the publication. Major contributors included Gold Star Investment Company of Monterey Park ($7,500), America Tsui of Mandarin Realty ($2,600), Concord Companies of Monterey Park ($2,000), Monterey Views and its partners Frank Venti and Mark Jabin ($1,000), and Bezaire Electronics ($750).[67]

On April 13, 1982, the so-called anti-crime slate of Chen, Almada, and Peralta were swept into office. The election drew 8,166 voters, over 39 percent of those registered and the largest number of citizens ever to go to the polls in a Monterey Park municipal election. The final tally showed that Chen led all candidates with 4,764 votes (22 percent), followed by Almada with 3,508 votes (16.6 percent) and Peralta with 3,505 votes (16.6 percent). In fourth place was Couch with 3,219 votes (15.3 percent), then Gilman with 3,033 votes (14.4 percent) and Gerlach with 2,275 votes (10.8 percent). Coming in last was Bill Feliz with just 730 votes (3.4 percent).[68]

The losers in what was clearly one of the most stunning upsets in local politics all complained bitterly about what they saw as dirty politics. Convinced that the *Chronicle* had stolen the election away from them, they threatened legal action. Gerlach called the mailer "slanderous" and charged that the public had been manipulated by "prodeveloper, pro-realtor and pro-Taiwanese" interests. An angry press release put out by RAMP expressed its members' feeling that "Monterey Park has been raped by the developers and real estate interests once again" and warned that these interests could "be expected to spread another blizzard of manure with [their] huge gold-plated shovel."[69] But Mancha Kurilich, who had been prominent in the pro–Proposition A campaign and now chaired Monterey Park Citizens against Crime, defended the mailer: "I don't believe that poker was a dead issue in this campaign. Everything in there is taken from the record. It's all accurate. What do they want to do, take away our first amendment rights?"[70]

To Richard Tretter, president of the Police Officers Association, the election results were no surprise: "A lot of hard work went into their campaigns and I'm pleased that all three won."[71] The association had endorsed Chen, Almada, and Peralta on the basis of their promise to "open communication" and "listen" to police representatives during any upcoming salary negotiations.[72] As many as twenty officers in civilian dress had walked precincts persuading residents to support their "anti-crime" candidates.[73]

Though most of the post-election contentiousness centered on the *Chronicle*, some commentators saw the mailer as having had only minimal effectiveness. "The combination of the Police Department out campaigning for Lily, David, and Rudy, concern with card rooms and crime, plus a message of quality development without racism, is what turned the election," Lloyd de Llamas believes. "One of the things that made Lily, David, and Rudy so attractive to the majority of the voters was that they said: 'Look, we don't have to take a meat ax approach to this. We don't have to pick on minorities, or stop retail development. All we need is to insist on quality development.'"[74]

Whatever the cause, the election results left the RAMP-backed candidates enraged. They vowed to come back from defeat, said they had learned a political lesson that would never be forgotten and went on the attack. On April 20, when the newly elected candidates were sworn into office and City Hall was full of festive supporters, the gala self-congratulatory mood quickly sobered as Gilman and Couch stood to give their farewell speeches. "The developers won a Pyrrhic victory," Gilman told the audience. "It is a matter of public record that developers and realtors donated $18,000 to bring us the *Monterey Park Chronicle*, $6,300 of which came from outside our community." He went on to predict that the new council majority would be beholden to monied interests. "In a way I feel sorry for this new council," he said. "They may find they have two masters to serve—the people of this community and the realtors and developers." Harry Couch, ousted after just one term as council member and just four months into his term as mayor, was equally combative. Referring to the upcoming June vote on Propositions K and L, he said, "The developers may think they have elected their own city council, but the people still have the initiative process."[75] These acid words cast a definite pall on the evening.

The new council members responded angrily, citing the voters' clear choice against divisive rhetoric as the reason for their victory. Peralta called the losers' attitude "sour grapes." Almada charged them with introducing race into the campaign: "I don't think it does this community any good when someone like Sonya Gerlach makes published statements about 'Taiwanese money' coming into this campaign." Chen declared that the *Chronicle* had little to do with her having received "the highest vote total in the history of Monterey Park."[76]

But for Chen and the other newly elected council members, the honeymoon would be short lived. Though the rejection of incumbents Couch and Gilman and candidate Sonya Gerlach dramatically restructured political power in Monterey Park, it was not long before RAMP began to regroup and put forth an all-out effort to pass initiatives K and L on the June ballot. In addition, RAMP's leaders became council watchdogs, constantly recalling the exaggerations in the April mailer and challenging the credibility of the three new members at every opportunity.

Political power and economic interests were at the heart of the battles fought in Monterey Park, as they are elsewhere. Political representation, taxation, accountability of government, and development are very much contested issues in any community, let alone one whose social fabric was already so frayed. Clearly, the Chinese immigrants became both players and pawns in a game between politically polarized groups as their numbers grew larger and their presence more visible. Chinese developers and speculators, lining up on the side of the pro-growth factions in town, were important players; others in the Chinese American and Chinese immigrant community were used as pawns by both sides to further their own political agendas. Though RAMP leaders focused primarily on development issues, they could not avoid allegations of racism by their detractors and were not consistent about divorcing themselves from those charges. These problems became even more apparent during the next four years.

A typical Monterey Park business sign (*Photo by author*)

Mr. Bob Peng leading daily morning Chinese exercise class in Barnes Park (*Photo by Larry Arellera, Southern California Community Newspapers*)

The bustling corner of Garvey Avenue and Atlantic
Boulevard in the late 1970s. Manny's El Loco and the
bowling alley were frequently cited by old-timers as
popular town gathering spots (*Photo by Aldo Panzieri,
courtesy of the City of Monterey Park*)

The corner of Garvey and Atlantic today, still bustling but considerably changed. The Landmark Center serves as the anchor for the new Chinese-owned and -operated businesses all along North Atlantic Boulevard (*Photo by author*)

An old-style Craftsman home, common in Monterey Park's
early days, dwarfed by a new condominium complex (*Photo
by author*)

One of the large, expensive luxury homes popular in
Monterey Park today (*Photo by author*)

Barry Hatch, former city councilman (1986–90) and mayor (1989). During his tenure Hatch drove a 1981 Datsun with a bumper sticker that read "CONTROL IMMIGRATION NOW!" (*Photo courtesy of the City of Monterey Park*)

Judy Chu, elected to the city council in 1988 and again in 1992 by running on a platform of racial harmony and controlled growth (*Photo courtesy of the City of Monterey Park*)

A young participant marches in the 1992 Chinese New Year's parade that began in Monterey Park and ended in the neighboring city of Alhambra (*Photo by Juan Ocampo, Southern California Community Newspapers*)

CHAPTER 5

Controlled Growth and the Official-English Movement

In May 1982 a *Monterey Park Progress* editorial headed "A Different City Council" pointed out that for the first time, four of the council's five members (Manibog, Chen, Almada, and Peralta) came from ethnic minorities. Also, for the first time, moreover, there were two Hispanics serving together (Almada and Peralta), a Chinese American (Chen), and two women (Davis and Chen).[1] The new council's new perspectives were soon evident as well; one of its first acts was to denounce federal raids on businesses that employ undocumented workers. After learning of an Immigration and Naturalization Service (INS) raid on a Monterey Park shoe manufacturing business, David Almada made a motion, seconded by Rudy Peralta, that the council send letters of protest to President Reagan and INS Commissioner Alan Nelson. The motion, passed unanimously, was lauded in the same editorial: "It is not unusual for a city council to take an official position on state and federal legislative proposals or programs. . . . And the *Progress*, for one, has no objections. As a matter of fact, we confess to some degree of admiration for the council's action. They showed some spunk. And that, too, is different from previous city councils."[2]

Initial harmony among the members, however, all too quickly became discord, bringing political turmoil that often pitted the council against the community. This chapter highlights events between 1982 and 1986, including the passage of controlled-growth propositions that were actively opposed by a majority of the city council, continued growth and change during which the council's efforts to assist newcomers were often misconstrued and resented by older residents, and finally an "official-English" movement that became entangled with development issues.

Propositions K and L

After the surprise results of the April 1982 city council election, heated community debate quickly focused on Propositions K and L. *Monterey Park Progress* "Publisher Emeritus" Eli Isenberg began the flurry in his May 12 "It Seems to Me" column: "Vote yes on K, and you limit the number of residential units that can be built to 100 a year for 10 years. Vote yes on L, and you require a vote of the people . . . on any zone change involving more than an acre. . . . Props. K and L were initiated by the Residents Assn. of Monterey Park, whose leaders include Planning Commissioner Sonya Gerlach and former councilmen Harry Couch and Irv Gilman. All three ran for election on 'no-growth' and were defeated for council. They hope to 'turn it around' on June 8." But, Isenberg added: "City Manager Lloyd de Llamas has said that the planned development of North Atlantic [on the table since 1980] would create $5 million in added municipal revenues within five years of its completion. Cities that fail to find new sources of revenue, de Llamas says, will cease to exist."[3]

Local commentator and muse Harold Fiebelkorn joined the fray in a May 26 column: "According to RAMP, all of the studies that have been made by experts in their field, all of the research that has been conducted by a competent and experienced staff, and all of the ambitions of reasonable people to promote Monterey Park are pure poppycock. . . . In promoting Props. K and L (many of us believe this stands for Kooks at Large), they [RAMP members] have made some astounding revelations. Firinstince, it is said that if we stop growth in Monterey Park, we would soon evolve into a society that no longer has bunions because people would no longer be forced to stand up on the bus. . . . if you believe all that, we have a very fine bridge in Brooklyn that we can let you have for a very low down payment and some very creative financing."[4]

The biggest controversy erupted when an opposition group, Monterey Park Citizens for Community Progress, published a mailer that quoted City Manager de Llamas as saying, "If these ballot measures are not defeated, Monterey Park will die." At the May 25 city council meeting de Llamas publicly denied having made the comment. "No, I didn't say it," he told the council and an audience of angry residents. Though acknowledging that he did not think the two initiatives were good legislation, "I don't feel that the city will fall in the ocean if [Propositions K and L] are passed."[5]

At the same meeting Mancha Kurilich, coordinator of the Citizens for Community Progress, defended the group and argued that the gist of the comments published was accurate. Kurilich—already a controversial figure because of her connection with the earlier mailer that had accused council candidates Harry Couch, Irv Gilman, and Sonya Gerlach of being the "pro-poker slate"—admitted only that the flyer had "paraphrased" de Llamas's statement, as quoted by Isenberg, that cities without new sources of revenue would "cease to exist." This flip response angered Louise Davis, who accused Kurilich of compromising the integrity of the office of the city manager by placing de Llamas in the middle of a controversy. Caught in a controversy of her own because her name had appeared without authorization on the ballot arguments opposing Propositions K and L, measures she supported, Davis wanted to know who was responsible for writing the campaign literature. Kurilich could not answer the question. Davis later expressed her frustration to a *Progress* reporter: "There are a lot of strange thing(s) happening. First we have my name on the ballot arguments without my consent or knowledge, and now we have them putting people's names on campaign literature without their consent."[6]

The Monterey Park Citizens for Community Development quickly returned with a publication that looked very much like the one used during the April city council election. The *Monterey Park Times* was a four-page "newspaper" claiming 35,000 readers. Under the headline "Ballot Measures Endangering $5 Million" the front page featured a cartoon showing a tied-up city council watching helplessly as Sonya Gerlach blows away money and essential services; the caption read: "Gone With the Wind—So Goes Monterey Park. An ill wind is blowing through our city. Its chief huffer and puffer is K and L founder Sonya Gerlach, still sore from her stinging loss during the recent City Council elections. If not defeated, Mrs. Gerlach's illegal measures will tie up the Council in red tape, cripple city services, and cost Monterey Park taxpayers millions in lost revenue and massive legal fees."[7]

Inside, the mailer was peppered with stories insisting "Monterey Park can become a slum if K & L are not defeated," "Slums breed crime," "This city will become a ghost town," and "City fights for its very life." One article went so far as to quote a psychologist who warned of a disruptive "extremist element" in the community. "If ballot measures K and L are not defeated, new life will be breathed into a dying divisive force that has been tearing apart the harmony and mental health of this city," said Dr. Jerome Silverman, clinical psychologist at Ingleside Mental Health Center. "The leaders of the extremist group are the same people who are the sponsors of the K and L ballot measures."[8]

For their part, the K and L proponents dedicated an all-out effort to passing their ballot measures. They continued to argue that uncontrolled growth and multiple-unit housing create traffic congestion, municipal service shortages, crowding in schools, and higher taxes for residents; they berated an uncaring city government and greedy developer interests. Following the defeat of its candidates in the April council election, however, RAMP made some changes in strategy. Instead of just one piece of campaign literature the "Yes on K & L" advocates, under the RAMP umbrella, produced several flyers. To exploit the credibility gap of their opponents, one brochure showed columns for "Lies" and "Truths." One statement under "Lies" read: "If these ballot measures are not defeated, Monterey Park will die." The corresponding "Truths" entry read: "City Manager Lloyd de Llamas at the May 25, 1982, council meeting publicly denied making this statement. . . . This is another instance of the opposition printing untrue statements to get votes." [9]

RAMP also prepared to counter any last-minute mailers by the opposition. Statements such as "Warning: Last-Minute Smears Are Dangerous to the Health and Well-being of Your City" recognized the effectiveness of having the last word, and members mobilized for quick responses. [10] Hence, when the *Monterey Park Times* appeared, RAMP was ready. "It was a Thursday evening (the election was the following Tuesday), and it was the same thing again," remembers active RAMP leader Joseph Rubin. "After they brought that over here, we made a pamphlet which responded to that, and we ran it off on some quick print . . . [and] spread it around town however we could. We handed them out, and we stood in front of the markets." [11]

RAMP's one-page, handwritten message began: "Who paid for the Developers 'newspaper'—'*The Times*.' According to their required disclosure statement they raised over $16,000 in a few weeks." There followed a copy of the monetary contributions statement submitted by the Monterey Park Citizens for Community Progress. The first three names on the list, each contributing $1,000, were Mandarin Realty, owned by Frederic Hsieh; Monterey Views, known in Monterey Park for its developer's support of Proposition A in 1981; and Operating Industries, owners of a controversial local dump site that had been accused of flagrant violation of sanitary regulations and the emission of offensive odors. The pamphlet ended by urging: "*You* may not have those kinds of bucks—*But you* have your *VOTE*! Use it! Vote *Yes* on K & L" (original emphasis). [12]

On June 8 both Propositions K and L passed by substantial margins—K by 7,447 to 4,294 votes, L by 7,174 to 4,263 [13]—despite active opposition from Mayor Monty Manibog and newly elected council members Lily Lee Chen, David Almada, and Rudy Peralta. RAMP leaders said they had expected the victory and expressed a sense of vindication for what had happened to them during the council election just two months earlier. Many residents hoped that the passage of Propositions K and L would settle any further development disputes and the city would return to a peaceful existence. Others hoped that RAMP would quietly disband or fade away.

But development and related issues were far from resolved in

Monterey Park. For example, how would the city council, four-fifths of which had fought the controlled-growth initiatives, work to enforce them? Would the worst-case scenario—crippling financial disaster—befall the city?

Continued Growth

Monterey Park's fiscal problems and demands for additional city services to meet the needs of a growing and changing community were critical issues that simply were not solved by the passage of Propositions K and L. Still convinced that the city's eroding tax base could be shored up only by pro-growth strategies, the city council took a series of highly controversial actions intended to bring more investment into the community.

The Lincoln Plaza Hotel

On June 30, 1982, the council approved plans to build a 150-room, six-story hotel and a three-level parking garage just behind the Garvey-Garfield business district—the first major project in that declining section of town in over twenty years.[14] The council majority and city officials were optimistic that the project would serve as the anchor for even further development in the area. The hope was to complete construction in time for the 1984 Summer Olympics in Los Angeles, expected to draw large crowds of tourists to southern California. Projections were that the hotel would generate $96,000 from room rates in the first year and increase to as much as $137,000 annually in five years. Because a variance was granted to allow the structure to exceed the four-story limitation in the city's building code, objections came primarily from nearby residents who feared that their view of the San Gabriel Mountains would be blocked by the height of the hotel; in addition, an increase in automobile and tour bus traffic would disrupt their residential neighborhood. In fact, construction was held up for several months because the city wanted the developer to build the hotel on another spot across the street, farther from residences, but the developer said that site was unacceptable and threatened to drop the project. In the end, the only council member who voted against the project was Louise Davis. The city's building code specified that a variance could be granted only if it was demonstrated that "the proposed project would be an improvement on an existing condition and that the project would be economically unfeasible without the variance"; in Davis's view the criteria for a variance had not been met.[15]

The South Atlantic Mall

The council majority also moved to replace Sonya Gerlach on the planning commission when her term expired in January 1983. When rumors circulated that such a change was imminent, thirty-five pick-eters carrying signs demanding Gerlach's reappointment marched in front of City Hall. The protest was organized by RAMP leaders Irv Gilman, Evelyn Diederich, and Betty Couch, wife of Harry Couch.[16]

The gossip began shortly after a January 18 planning commission meeting at which two architects, representing developers of a proposed 122,000-square-foot commercial shopping mall on the dilapidated southern portion of Atlantic Boulevard, requested that their hearing be continued until February 15—in order, they said, to allow them to prepare responses to questions posed by the commission and possibly to revise the plan. The extension was granted. But at the January hearing three commissioners, Gerlach, Patricia Chin, and Chair Yukio Kawaratani, were prepared to vote against the project because developers sought a variance to allow a six-story parking structure that would significantly affect two nearby homes.

Opposition to the project came from one of these homeowners and a large turnout of people led by RAMP members. Joseph Rubin cited the increased traffic, noise, and view obstruction as sufficient cause to halt the proposed development, adding that the shopping mall was not worth the estimated $120,000 annual tax revenue to the city. Evelyn Diederich, opposing the requested variance, called the situation all too common in Monterey Park: "The developer gets the gold mine, and the homeowner gets the shaft." Irv Gilman argued that the proposed mall went against the controlled-growth spirit of Propositions A (1981) and K and L (1982). "What we need is moderation, but we're always going for overkill," he said. And after the meeting a suspicious Sonya Gerlach told the *Progress*: "I think that it's very likely and very possible that someone whispered into the ear of those [architects] that I wouldn't be a member of this commission come February 15, and with a new commissioner it's likely that they'll get the approval." [17]

On January 24 the city council selected Fred Rivera, a retired construction supervisor, to replace Gerlach on the planning commission. Again, Louise Davis cast the lone "no" vote. RAMP leader Joseph Rubin angered Mayor Manibog by calling the appointment "a reward for political friendship."

Rubin and Manibog exchanged harsh words, and the mayor challenged Rubin to prove that commission appointments were being used for political purposes. Rivera himself conceded that he had worked in Manibog's political campaigns, but as he had also worked to elect Louise Davis and Sonya Gerlach's husband, John, to various offices, he found the accusation unfair.[18]

A *Monterey Park Progress* editorial defended the actions of the city council shortly thereafter: "Commission appointments made with political motives are an unfortunate sin of our politics, but nevertheless a reality of the game. . . . If Mayor Manibog harbored political motives in appointing Rivera, it should surprise no one. That's the way politics is played. Lest we forget, it was little more than one year ago when talk was circulating throughout Monterey Park that RAMP member Patricia Chin would be appointed to the commission by political cohort Harry Couch, who was then mayor."[19]

Gerlach seems to have read the situation accurately: on February 15 the newly formed planning commission approved the mall by a vote of three to two. Katherine Cutrell, William Kenneally, and Fred Rivera voted in favor of the project; Patricia Chin and Yukio Kawaratani continued to oppose it. Commissioner Chin, who had voted in favor of the hearing delay, was infuriated after reviewing the "revised" plans. She charged the architects with making only "token" changes and said she felt the commission had been hoodwinked: "I was criticized . . . for agreeing to such an extension, but I believed that you were honest and sincere in your desire to try and make a project that was livable in this community. . . . I thought you would come back with a better project, with a project that was more suitable to this area. And the reason I gave you that extension was because I knew if we turned you down, you would go to the city council and, viewing some of their past decisions regarding planning, I don't think you'd have [had] a problem getting it through."[20]

On March 28 the Monterey Park City Council unanimously approved the $20 million mall project—with several modifications—during a rancorous meeting that lasted until 1:30 A.M. The approved plans called for the parking structure to be moved twenty-one feet away from the nearest home and to be one and a half stories lower than originally designed. A proposed 400-seat theater—the leading source of revenue, according to developers—was deemed excessive for the property's space, and likely to create traffic congestion and parking problems. The developers agreed to the size reductions and promised to beef up nighttime security for the mall.[21]

Opponents reiterated their concerns about increased traffic and density in the area, but Hal Mintz, consultant to the developers, cited an Environmental Impact Report that projected an acceptable level of impact. And Councilman David Almada, while also concerned about traffic problems and the effect of the project on surrounding homes, cautioned that Monterey Park "mustn't fall into the hands of people who would capitalize on emotional issues for the detriment of the city. . . . There are demagogues out there who would like to see no development and use an issue like this as a political football without ever being mindful of the city's financial situation."[22]

The North Atlantic Boulevard Plan

Toward the end of 1983 civic leaders gave serious consideration to a fifty-six-acre development project intended to convert North Atlantic Boulevard into a major retail area. This was the plan that City Manager Lloyd de Llamas had been working on since 1980 and had projected would bring the city $5 million in revenue. It passed its first hurdle on September 13 when it was unanimously approved by the Monterey Park Planning Commission with surprisingly little resistance.[23]

The proposal called for upgrading a six block area of Atlantic Boulevard, between Hellman and Newmark Avenues, to provide sites for new offices, retail stores, a large hotel complex, and other commercial enterprises. According to de Llamas, the idea was to encourage consolidation of properties to bring in much-needed large-scale retail stores before commercial property in the city became too expensive for economical investment. Land speculation in Monterey Park had been parceling properties into ever smaller units of strip development so that low-profit Chinese-owned and -operated enterprises and small-scale professional offices were the only new businesses coming to the city. The results were more competition, density, signs, and traffic but less open space and landscaping—and little contribution to the city's treasury.

The North Atlantic Boulevard Plan not only allowed for six-story buildings, but permitted a developer who could bring in a large, high-volume retail store to add an *extra* floor. "In my view it was really the last opportunity for Monterey Park to take advantage of the investment interest and guide it," explains de Llamas. "In the late 1970s, property was being purchased for $6.00 a square foot. Six months later it would turn over at $12 a square foot. Eight months later they'd sell it for $22 a square foot. It actually priced us out of the position to be able to create the kind of retailers you'd like to build on in a balanced economy and that would help finance the type of quality environment that the community wants."[24]

A November editorial in the *Progress* wholeheartedly endorsed de Llamas's assessment; recognizing the need for judicious change concluded, "The North Atlantic area is too large and too important to be neglected or carelessly developed. Change can't be stopped, but it can be controlled. The North Atlantic plan offers the best means of bringing about that control." [25]

With the backing of the planning commission, the city staff, and the entire city council, the plan needed only public approval. Because it called for a zoning change in an area larger than one acre, the North Atlantic Boulevard Plan had to come before the voters. The election was scheduled for June 1984.

Continued Change

Despite the controversies over development throughout 1983, Monterey Park did enjoy some positive media attention from the outside. In June, thanks to the election of Chen, Almada, and Peralta, *Time* magazine hailed the "majority minority" city council as representative of a harmonious middle-class melting pot.[26] But by that time, however, the full impact of demographic, economic, social, and cultural change in the community was being felt and increasingly resented. Later in the year a blatantly anti-Chinese letter signed "W.G." appeared in the *Progress*.

> I am writing this letter knowing that I have a lot of support from the citizens who have lived here for some time, and no support from the ones who invaded our city three or four years ago. . . .
>
> The people I am referring to are the Chinese and to come right down to the nitty gritty, what have they contributed to the world or the United States? If you study that question for a while you will come up with the answer, "Nothing." . . .
>
> So to all the good citizens of Monterey Park . . . don't let the invaders push you around, push in front of you while shopping, cut you off while driving, and run you away from eating in peace and quiet. After all, enough is enough, and they have to obey our laws and adapt to our customs, not theirs. So if anyone reading this letter is guilty of any of the above, remember there are people here other than you, and they have their rights, too.[27]

Ironically, and perhaps intentionally, W.G.'s letter was written just before Lily Lee Chen was to become mayor of Monterey Park. Her November 28 installation as the first Chinese American woman mayor in the United States brought unprecedented fanfare and became an international media event.

The "Coronation" of Lily Lee Chen

Having received the most votes of any candidate in the April 1982 city council election, Chen was first in line to become mayor (a rotating position) when Louise Davis's term expired. For Chen, it was a culmination of years of hard work, dedication, and passion for center stage. Many predicted that her political prominence was just beginning.

Lilly Lee was born in 1936 to a powerful and privileged family living just outside Beijing. After her family escaped the Chinese Communists and fled to Taiwan, her father became chancellor of a teacher's college there and a member of the Taiwanese legislature. He was a dominating figure who expected nothing less than excellence from his children. With this kind of influence, it was not surprising that she showed leadership potential early in her life. When she was just seventeen she represented the Republic of China (Taiwan) at an International Youth Leaders Conference sponsored by the U.S. State Department, was elected chairperson by delegates representing some sixty countries, and later served as their Goodwill Ambassador on a world tour.

Lily Lee came to the United States in 1958 to attend school at San Francisco State College (now University). There she met Paul Chen, an engineering student; the two were married in 1960 and moved to Seattle, where Paul had a job in the aerospace industry. Lily Lee Chen continued her education at the University of Washington, earning a master's degree in social work in 1964. While attending graduate school, Chen worked as a correspondent for Voice of America and later hosted her own talk show.

After the family, which now included a son and a daughter, moved to Monterey Park in 1970, Chen landed a job with Los Angeles County and quickly became active in the PTA and the Monterey Park Boys' Club. She then went into politics, working for various issues and candidates and becoming a candidate herself for the first time in 1981. Before her election to the city council she was appointed to two presidential committees: Gerald Ford named her to the Department of Health, Education and Welfare's Advisory Committee on the Rights and Responsibilities of Women; Jimmy Carter appointed her to the National Advisory Council on Adult Education.

Chen was seen as a up-and-coming star within the Democratic Party even before she became mayor of Monterey Park. She said she did not want to be seen as a "Chinese" representative but as a representative of the entire community. "The major theme of my campaign was to reflect the ethnic diversity of our city," Chen says. "My interest and commitment was to represent all people, and to make Monterey Park a city of tomorrow."[28]

As early as February 1983, Chen tried to stem the tide of anti-Chinese sentiment in the community. She announced that she would encourage Chinese business owners to put up multilingual signs voluntarily. She also wanted to crack down on merchants who had erected signs without obtaining proper permits. Chen offered her "personal assurance" that the problem would be corrected, predicting that within 100 days there would be no business signs displaying only the Chinese language in Monterey Park. To defuse the issue further, she pointed out that of the four businesses displaying Chinese-only signs in the city, two had already changed them and the other two were in the process of doing so.[29]

Chen's critics charged that she was vain, petty, and ambitious to a fault. Stories of her obsession with living up to her prominent family's high expectations were common throughout the community; Chen acknowledged that she maintained the family name Lee as a sign of respect to her father because he did not have male offspring.[30] Her mayoral installation—or coronation, as many residents recalled it—drew wide attention and criticism. The council chambers were packed solid with invited guests, and more people crowded outside to see Lily Lee Chen become the first Chinese American woman to lead an American city. The evening's pomp and circumstance included introductions of visiting dignitaries, long speeches, and music performed by the Mark Keppel High School marching band. Former city attorney Norman Lieberman vividly remembers that evening of November 28, 1983: "She had a ceremony like we never had [and] I was embarrassed just sitting there watching what was going on. I saw her . . . taking an oath of office that didn't exist from a federal judge who should have known better."[31]

The event was unabashedly touted as an example to the nation and the world that Asian Americans had finally made it into mainstream American life and politics. Chen's career was profiled in China's *People's Daily*; the *Washington Post* carried the installation on the front page; the Associated Press sent the story on its news wires. Without doubt, with the *Time* magazine feature, the installation of Lily Lee Chen, and the upcoming 1984 Summer Olympics in nearby Los Angeles, Monterey Park gave notice that it was now an international city, that this formerly sleepy bedroom community was indeed becoming the cosmopolitan city of tomorrow.

Proposition Q

Probably the council's biggest challenge during Chen's term as mayor was to get voter approval of Proposition Q, the citywide ballot initiative that would authorize the rezoning necessary to make the North Atlantic Boulevard Plan a reality. The North Atlantic plan was seen by a majority of council members and city staff as Monterey Park's last chance for a major planned development project that could bring in significant revenues. For years Monterey Park had lagged behind the neighboring cities of Alhambra and Montebello, which were already breaking ground on their retail redevelopment plans.

Not surprisingly, then, Proposition Q was the major topic of debate during the April 1984 city council campaign. Incumbent Monty Manibog was running for a third term; Louise Davis's seat was available because she had decided to retire from the council. At a public forum first-time candidate Cam Briglio, a sales and service technician for a pest extermination company, came out strongly against Proposition Q: "Where are all those cars gonna park? Where's this traffic going?" As one of the founders of the Monterey Park Taxpayers Association and a resident of the city since 1968, Briglio prided himself on being a blue-collar "people's candidate." At the same time, he had a reputation for crass behavior and thoughtless comments in public (for example, addressing a female candidate for the same seat as "sweetie").[32]

In an interesting split decision the residents of Monterey Park re-elected Monty Manibog, a strong proponent of Proposition Q, and brought into office Cam Briglio, an avowed opponent of the same measure.[33] Such an outcome kept the issue of Proposition Q active in residents' minds, and as June 5, the day of the vote, drew near, the debate in the community became sharp. Eli Isenberg wrote in favor of Proposition Q in a May 23 column and contrasted the pro and con factions: "If approved, 'Q' would permit the City of Monterey Park to develop North Atlantic Boulevard on a 'planned' basis. Defeat the issue and you build as you please. The city council majority approves 'Q' because it is 'better' economically and visually. And it will net more taxes. . . . the Residents Assn. of Monterey Park . . . claims that approval will mean less tax benefits. It gets down to whom you believe— City Manager Lloyd de Llamas and the majority of the council, or Irv Gilman and RAMP."[34]

On the same day Harold Fiebelkorn's bitingly sarcastic column compared RAMP leaders to the spoiled child "who picked up his ball and went home because the rest of the kids wouldn't let him pitch. . . . Monterey Park has several of these kids who really don't give a damn about the city, all because the voters wouldn't let them be the pitcher. Remember Harry Couch and Irv Gilman, who didn't get reelected to the city council, and Sonya Gerlach, who didn't get reappointed to the planning commission?" Fiebelkorn accused those three of trying to "stop the game" by telling residents that Proposition Q would result in unsightly skyscrapers and traffic gridlock on Atlantic Boulevard.[35] In addition, the June issue of *Monterey Park Living*, the city's own quarterly publication for residents, carried stories exclusively favoring Proposition Q[36]—even though opponents contended that a taxpayer-supported city magazine could not ethically be used as a political vehicle.

Despite an all-out effort by proponents, however, Proposition Q was defeated by the voters: 6,028 (59.3 percent) opposed the rezoning measure; 4,145 (40.7) voted for it.[37] RAMP leaders had had difficulty getting people to work actively against the proposition. "We had a lot of people on our side, but it was hard to get workers," remembers Evelyn Diederich.[38] Nevertheless, the small donations that allowed RAMP to put out one mailer and the small cadre of fervent volunteers who walked the streets and put up hundreds of signs apparently had their effect. For Lloyd de Llamas, who had dedicated four years to the project, seeing it go down in defeat was a crushing blow. "I remember Betty Couch walked door-to-door with signs saying: 'They'll condemn your property, it'll mean higher taxes, there will be twelve-story buildings in town, and they'll ruin the city,'" he says. "They absolutely killed it."[39]

The Widening Credibility Gap

After the defeat of Proposition Q, RAMP members and other residents sent letters accusing everyone in the city's leadership of having bowed to special interests. "There could be a nice development on North Atlantic if the city council would refuse to grant variances and conditional use permits," wrote Evelyn Diederich to the *Progress*. "But then how can the council repay the developers that were instrumental in getting the majority of the council elected?" James Ashley attacked the *Progress* itself: "This local newspaper has sold out to outside 'developers' in exchange for increasing advertising revenue at the expense of the local citizenry it has a responsibility to serve through truthful reporting." Irv Gilman, who had been a regular writer to the *Progress* since his electoral defeat in April 1982, asserted that "Monterey Park is divided into two parts. The largest part is the voter who keeps sending loud, clear, unmistakable messages to city hall about development in our community. The second part is the misguided city council, an insensitive chamber of commerce, greedy developers and a bunch of good old boys. Actually, the second group can be bunched together as the establishment—an elite group that is either deaf or has decided the voters are just too dumb to vote right."[40]

Lily Lee Chen and David Almada both denied being controlled by developer interests. Instead, they blamed RAMP and its "no-growth" policies for ruining the city. Chen called Propositions K and L ill-conceived measures because all they did was "limit growth only by number and not demand quality." She insisted that her decisions were based solely on her desire to meet the needs of a growing city: "I think there has to be a balance in terms of commercial development that would generate enough revenues to pay for the services that the citizens demand."[41]

Almada agreed that uncontrolled development was a problem but maintained that RAMP had stirred up racism to fuel anti-development sentiments in the community: "People who normally are espousing a 'free-enterprise system' and capitalism . . . now are turning around and telling Asians that they can't participate in capitalism in this country." He added that people forgot what Monterey Park was like before Chinese investors brought money to the community when no one else would and "redeveloped blighted areas, including Garfield and Garvey, the old downtown area. If you had seen it ten years ago [mid-1970s] and look at it today [mid-1980s], there is no one who can tell me that it's worse today."[42]

Lloyd de Llamas, while certainly no friend of RAMP and its policies, acknowledges that the council increasingly lost credibility with residents. In his view, the open interest of Chen, Almada, and Manibog in running for higher office affected their public policy decisions. "It's pretty heady for someone who is suddenly sitting at the head table of banquets getting introduced as the councilman from Monterey Park and a potential candidate for [the California State] Assembly," he explains. "The council became variance happy. They supported quality development, but the more they were lobbied by developer interests, the more their view of . . . quality was influenced by who was making the proposal. For example, they would say, 'Well, we still want quality development, but maybe the parking restrictions don't have to be so tight on this particular project being proposed by our friend. . . . Suddenly it became, 'How does this help my political career?'"[43]

The Language Battle

As mistrust grew, residents began to look suspiciously at every action the council took. Still, "in all fairness to them," de Llamas points out, "they understood that they had to bring people together—if for no other reason than to build up their own political constituency. They did make a tremendous contribution in encouraging and making opportunities for new residents to become involved in the community and making sure that our services met the needs of immigrant residents." Among other things, the council initiated police-citizen translator service whereby bilingual individuals were on call as interpreters, hired a Chinese-speaking librarian, sponsored cultural events, and established English-as-a-second-language classes run by volunteers in virtually every church, as well as the senior citizens' and recreation centers. Such programs helped Monterey Park win an "All-America" city award from the Municipal League and *USA Today* newspaper in 1985. "Unfortunately," adds de Llamas, "we were concentrating so much on the newcomers' needs that we hadn't really thought about the old-timers and their growing resentment."[44]

The Business Sign Controversy

The increase of Chinese-owned and -operated businesses throughout the late 1970s and into the mid-1980s brought on a ground swell of discontent among many long-time residents in the community. From the early 1980s their foremost cause for complaint was that many businesses displayed signs in large Chinese characters with minimal or no English translation. Criticism first couched in terms of concern for public safety and public information later blew up into clearly anti-Chinese sentiment. As Norman Lieberman, former city attorney, puts it:

> The justification for English on the signs was that the police and fire [departments] had to know what was going on there and . . . where it was to answer a call, [and the public should know] what business is going on so they can shop if they choose to, and to some extent the city gets revenue from it. . . . [But] I can assure you that the police and fire know what is there, no matter what language you put on it. As [for] people knowing what business is being conducted, . . . a merchant can decide for himself. Because, in fact, if they don't want to cater to Caucasians, they don't have to. . . . It was just absolute nonsense to suppose that there was some public welfare reason for the fight that went on; it was political. [But that argument] was effective because . . . a tremendous number of voters out there—I'm not talking about bigots— [would] say, "Gee, that sounds right."[45]

Despite her promise in 1983 to relieve such tensions in the city, Lily Lee Chen's results were desultory. As investment in Monterey Park continued and the number of Chinese businesses grew, the number of Chinese-only signs increased to about a dozen, and those that did include English offered little more than a token translation. Rapid turnover of small businesses also made it difficult to achieve voluntary compliance.

By 1984 a group of frustrated residents and a few long-time merchants were calling for a strict city ordinance requiring at least 50 percent English on all business signs in town. The movement stalled when then City Attorney Lieberman expressed his legal opinion that any language ordinance would be a violation of constitutional free speech. A proposed ban on roof signs and projecting signs was strongly opposed by most merchants, both Asian and non-Asian. But because of political pressure from residents, a committee made up of city staff, merchants, and residents was formed to study the matter. In addition, the city council sponsored "Town Hall" meetings to hear residents' complaints about signs, traffic congestion, and commercial development.

Sensing that the growing political controversy might be getting out of hand, in April 1985 Lily Lee Chen gave up the idea of voluntary compliance and, ignoring the city attorney's opinion, proposed an ordinance requiring that English be added to Chinese signs. Chen was hopeful that a formal ordinance, if approved by the planning commission, would finally quell the growing complaints.

But her effort proved futile, and the issue exploded when the *Monterey Park Progress* published a fiery letter from Frank Arcuri, a resident who unabashedly stated publicly what many people were thinking privately. "The proposed Monterey Park law that English be included in business signs so that police and firemen can find these locations in emergencies does not address the real issues. The problem is that Asian businesses are crowding out American businesses in Monterey Park and Alhambra. . . . Stores that post signs that are 80 percent Chinese characters make us feel like strangers in our own land. . . . I will go a step further than the proposed law and say that all signs must be completely in English."[46] Chen's proposal did not go over well with Chinese merchants, either; they claimed that the English requirement would be a violation of their freedom of speech and that putting up new signs would impose a financial hardship.

In June 1985, amid these conflicting interests, the planning commission recommended approval of an ordinance that would impose the least restrictive requirements possible, hoping thereby to preserve freedom of speech. Citing public safety, the law would have required minimally that the address of each business establishment should appear in English and arabic numerals visible 100 feet from the main entrance. But none of the twelve people attending the planning commission hearing supported the proposal. Irv Gilman reminded the commission that the initial intent of a sign ordinance was to ensure that people would know what business was being conducted. Frank Arcuri complained that the proposed ordinance would only add to visual clutter and create confusion among residents and shoppers.[47]

On July 22, 1985, when the city council gave preliminary approval to an ordinance requiring only that a business add its address in English, the outspoken Arcuri denounced it as "useless" and threatened to place an "English only" sign ordinance on the ballot as an initiative.[48] "Monterey Park is not the All-American city that its public relations people are trying to create," he shouted. "It is the new West Coast Chinatown that excludes other ethnic groups in shopping districts. . . . The [slogan] 'Will the Last American to leave Monterey Park please bring the American Flag' is a valid description of the problem." When Manibog asked how he defined an "American," Arcuri responded, "If you don't know what 'American' means, you have no right representing us."[49]

Manibog, a Filipino American veteran of the Korean War, bitterly resented this challenge to his patriotism and called Arcuri a bigot. Councilman Almada agreed that Arcuri's comments were irresponsible: "I can't condone his method of solving this problem. To say that Asians are not American, I cannot accept." Lily Lee Chen, who had originally proposed a more stringent ordinance, was clearly taken aback by the tone the discussion had taken; she too accused Arcuri of bigotry and of unfairness to "so many old-timers and new-timers who are trying to promote understanding in the community."[50]

No ordinance on business signs came to a city council vote until early 1986. The issue became sidetracked by an emerging movement for "official English."

English as the Official Language

Arcuri made good on his threat. To start a local ballot initiative he enlisted the technical assistance of U.S. English, a Washington-based group founded by former U.S. Senator S. I. Hayakawa and dedicated to making English the official language of the United States. In August 1985 he and fellow resident Barry Hatch filed a legal notice of intent to circulate a petition: "English is the language we use in Monterey Park when we want everyone to understand our ideas. This is what unites us as Americans, even though some of our citizens speak other languages. Let us make English our official language as a symbol of this unity."[51]

Arcuri and Hatch had met earlier with twenty-five supporters to map out a strategy. "If the city council does not solve the problem, then we can take it out of their hands," Arcuri told the gathering. "That's what is great about being an American."[52] The group had to gather 2,000 signatures—10 percent of the registered voters in Monterey Park—by November 11, 1985, in order for the city clerk to verify the names and put the issue on the ballot.

That Arcuri and Hatch had tapped strong feelings in Monterey

Park was attested by a letter from resident Bill Marticorena to the *Progress*: "I am American. I think American. And I act American. I volunteered into the U.S. Army 10 days before the U.S. first military draft law. I . . . served in three theaters of World War II. I have been in foxholes and so therefore they are going to have to drive me out of one before I sell my home, as many old-timers of Monterey Park have done in the past. . . . It takes a lot of guts for Americans like Frank Arcuri and Barry Hatch to stand up. I am going to stick with [them] whatever."[53]

Frank Arcuri, the self-appointed protector of American culture, moved to Monterey Park with his wife in 1972. He was earning his living as a commercial photographer and sculptor, but what he enjoyed most was being a political activist. "I think about it," he told the *Los Angeles Times*. "I dream it."[54] Short and stocky, he looked like a pugilist and fancied himself the underdog Rocky Balboa of Monterey Park. One of his campaign flyers pictured him in a fighting stance, wearing boxing gloves and a smirk.

Born and raised in New York City in an Italian American family, Arcuri joined the army at seventeen and served for three years. After his military stint he became an apprentice photographer and then studied art in college, earning a bachelor's degree in 1972 and a master's in 1973 from California State University, Los Angeles. Arcuri says he has exhibited his artwork in galleries and museums across the country. He moved to Monterey Park because it was close to the university and because he liked its diversity: "I've always lived in cities that had mixed communities. I've avoided ethnic communities, I never would have felt comfortable. . . . Now all of a sudden, to have a group come to our city, which in this case is Chinese people, with enough money so they can buy our city, buy our economy and force their language and culture down our throats, this is what's disturbing to people in Monterey Park."[55] Both critics and supporters found Arcuri as tough as nails and as self-righteous as a fist. His aggressive confrontational style brought him far more foes than friends, but that didn't bother him. "Never did," he said. "I hear a different drummer."[56]

Co-petitioner Barry Hatch, one of six children, was born and raised in Monterey Park and has lived there most of his life. Old-timers in the city remember young Hatch as reliable and always willing to help neighbors paint their fences or run errands. In high school he worked at the downtown Star Market, which has since been replaced by the Chinese-owned Quang Hua Supermarket. His ancestors came to this country from Wales and England in the eighteenth century. His family is Mormon; his great-great-grandfather reportedly was the scout who first came upon the Salt Lake Valley and told Brigham

Young, "We are there," and Barry is also said to be a distant cousin of Utah's Senator Orrin G. Hatch.[57] His parents moved from Salt Lake City to Monterey Park in the 1930s.

Hatch graduated from high school in 1954 and attended nearby East Los Angeles Community College for one year before becoming a missionary in Hong Kong; he spent three years in Asia, and learned to speak and read Chinese. In 1960 he was drafted into the army and served two years in Germany, where he was married briefly. For the next ten years Hatch worked as a Los Angeles County deputy sheriff and went to school part time; for a short time he also was a cadet at the California Highway Patrol Academy. Hatch left Monterey Park to attend Southern Utah State and graduated with a degree in education in 1973. After teaching for five years, he returned in 1978—just as the Chinese influx was reaching its peak—to take care of his ailing parents. Since that time he has earned a master's degree in educational counseling from the University of La Verne and has taught American history at a junior high school in nearby Bell Gardens. Tall, handsome, and husky-voiced, Hatch, physically strong and firm in his convictions, epitomizes the "John Wayne" American. "I promote speaking a language we can all understand," he said. "All people in this city have a stake in this issue. I pay a mortgage, others pay mortgages, so to that degree we own this city. Then when we look up and see all these Chinese characters on signs—why, it feels foreign to us. It is one bold slap in the face, which says to us, 'Hey, you're not wanted.'"[58]

Just one week after Arcuri and Hatch announced their intention to make English the official language in Monterey Park, several residents came to City Hall to oppose the measure. "What is this guy [Arcuri] talking about?" one Chinese protester asked. "In Hong Kong, the official language is English and nobody speaks it. What really doesn't make sense is when he says he's doing it to unite the community." A white resident said the move was unnecessary and called it "a Pandora's box"; he suggested that its sponsors could do more good by getting involved in a literacy program. A representative from the Mexican American Political Association asserted that "those who speak two languages have a right to speak the second language." And a Japanese American resident pointed out that classes in English as a second language (ESL) already had long waiting lists: "I question whether government needs to tell the people they need to learn English. Don't we give these people credit for taking the initiative?"[59]

Despite these multi-ethnic efforts, within a month the measure's proponents had 3,200 signatures on their petitions—more than enough to qualify for the April 1986 ballot. In a meeting with the Monterey Park Community Relations Commission on October 16, Hatch proclaimed that the movement to make English the city's official language was receiving broad support. In a sample of 10 petition sheets with 280 names, he said, "about 25 percent were Hispanic and 15 percent Asian, with one-third of those Chinese." Asked how he could tell the Chinese from the Japanese, the former missionary in Hong Kong replied, "I speak Chinese, so I can tell those from Japanese." Hatch went on to argue that the many dialects in China had ruined that nation and pointed out that the Communist government was trying to unify the country with one language. "The Chinese, of all people, should understand that one language unites this country," he said. "English is a vital issue. There are parts of Florida where only Cuban [Spanish] is spoken and Monterey Park could easily become a Chinese-speaking community."[60]

The Community Relations Commission meeting, relatively civil at first, turned hostile as the evening wore on. Commissioner Francis Hong, who had suggested inviting Arcuri and Hatch, was incensed when Arcuri asked him if he was an American citizen. "I am a good American, law abiding, and just as educated as anyone in this room," stormed Hong, who had come to the United States in the mid-1960s. "Why do I have to be singled out for such a question? You didn't ask any of the other people. . . . Is it because of the color of my face?"[61]

In direct reaction to the movement to make English the official language, an ad hoc opposition group formed, made up of Asians, Latinos, and whites who called themselves the Coalition for Harmony in Monterey Park (CHAMP). In a press conference held November 1, 1985, its leaders said they wanted to place a rival resolution on the April 1986 ballot, calling for acceptance of cultural diversity and more funds for ESL classes. "We are concerned that some in this community are using the [official-English] petition drive to promote unity by disunity and harmony by dissension and by enlightening us back to the Dark Ages," said CHAMP co-chair Michael Eng. "They would twist the meaning of patriotism and Americanism. Our purpose is to foster and maintain a spirit of citywide harmony, acceptance, and cooperation among the culturally diverse members of the community."[62]

On November 11 the proponents of official English handed in their petitions to the city clerk with great fanfare. Their mood quickly turned sour, however. City Attorney Richard Morillo unceremoniously ruled that the proposed initiative was invalid because, ironically, it lacked the proper wording: it contained the reasons for adopting the ordinance but not the full text of an ordinance. "We can't guess at what it's supposed to say," Morillo told the press. Declaring that his decision had nothing to do with the constitutionality of official English or any personal feelings, he ordered proponents to collect signatures all over again.[63]

Arcuri branded the city attorney a "tricky lawyer" and vowed he would fight the ruling. But Marcus Crahan, an attorney who had advised the official-English proponents, admitted that the petition was technically incorrect. Noting that the petition did clearly state its purpose—the enactment of an ordinance to declare English the official language—Crahan advised the initiative leaders to refile their documents with an attached ordinance, in the hope that this would satisfy the legal requirements.[64] The council, though a majority vigorously opposed the official-English initiative, did not wait for the city attorney's new ruling; on December 3 it unanimously approved the draft of a proposal that would further restrict Chinese-language business signs. Frank Arcuri, clearly enjoying his newfound celebrity status and still advocating English-only signs, blasted the proposed ordinance, charging that it would not change the "Asian marketplace look" of the city: "They're putting their signs in Chinese because they think their language and customs are superior to ours."[65]

When the city attorney rejected the refiled documents, the supporters of official English were prepared and immediately brought suit against Monterey Park in Los Angeles Superior Court, seeking to force acceptance of the petition. In a well-orchestrated media event, Arcuri watched as retired thirty-five-year resident Clifford Sharp served the city clerk's office with the lawsuit. Under the bright glow of television lights Arcuri, who had already announced his intention to run for city council in 1986, denied any attempt at grandstanding: "I care about issues, not about personal publicity."[66]

In late December Superior Court Judge Jack T. Ryburn ruled against the official-English supporters and upheld the city's action in refusing to accept the petition. The verdict ended five months of bitter fighting over the controversial measure. "Technicality in the law is the last refuge of scoundrels," Arcuri said bitterly. But supporters quickly vowed to shift their focus. Arcuri announced that rather than appeal the decision, he would start a new petition drive to restrict Chinese-language signs and also help gather signatures for a statewide initiative seeking to make English the official language of California.[67]

The official-English movement thus grew out of the frustration caused by seemingly uncontrollable development and the anxiety over the influx of Chinese immigrants moving to Monterey Park. Within this multicultural "majority-minority" community, the overt linkage between language and development issues forcefully challenged residents to choose their loyalties. The small percentage of whites living in the city were overwhelmingly on the side of preserving the community as they had known it in the past; Latinos and, especially, American-born Asians were torn by the broader political choice between ethnic solidarity, individual self-interest, and community control. How these loyalties played out is the focus of the next chapter.

CHAPTER 6

"City with a Heart"?

The movement for English as the official language was not
unique to Monterey Park. As early as 1980, voters in Miami,
Florida, a city where large numbers of Spanish-speaking
Cubans have settled, overwhelmingly approved a law (since reversed)
restricting the use of Spanish and Creole. In November 1984, voters
in California passed by a 71 to 29 percent margin Proposition 38,
an advisory ballot measure recommending that all election materials
be printed in English only.[1] Fillmore and Alameda, two small California
communities, passed official-English ordinances in early 1985,
and several others considered similar actions later on.[2] But Monterey
Park, had the proponents of official English succeeded in placing
the measure on the municipal ballot, would have been the first city in
California to put it to a vote of the people.

Despite opposition from civil rights groups and ethnic organizations,
efforts to declare English the official language quickly gained
momentum throughout the nation. Spearheading the effort was U.S.
English, the organization that assisted Monterey Park's initiative attempt,
which by 1986 was seeking to pass laws or voter-initiated ballot
measures in Alabama, California, Florida, Idaho, Iowa, Kansas,
Maryland, Massachusetts, Missouri, New Hampshire, New Jersey, New
York, Washington, and Wisconsin. Until that time only six states—
Georgia, Illinois, Indiana, Kentucky, Nebraska, and Virginia—had
official-English laws, passed years before. With a goal of making
English the official language of the nation, advocates acknowledged
that interest in the idea had been renewed by the large influx of Latino
and Asian immigrants. "Communities are changing very, very quickly,
and I think . . . there is a great deal of frustration about it," said Gerda
Bickales, executive director of U.S. English.[3]

In early 1986 a group called California English Campaign, the
California arm of U.S. English, began circulating a petition to place
an initiative on the November 4 statewide ballot. By July members
had collected over a million signatures. California English Campaign's
Proposition 63 was intended to amend the California constitution to
declare English the official language of the state; it would also require
that the legislature "take all steps necessary" to enhance the role of

English, and allow any citizen to sue the state to force such actions. Proposition 63 was the first of such laws actually submitted to the voters by the initiative process. According to Frank Arcuri, Monterey Park had been "sort of a dry run for the state."[4]

Throughout the United States, heightened opposition to immigrant Latinos and Asians and to their impact on the social, cultural, economic, and political landscape was at its peak in the middle to late 1980s. While the nation was debating the merits of official English, Congress was preparing to pass the sweeping 1986 Immigration Reform and Control Act, aimed at controlling the flow of undocumented immigration.

It is against this backdrop that events in Monterey Park in 1986 and 1987 need to be understood. This chapter discusses the 1986 city council election, which swept two Latinos and a Chinese American out of office and replaced them with white advocates of controlled growth and official English; the actions initiated by the new council majority, which many critics called "anti-Chinese"; and the attempt in 1987 to recall two of the three newly elected council members.

The 1986 Election

When the official-English ballot initiative was voided by the city attorney and the city council, its supporters charged that the council had been bought out by Chinese developers. Their accusations fell on receptive ears, and four candidates emerged—Frank Arcuri, Barry Hatch, Chris Houseman, and Patricia Reichenberger—to challenge incumbents in one of the most hotly contested and highly publicized council elections in recent memory.

Chris Houseman, a twenty-seven-year-old UCLA law student born and raised in Monterey Park, was a strong controlled-growth activist; he had been a member of RAMP, but during the 1982 campaign for Propositions K and L he worked independently for their passage. In 1986, when he had just entered his first year of law school, he decided to run for city council not because he thought he could win but because he was disturbed that the focus was moving away from development and land-use policy toward official English and ethnic divisiveness: "I reached a conclusion that somebody had to go out and run in the election and articulate what he or she would feel were the real problems in the community." Basically, he said, "you had three incumbents who had stinko records in terms of development policies," yet the only credentials of the three people running against them seemed to be based on "this English issue."[5]

Houseman's hyperactive personality and thought processes were apparent: he spoke in rapid bursts that often went off on long tangents. Critics said he was brash, prone to temper tantrums, and not much of a team player. Nevertheless, his independence and sincere passion for the issues in Monterey Park earned him the endorsement of popular Louise Davis; moreover, residents seemed to like his candor. "I used to walk around and knock on people's doors during the campaign," he says, describing his election strategy. "I had to spend a lot of time talking to people on their doorsteps. Other candidates could go around and say, 'Hi. Blah. Blah. Blah.' They'd be gone in one minute and maybe get a sign up on the front lawn. I ended up spending a half-hour on everybody's porch."[6]

Patricia Reichenberger, a gregarious woman with an easy laugh and a raspy smoker's voice, had a more deliberate approach. A long-time RAMP member and active supporter of the official-English initiative, she had moved to Monterey Park with her family when she was eight years old and had lived in the community for thirty-three years at the time of the election. She ran for the council because she believed that the community was being taken away from its residents: "Certain investors and developers came in with the idea of making a multi-million dollar situation, which they did. I really relate to it as a rape of Monterey Park." In her door-to-door campaigning she found that people of all ethnic backgrounds "felt that we were lacking department stores, we were lacking grocery stores, we had traffic problems; everyone agreed what the problems were."[7]

As for official English, "it was a very well-known fact that I supported it and worked on it, but it was something that I never really campaigned on. When I went to the door, I would talk about development; I would not talk about English unless I was directly asked." She and Barry Hatch had both broken away from Frank Arcuri because they thought his methods and statements were too extreme to gain widespread support: "I found that his ideas were racist and bigoted and they were not the reasons that I became involved in English, so I chose to go my separate way, along with Mr. Hatch," recalled Reichenberger. "We bailed from Frank Arcuri; we never bailed out from the U.S. English. In other words, we supported the English movement but not on Frank Arcuri's level." Community resentment over Chinese-language signs, she thought, was not "resentment towards the Chinese as much as it was the fact that, hey, we want some English. I don't think that people here really want all English, I really don't. . . . I would like to see 50 percent English, 50 percent Chinese, which is fair to everyone."[8]

In a somewhat surprising move, the *Progress* endorsed incumbent Lily Lee Chen plus Houseman and Hatch for city council. Not so surprisingly, RAMP endorsed Houseman, Reichenberger, and Hatch. Though they did not run as a single slate, RAMP campaigned on behalf of the challengers and, as if to avenge the defeat of their candidates in 1982, mobilized against the incumbents. In a last-minute campaign mailer called the *Record*, it cited campaign statements showing that Chen, Almada, and Peralta had raised ten times as much money as their challengers, accused the incumbents of being bought by developer interests, and pointed to questionable items in their expense records during their time in office.[9]

The mailer used headlines shouting "Big Buck Developers Pay for the Election of the Developer Candidates," and "Developer Candidates Chen, Almada, and Peralta Have Put People Last and Developer Greed First." It retold the story of the Townsend family, whose home was "ruined" when the city council approved a variance for a parking structure less than ten yards away, and the Ornelas family, who were denied permission to add on an extra bedroom because of a building code technicality. Without stating anything specifically anti-Chinese or referring to the official-English issue, the *Record* featured photos of closed storefronts that had once housed old favorites J. C. Penney, Safeway, Ed Kretz Motorcycle. These, it said, were being "pushed out" and "replaced" by banks. The banks pictured included the East-West Federal Bank, Cathay Bank, Bank of Canton, and others that prominently displayed Chinese-language characters.[10]

The incumbents running for reelection based their campaigns on high-powered endorsements and slick professional mailers. One of David Almada's flyers featured a letter signed by Congressman Matthew Martinez, State Senator Joseph Montoya, and Assemblyman Charles Calderon, all urging citizens to vote for their candidate.[11] Other prominent Latino politicians such as Los Angeles Councilman Richard Alatorre and State Assemblywoman Gloria Molina also campaigned for him, but these efforts seemed to backfire and create resentment among Latinos and non-Latinos alike. "Almada likes to talk about the 'All American [*sic*] City—Monterey Park' while at the same time he exploits his race and uses Hispanic politicians to head up a twenty-five-dollar per person reception to fatten up his political war chest," wrote enraged resident Trini Estrada. "I am tired of the attempts by Mexican-American politicians to exploit us for their own selfish reasons. Let's vote for a city council candidate regardless of race."[12]

Lily Lee Chen raised $61,415 for her campaign; she spent $42,353 to rent a large office that served as her headquarters, hired a "professional" staff to manage her reelection bid, and printed glossy campaign flyers.[13] Most of her mailings featured glowing photos of the candi-

date. One that read "Re-Elect Lily Chen City Council . . . Striving
for a Monterey Park with Liberty and Justice for All" had photographs of her waving an American flag and posing with United Farm
Workers organizer Cesar Chavez—perhaps an attempt to ingratiate
herself with Latino residents in Monterey Park.[14]

On April 8, 1986, in what many local pundits agree was a surprise
result, the three city council incumbents were decisively ousted from
office. The leading vote-getter was Chris Houseman with 4,948 votes
(21.2 percent), followed by Barry Hatch with 3,990 (17.0 percent), and
Patricia Reichenberger with 3,778 votes (16.1 percent). In fourth place
was Lily Lee Chen with 3,125 votes (13.3 percent), followed closely by
David Almada with 3,019 (12.8 percent), and then Rudy Peralta with
2,583 (11.0 percent). In last place was fiery Frank Arcuri, with 1,992
votes (8.6 percent).[15]

This election drew one of the largest turnouts for a city council race in the city's history: according to the city clerk's records,
8,770 residents, or 39.2 percent of 22,375 registered voters, came
to the polls. It had also been the most expensive campaign to date:
together the incumbents spent a total of $92,537 for jobs that paid only
$200 a month. Chen was by far the top spender, followed by Almada
($29,508) and Rudy Peralta ($20,676). Houseman spent $10,428 from
donations of $11,860, but the bulk of his contributions came from his
parents and from loans made to him by his sister.[16]

The results of the election drew a bitter response from the incumbents. Chen accused Arcuri, Hatch, and Reichenberger of fueling
racial tensions: "They used this particular issue [of 'English only']
to generate an emotional response from the local residents and they
linked the issue . . . with development."[17] Chen had been the direct
target of considerable ugliness during the campaign; under the caption "Chen's Laundry," grotesque caricatures of her washing dollar
bills against a backdrop of banks with names in Chinese characters
had been widely circulated.

"It was a backlash primarily against the Asians and ethnic people
in general," said David Almada. "What happened was our old-timers
went out and voted in droves. . . . just look at the names Reichenberger,
Hatch, and Houseman and tell me how they voted. They didn't vote
for Peralta, Chen, and Almada!"[18]

The New Council and Resolution 9004

On April 28, just weeks after the election, Barry Hatch publicly announced that rather than raise the official-English question again he
would let statewide Proposition 63 settle the matter in November.

The issue had become too divisive, he said, and "forces that got involved did more damage than good." He promised, however, that if Proposition 63 failed, he would ask the council to declare English the official language of Monterey Park. Three members—Hatch, Reichenberger, and Cam Briglio—openly supported official English, and Hatch claimed that most people in Monterey Park wanted it, but "nobody wants to go to war" over it.[19]

At the same meeting the Monterey Park City Council made some bold and highly controversial decisions. First, in order to review development standards and make recommendations for change, its members voted unanimously to place a moratorium on construction of commercial buildings, apartments, and condominiums for at least forty-five days; some members said it might last from six months to a year. Development Director Henry Terashita objected that the moratorium would halt the construction of seventy-four residential units already under consideration by the city. Other speakers charged the council with racism; Paul Yen, whose plans to build ten condominium units were now blocked, said that the decision was a result of "race conflict" in the community and that "a lot of people don't want to see too many Orientals move in."[20]

The council also voted four to one against a proposed forty-three-unit senior housing project in the northeastern section of town. Sponsored by Taiwanese developers, the project had initially been planned as seventy-five units with parking in the neighboring city of Rosemead but was entirely redesigned after the Rosemead planning commission denied permission to build the parking structure. The Monterey Park Planning Commission had voted to approve the revised plans with a conditional use permit (CUP) but required additional changes for full approval. Now the developers appealed to the city council to override the planning commission's recommendations. But dozens of residents who lived near the proposed site came to the meeting to oppose such a development in their residential neighborhood. "The day of high-density projects should be over," said one.[21]

The passage of the moratorium and the rejection of the senior housing project certainly heightened tensions in Monterey Park but did not on their own create the firestorm of protest that erupted after the passage of Resolution 9004. Adopted at the end of the June 2, 1986, council meeting, this resolution brought Monterey Park unwanted and unflattering national media attention.

Throughout his election campaign, Barry Hatch had never hidden his deep concerns over the numbers of undocumented immigrants entering the United States and the fact that, in his eyes, our country was "losing control" of its borders. Once in office, he openly expressed his complete opposition to the growing "sanctuary" movement intended to protect the civil and human rights of the undocumented. In a number of cities across the country, including nearby Los Angeles, church groups and others were advocating greater recognition of the U.S. economic, political, and foreign policy which, they claimed, were pushing people from their home countries—particularly war-torn Guatemala and El Salvador, whose repressive right-wing governments were supported with U.S. money and arms. These activists argued that people entering this country because of life-threatening circumstances at home should be considered economic and political refugees, not treated as criminals. "Sanctuary cities" acknowledged these factors and promised not to use municipal resources to apprehend or deport "illegal" aliens.

Horrified by that trend, Hatch asked for a draft resolution whereby Monterey Park would affirm that it opposed "the so-called Sanctuary Movement as a violation of the United States immigration law"; that it would "never become nor support any city that does become a 'sanctuary' city"; that its police department would "cooperate with the INS in regard to illegal aliens"; that the city "urgently" requested Congress to "pass legislation to control United States borders and to remove aliens who are residing in the United States illegally"; and finally, that Monterey Park would support "legislation to make English the official language of the United States."[22]

Hatch originally wanted to delete the official-English clause but during discussion on June 2 Cam Briglio threatened to withhold his support of the entire resolution if it was not included. Briglio, who had been heavily criticized the year before for calling construction workers in town "ignorant illegal aliens," was steadfast in his position and would not back down, though Mayor Manibog accused him of bringing the official-English issue "in the back door" and "opening wounds."[23] Eventually, Hatch, Briglio, and Reichenberger voted to support the full resolution; Manibog voted against it, and Houseman abstained.

Though Resolution 9004 was purely symbolic and carried no legal weight, many in the community were offended and immediately seized upon it as another example of the council's behind-the-back, xenophobic, nationalist, and anti-immigrant agenda. CHAMP reorganized with renewed vigor and called a series of press conferences to plead for community unity and to argue that the measure was mean-spirited and served only to create divisiveness. On June 9 forty-five people expressed their opposition to Resolution 9004 and urged the council to rescind its action, but despite four hours of heated testimony its council supporters refused to budge.

Patricia Reichenberger said later that she had wrestled with herself about reversing her vote but became convinced that the protesters were just fronts for developer interests. Her mail overwhelmingly supporting Resolution 9004, and only a few letters called the measure racist or discriminatory. "You know what it is really about?" she asked. "It is about the development, the moratorium, that is what it really is all about. Not the resolution. The resolution was ammunition that we gave them to use on us, and they chose to do that. That I regret; if I had to do it over, I would have definitely waited on the timing. You learn your lesson the hard way."[24]

Chris Houseman agreed with Reichenberger that developer interests were using the issue to attack the new council, but he also insisted that the residents who were genuinely hurt by the council's action should not be ignored: "A number of people in Monterey Park . . . were sincerely concerned about that resolution, sincerely worried . . . that it would open old wounds in the community and tear at the [social] fabric here. Their sincere feelings against it were disguised by the fact that the developers were running around screaming about this resolution, and everybody knew they didn't really care one way or the other. They just wanted something to clobber the new city council with."[25]

Resolution 9004 set neighbor against neighbor in a way never seen before in Monterey Park. A flurry of letters published in the *Progress* expressed all views on the issue. George Rustic, a retired public school administrator who supported the resolution, soon became a regular letter writer to the paper:

> Even though seven out of 10 Monterey Park citizens support the idea of English as the language of our country and city, a handful of weirdos [are] telling us we are unAmericans, racists and wrong. . . .
>
> Now, this anti-English group is going on record as supporting sanctuary movements and also supporting the resultant violations of United States laws pertaining to immigration. . . .
>
> I believe it's time we seven out of 10 got off our duffs and wrote to both our city council and the local newspapers about how we feel. Our complacency and good-neighbor attitudes have allowed this handful of bigoted unAmericans to dictate social and political order in our city. I believe it is time the thousands of us tell the few racist unAmericans to shut up.[26]

Maxine Vogeler agreed and professed shock at "the abuse our new neighbors from across the Pacific heaped on Barry Hatch simply because he is trying to keep Americanism alive and well. . . . Americanism is a condition of the heart and from what I heard, perhaps the people who spoke with such hatred should return to whence they came because I doubt Americanism will ever dwell in their hearts."[27]

Marjorie Kemmerer responded directly to Rustic: "I am shocked to the core by the waves of exaggerations, mis-representations, lies and villifications [sic] which have been proliferating in Monterey Park in the last few months. A lot of people seem to forget that the right to disagree is a constitutionally protected, very American right in the U.S. But it is morally wrong to lie." Accusing Rustic of being "one of the most blatant in this anti-social mudslinging," Kemmerer challenged his "seven out of 10" as a dubious and unsubstantiated statistic and denied that those who opposed official English did not love this country or respect the law. "Loving our country is not a matter of lip service," she wrote tartly. "It is a matter of working to keep it true to its traditions of fairness to all."[28]

Rustic fired back the following week, bemoaning the city's "Anglo exodus." Within the previous ten years, he asserted, "close to 28,000 Anglos have fled from this city"; he blamed condominium construction, increased traffic congestion, and Chinese-language business signs. He also complained that with the arrival of so many immigrants, "There has been an appreciation for every individual culture" at the expense of "the total American culture. There's no justification for the absence of a [city] Fourth of July celebration for nearly a decade."[29]

The war of words continued, as did protests and lobbying by CHAMP to overturn Resolution 9004. On July 14 the Taiwanese American Citizens League (TACL), a coalition of four Taiwanese organizations, called for a protest march against the city council for its rejection of the senior citizens' home and passage of the resolution. Some four hundred people—mostly elderly Chinese joined by CHAMP supporters—picketed City Hall before the regularly scheduled council meeting, carrying signs reading "Be Kind to the Elderly," "America, Land of Oppression," and "End Monterey Park Apartheid." The demonstrators also sang the civil rights anthem "We Shall Overcome" in front of television cameras and newspaper photographers. Li Pei Wu, president of TACL and head of a group called the Committee against Age and Racial Discrimination, told reporters that the recent actions by the council were racially motivated. "I have no doubt that it is racism," charged Wu, a bank president who actually resided in nearby Glendale. "There is an undercurrent [in Monterey Park]."[30]

Unmoved, the city council refused again to change its position on Resolution 9004 and would not discuss the senior housing project it had turned down earlier. The high-profile protest failed to impress Reichenberger because "only about 25 to 50 of those people were residents of Monterey Park." Before the council meeting began, she had asked a Chinese-speaking friend to find out where the protesters were from and what they were doing in Monterey Park. Her friend reported that they were from Glendale and didn't know what they were there for; they had just been brought to the city by bus.[31]

The Recall Effort

When demonstration proved ineffective, more drastic measures were planned. CHAMP leaders decided to wage a citywide petition drive to demand that the council rescind Resolution 9004 and to prove that the council's actions were arbitrary and divisive, not the result of a mandate from the community. Before CHAMP could line up its first signature, however, a pro-growth faction split from the group and took action on its own. On July 28 Kevin Smith, the twenty-seven-year-old son of one of the largest developers in town, formally notified the city council that an effort would be made to recall Hatch, Reichenberger, and Briglio. The notice was signed by Smith and four other Monterey Park residents, including David Almada, the former councilman who had been defeated in April. Proponents of the recall had first to publish a legal notice of their intentions and then allow seven days for the officeholders to respond. After that, the charges and responses could be printed on petitions and circulated to registered voters; 4,536 signatures (20 percent of the total) were required to force a recall election.

The recall sponsors specfically blamed each of the targeted council members for inciting tensions in the community and failing to provide "responsible and fair representation for all the residents of Monterey Park." They charged that Resolution 9004 was "racially motivated" and likely to "subject every Hispanic and Asian to immigration checks by the police department." Their statement also cited the rejected senior housing project as an example of "insensitivity towards all of the senior citizens of Monterey Park." Kevin Smith denied all accusations that the recall effort had anything to do with development interests; although his family firm had erected numerous residential and commercial buildings in Monterey Park, he contended that his primary objective was to end racial division. Smith said he was particularly sensitive to racism, having grown up in the community, married a woman of Mexican descent, and developed many working relationships with the Chinese; he simply could no longer sit back while "my friends are being attacked." Smith emphasized that the recall petition made no mention of the moratorium, but when pressed, he told reporters he was against a ruling so rigid that it prevented a nursery school from building a fence, and a pizza parlor from remodeling its premises.[32]

As months passed and the bickering continued, the Taiwanese American Affiliated Committee on Aging filed a lawsuit against the city, alleging that the council had illegally rejected the senior housing project "in the midst of racial conflict." The suit noted that the project had been approved by the previous council in March but was turned down by a new and hostile council "after a racially charged election." An exasperated Cam Briglio adamantly denied the charges: "We haven't turned [the project] down. We turned the location down." Patricia Reichenberger, noting that the project was planned for the far edge of town, away from city services, said the council would be more than willing to accept it if it were relocated to a more appropriate site. "I voted against the project for very honest reasons," she insisted.[33]

The Fall of 9004

While the city council was busy fighting off the lawsuit and negative press reports, CHAMP leaders made a point of distancing themselves from the recall effort. Though the group did not openly oppose the recall, leader Pete Hollingsworth called the attempt "premature to say the least"; he would want some assurance, he said, that any city council successors would be better than the ones removed.[34] CHAMP members chose to focus instead on collecting signatures for their petition to repeal Resolution 9004, and at a Monterey shopping mall one evening Michael Eng was clearly excited about the response: "Even though I just got here, I am averaging one [signature] a minute," he beamed. An older Chinese man who stopped to sign the petition remarked: "This [resolution] is discriminating against the Chinese, or the minorities, who live in this community. . . . I think it's not really nice, because the Chinese did very good for the city."[35]

After gathering over 4,500 signatures, CHAMP returned to City Hall on October 27 to present the petitions to the city council and again asked that Resolution 9004 be rescinded. Unexpectedly, following more than three hours of emotional testimony and heated debate, the council did rescind the four-month-old resolution—and Cam Briglio, who had insisted on retaining the official-English clause, made the motion to do so. "Whether I agree or not," he told the capacity crowd, "let's cut out the divisiveness."[36] At the time Briglio changed his vote, he was under tremendous political pressure. He later said he had been harassed over the phone and on the street because of his position on the issue. (Briglio was also the butt of many jokes because of an incident at a Chinese restaurant when he shot a tank full of live fish to foil an alleged robbery attempt.) Acknowledging his shoot-from-the-hip style in both words and deeds, Briglio later confessed to a reporter that he had been confused when he originally voted for Resolution 9004: "I didn't even read half the stuff [in it]."[37]

A chorus of both cheers and boos rang out from the audience after the three-to-two vote to rescind. Though Hatch and Reichenberger had held to their positions and voted against overturning the resolution, a relieved Chris Houseman gave an impassioned speech calling for unity in the community. Everyone must recognize, he said,

> that there are genuine fears among people about rapid demographic changes. . . . And these people cannot be dismissed as racists. . . . They're not racists, but they're fearful. . . . Changes have come so fast to this community that they haven't been able to adjust, and they feel lost about it, and we need to understand that. . . .
>
> I'm so glad that 9004 is off the books and behind us, because . . . it clouded the positive efforts and made it more difficult for people to come forward and join together. . . . there's agreement now that the basic problems in Monterey Park [are] economic, land-use policies, [and] not listening to the concerns of residents about development in this community. Those [are] the real things that were dividing us. . . .
>
> The future is here today in Monterey Park. What you see around you is the future. If we're smart, we're going to meet it with open eyes, we're going to grasp it, we're going to give it a good handshake, and we're going to all work together.[38]

But even though the city's Resolution 9004 had been overturned, the controversies were far from settled. On November 4 the ballot initiative calling for English to be the official language in California was passed three to one by voters across the state. Interestingly, Monterey Park voters supported Proposition 63 by only 56 percent to 44 percent, far short of the statewide margin and the average 73 percent "yes" vote throughout the San Gabriel Valley. CHAMP credited the narrower margin to its opposition to Resolution 9004 and to the 10,000 mailers it had sent out to city residents denouncing Proposition 63 as racist and divisive. Buoyed by the statewide success, however, and still interpreting Monterey Park's vote as a mandate from the people, Councilman Barry Hatch crowed, "We're going to return Monterey Park as an English speaking city." He vowed to renew efforts to bring down the Chinese-language business signs and to halt Chinese translations of articles in the city-funded quarterly, *Monterey Park Living*.[39]

Also in November the Monterey Park City Council voted three to one (Manibog was absent) to propose an ordinance that would prohibit the flying of foreign flags from the two flagpoles in front of City

Hall and reserve their use "exclusively for the flag of the United States and the flag of the state of California."[40] Such an ordinance would ban the raising of the Taiwanese flag every October 10 in recognition of the "Double 10" celebration sponsored by the Yung Ho Sister City Association. That practice had met with no objections until a few months earlier, when the Chinese consul in San Francisco wrote to protest Monterey Park's participation in a Taiwanese national holiday celebration as deeply offensive to the People's Republic of China, the sole government of China as established by the United Nations in 1971. Houseman was suspicious about the timing of the policy change and accused his colleagues of "playing a big, phony game." He criticized the proposed ordinance as "completely unnecessary" and said it would prohibit Monterey Park from honoring visiting foreign dignitaries by flying their flags at City Hall. His attacks were so vehement that Reichenberger left her seat, and the council adjourned briefly to give her time to regain her composure.[41] But two weeks later the ordinance to ban the flying of foreign flags in front of City Hall passed by four votes to Houseman's one.

Recall Wrangling

Not surprisingly, Hatch's post–Proposition 63 statements and the council's new flag policy helped to fuel the recall movement. The pro-recall group adopted the name "A Better Cityhood," or ABC for short, co-chaired by Kevin Smith and Steven Tan, owner of an insurance company. By January 1987, ABC had gathered enough signatures to force a recall election against Barry Hatch, Patricia Reichenberger, and Cam Briglio. Former council member David Almada, an active proponent of the recall movement, told reporters that "people don't like the racial intolerance [that the three council members] have generated by their own actions," including the recently adopted flag policy: "People reject that extreme radicalism, almost neo-Facist point of view."[42] Hatch and Reichenberger countered that the recall effort was merely the work of disgruntled developers and defeated council members. "That's what it looked like and based on that, RAMP decided to fight against it," says Joseph Rubin.[43]

Rubin, a native New Yorker who owns a tool manufacturing business in Orange County, moved to Monterey Park with his wife, Maxine, in 1960. They quickly became involved in local Democratic Party activities and joined the picket lines in 1962 to help integrate the Monterey Park Highlands after a black family was denied housing. Rubin became an enthusiastic supporter of Eugene McCarthy for president in 1968 and calls himself a "Jesse Jackson Democrat." He acknowledges that RAMP was split on the issue of official English but in general agreement that Resolution 9004 was a mistake. Rubin, who had served as Patricia Reichenberger's campaign manager, tried to talk her out of supporting Resolution 9004, which "was perceived by Asian and Hispanic residents as an attack." Nevertheless, Rubin and RAMP took on the fight against the recall. "We had elected those candidates based on their positions on slow growth. . . . We didn't want to get shot out of the saddle on slow growth because of their other positions," he says emphatically.[44]

The recall campaign soon became a rough-and-tumble brawl. On February 2 the city council fired the entire five-member planning commission, saying they wanted to open up the body to new people with fresh ideas. "This Planning Commission has never related to the people of the community," stated Reichenberger, who voted with Houseman and Hatch in favor of the action. "They do not reflect the feelings of the council," she said. Monty Manibog, who voted against the dismissal, argued that the new council majority was going too far in trying to shape the commission in its own image: "You don't [fire] commissioners who have served honorably and in a dedicated manner." Briglio abstained from the vote, saying that he would like to see one (unnamed) commissioner let go but not the entire body.[45]

Those fired were second-term commissioners Patricia Chin and Yukio Kawaratani, and first-term commissioners Johnny Li, Fred Rivera, and David Barron. Chin and Kawaratani were generally seen as sympathetic to the slow-growth goals of the new council majority and immediately sought reappointment to the commission. Barron was considered middle-of-the-road, but Rivera worked for developer Gene Smith, father of recall leader Kevin Smith, and Li was involved with the pro-recall group. "I attended the very first meeting of ABC and I am the one who came up with the name," Li admitted, adding that he agreed with the group's basic concerns but "not necessarily the timing and their methods."[46]

Just three weeks later the city council appointed a new planning commission. As expected, Chin and Kawaratani were reappointed. The new members were Ken Fong, J. J. Rodriguez, and outspoken letter writer George Rustic.

While the city council was replacing the planning commission, the Los Angeles County district attorney's office was receiving allegations of improprieties in the recall effort. Complaints signed by residents charged that the petitioners included under-age, unregistered voters and people from outside of the city, and that some were misrepresenting the petitions they were circulating. Activist Irv Gilman wrote to the *Progress*: "The latest ploy to come to light is a knock on the door and someone asking for a signature on a petition for a better police department, but in reality the petition is for the recall. And we were approached by a youth who told us the city was losing police and firemen because the city could no longer pay them. That's not just a plain lie—that's a grade AAA fancy lie."[47] Larry Landreth of the Monterey Park Police Officer's Association also wrote to deny reports, attributed to the petitioners, that the association favored the recall drive: "The police association has no reason to take any position or become involved. Further, the police association has no reason to be dissatisfied with the current city council."[48]

In March, City Clerk Pauline Lemire announced that although petitions to recall Barry Hatch had amassed 6,902 signatures, 2,183 were invalid. Still, the remaining 4,719 signatures exceeded the number required to force a recall election, as did the total of valid signatures against Patricia Reichenberger. But those against Cam Briglio, once the invalid signatures were subtracted, fell short.[49] Widespread rumors in the community claimed that Briglio had switched his vote on Resolution 9004, in exchange for being dropped in the recall attempt and in order to gain developer support for his reelection in 1988.

The antagonism created by the recall attempt ushered in one of the most tumultuous periods in the city's history. On April 10 the Monterey Park Chamber of Commerce, still the center for conflict between old-time slow-growth merchants and aggressive pro-development investors, rejected six out of seven Chinese candidates running for the organization's board of directors, among them the vice-president, Anthony Chen, who would have been the next president if elected to the board. Charges were immediately raised that several reelected and incoming board members had formed a voting block to remove three incumbents—two of whom were Chinese—and to keep the six Chinese candidates out of office.[50] The chamber's president, George Ricci, resigned to protest what he called the "anti-Asian" vote of those members who did not believe that the organization "should represent the full ethnic spectrum of the business community." The chamber, Ricci declared in his resignation statement, should "represent the business community as it is now, not as it was in the past." Instead, he told the Los Angeles Times, it had "broken faith with a moral commitment to help assimilate the immigrant population into the community."[51] At the time, it was estimated that Asians owned and operated more than two-thirds of the businesses in the city but represented only 25 percent of the chamber's membership.

In May, City Manager Lloyd de Llamas announced his resignation after eleven years of service. He planned to join a private consulting firm, a move he said he had been contemplating for several years.

He called his position with Monterey Park "a plum job" and cited the city as "a laboratory for everything going on in California." He also added: "Monterey Park is on the cutting edge of some intense and very rapid social and economic changes that will impact all of California through the rest of the century. This city is openly dealing with state-wide issues better than other cities."[52] De Llamas now acknowledges that although a career change was his primary reason for leaving, the work environment in Monterey Park at the time was extremely diffi-cult because of the "continuous negativism" displayed in the council and the community. "After a while you get tired of working in that atmosphere."[53]

As if to illustrate his words, on the same day that the *Progress* announced de Llamas's resignation, it printed a letter from Bill Marti-corena: "Can you believe it? Asians inviting themselves illegally to the U.S., enrolling themselves on welfare—and then have the guts to moonlight in sweat shops and not report earnings to the IRS, and more guts to call it a bonus to send their children to college. . . . My parents came to America in 1915, along with the Italians, Polish, Germans, Jewish and the Hispanics. These people didn't hang their language signs all over American cities. They did not say 'get out of the way, we are coming.'"[54]

The Recall Vote

As the recall vote drew near, tensions heightened and rumors flew. Exploiting the city council's denial of a permit to raise the height of a protective fence for a local child-care facility from three to six feet, one pro-recall mailer was headlined "Kidnapping Is a Problem . . . But NOT to Hatch and Reichenberger" over staged photographs of an unsavory character enticing children with candy and dragging a strug-gling child into his car. The text ended: "Say Yes to Our Children" and "Vote Yes on Recall." Another flyer featured a defaced picture of Kevin Smith allegedly sent to the ABC office and a copy of the scrawled note that came with it, addressed to "You jackass Kevin Smith": "Get the hell out of Monterey Park, and take your stinking Mexicans, Chinks and Japs with you, out of California too." Asking "Is development the real issue?" and "Who do they represent?" the mailer urged voters to support the recall.[55]

But just one week before the recall election the *Monterey Park Progress* reported that two former ABC workers had filed sworn affida-vits at the city clerk's office alleging that they and others had been paid to collect and complete absentee ballots and to instill fear in Asian and Latino voters in order to gain support for the recall effort. Resident

Louis Wang told the *Progress* that a campaign worker said to him, "We cannot afford to have persons [on the city council] who cause trouble to disrupt the harmony [in the community]." Wang also stated that he gave his absentee ballot to the worker, not realizing that such a ballot can be legally received only by an appropriate election official. ABC leaders categorically denied the charges and insisted they were being disseminated by the council itself.[56]

Using rumors of similarly outrageous campaign activities to its own advantage, RAMP revived the *Record* to refute ABC's arguments for the recall. For example, to rebut the ABC charge that Hatch's and Reichenberger's policies and racist attitudes had cost Monterey Park $34 million in lawsuits, the *Record* quoted a May 29, 1987, memo from City Manager de Llamas: "We average 50 to 60 claims each year. These range from 'trip and fall' to disputes with contractors. The average amount of claims each year range from $15 million to $20 million. Less than 30% go to litigation, and our actual payout rarely exceeds one or two percent of the total [claims] received. . . . I researched the files and find that we recently had a claim filed by a family who was injured in a traffic accident and claimed the accident occurred because of a poor street design. Their claim is $30,000,000."[57]

The *Record* was filled with bold print asserting "RACISM IS A TOOL OF THE DEVELOPERS," "RACISM IS THIS YEAR'S BIG LIE!!" and "WORST OF ALL—The Developers are telling Hispanics and Asians that they will be arrested and deported . . . for having brown skin if NO-on-Recall wins. This is an attempt to strike TERROR in the hearts of community residents. Think of the person who believes this foul lie!" A lengthy quotation from resident Irene Huerta followed: "We were visited by 2 precinct walkers who said that we were on their list for a Yes sign. I told them I had not spoken to anyone about it. They said we were 'Mexicans' and should have a Yes sign. I told them I was an American—I'm proud of being an American, and I'm proud of my Mexican heritage too. They turned to my daughter and said, 'How would you like it if your mother walked to the corner store, was arrested and didn't come back?!' "[58]

The final blow to ABC occurred when the *Progress* came out strongly against the group and its recall effort: "[ABC's] allegations are either sour grapes from the people Hatch and Reichenberger defeated for their council seats or from special interest developers who fear they no longer will have their projects rubber-stamped by the council. . . . By bringing racial issues into the recall, ABC has succeeded in doing just what it accuses Hatch and Reichenberger of doing—inciting fear and prejudice."[59] After months of heated campaigning by both sides, the result of the June 16, 1987, special election was an overwhelming defeat for ABC: 5,136 to 3,211 votes against Hatch's recall 5,163 to 3,222 against Reichenberger's. The turnout for this special election was 35.5 percent of the city's registered voters, the highest for any special election in the city's history.[60]

Clearly, ABC had erred in several ways and failed to convince Monterey Park's residents of the merit of its arguments. First of all, ABC was in fact a thinly disguised vehicle for development interests. "I saw that . . . there was not a real cross section of people, there was not a real grassroots effort," admitted long-time resident Alice Ballesteros, an initial supporter of the recall. "It was really an effort put on by developers that injected a lot of money into it."[61] According to records, ABC had raised $26,203 in support of the recall, 90 percent of it from developer-associated individuals and companies and nearly half from out of town.[62]

Second, members of ABC convinced themselves that people of color in Monterey Park would band together against whites. This assumption became a liability after disgruntled campaign workers publicly stated that they had been instructed to spread fear in the community in order to gain support for the recall. Besides, because Ballesteros and others knew Patricia Reichenberger and her family through community sports programs, they were not convinced that she was the racist she was painted to be. In fact, Reichenberger's husband coached Ballesteros's daughter in the girls' basketball league, "and I think when you know people from that aspect it is harder to just accept what people say about them and a lot of the untruths that go on." Though Ballesteros was clearly offended by Barry Hatch's rhetoric and thought Reichenberger's close alliance with him was a disservice to the community, the recall campaign became a real political education for her and "opened my eyes to those causes I would support," she said. "You have to see it for yourself."[63] Nor could Monterey Park's large, well-assimilated, middle-class Latino population and a smaller group of U.S.-born Asian Americans be hooked or swayed by ABC's claims that Hatch and Reichenberger were racist and anti-immigrant. When these second- and third-generation, English-speaking Latinos and Asian Americans were asked to choose between whites and immigrants, they allied with the whites on the basis of the issues. Racial and ethnic solidarity were not the overwhelming factors for them that the recall proponents had anticipated.

Third, ABC was simply not able to prove that Hatch and Reichenberger had done anything illegally. CHAMP leader Michael Eng expressed these concerns long before the election took place: "Usually," he said, "officials are turned out for allegations of sexual misconduct, bribery, or malfeasance."[64]

On election day itself, both sides traded charges and counter-charges of voter harassment and improprieties. "It was a horror," said City Clerk Pauline Lemire. On four occasions police officers had to be dispatched to polling places to resolve disputes. People were "turned away from the polls and denied their right to vote," said an angry Kevin Smith, citing reports by ABC representatives who were sent to monitor the polling places. "If you were Asian or Hispanic you were treated differently than if you were Anglo."

Smith said he personally witnessed a young Chinese male, perhaps eighteen or nineteen, who was harassed by poll workers who "insisted on looking at his identification; they scrutinized it carefully and were very rude to this kid. Right afterward, an elderly Anglo lady came in to vote and was not asked for an ID." On the other hand, Lemire said precinct workers complained that poll watchers initiated contact with Chinese voters. Though most of the precinct workers couldn't speak Chinese, they suspected that attempts to influence voters were being made.[65]

Victorious council members Hatch and Reichenberger expressed deep concern over what they saw as abuses in the absentee ballot system. The city received requests for 3,775 absentee ballots, of which over 2,300 were cast. Targeting non-English-speaking Chinese, ABC had been instrumental in assisting voters to obtain absentee ballots, and the results of their efforts were clear: though the recall attempt lost by a two-to-one margin or more in most precincts, absentee voters overwhelmingly favored the recall of Hatch 1513 to 830, and of Reichenberger 1505 to 824.[66] Smith expressed his own concerns about the entire electoral process; he wanted to see reforms that would make non-English speakers more comfortable at the polls and reduce the animosity of election workers toward newcomers.[67]

The years 1986 and 1987 were clearly the most turbulent times in Monterey Park's history. In the end, RAMP successfully exposed developer interests and efforts to control the city. RAMP's leaders had learned a valuable lesson in 1982 when they were blindsided by the notorious *Monterey Park Chronicle* "hit piece," which they believed was responsible for knocking their city council candidates out of contention. In the 1986 council election, RAMP took the initiative and seized the moral high ground by discrediting opponents with their own words, actions, and excesses; it proved an extremely effective strategy in rallying support. When ABC accused Hatch and Reichenberger of racism and forced a recall vote, RAMP stood up for its candidates, turned the issue around, and made ABC instead look like the racists for attempting to divide the community.

After crushing the ill-conceived and politically naive recall attempt, RAMP and its supporters seemed omnipotent in Monterey Park. With the three candidates it had helped to elect in 1986 firmly in place, the organization was looking forward to the 1988 city council election. Both erratic Cam Briglio and pro-growth Monty Manibog were on shaky ground with voters, and RAMP fully anticipated driving them out of office.

The heady prospect of sweeping the upcoming election and placing five growth-control loyalists on the city council was too good to be true. On the surface RAMP seemed unbeatable, but in reality its hold on the community was precarious. For years the organization had walked a fine line, advocating controlled growth while ignoring accusations of nativism and anti-Chinese sentiment within its own ranks. The passage of Resolution 9004 was an embarrassment to its leadership and exposed fault lines that could shift again at any time. Not unlike CHAMP, which started out advocating harmony in the community but was quickly tainted by pro-growth elements, RAMP would soon face a challenge from nativist and staunch no-growth elements that, for their own reasons, had hopped on the RAMP bandwagon.

CHAPTER 7

The Politics of Realignment

The resolution of the recall effort in Monterey Park by no means ended the city's contentiousness. The 1988 city council election brought to the fore another Chinese American woman candidate whose campaign themes of racial harmony and controlled growth received a warm reception, but the old divisions were still apparent, and new ones developed. One was the split between recall survivor Barry Hatch and his former supporters. RAMP's slate of city council candidates performed poorly in the 1990 election and were replaced by a new pro-growth majority that quickly changed the policy direction of the city. Two years later the city council election brought about a complete realignment of political interests in Monterey Park and the apparent beginning of a period of conciliation and coalition-building.

Toward the 1988 City Election

After the failed recall, residents in Monterey Park hoped for a period of calm, and they had it for a short time. In an October 20, 1987, special election voters overwhelmingly supported four council-endorsed ballot propositions based on a redevelopment plan formulated by a Community Design Advisory Committee, a group of fifteen residents who worked for several months with city-hired development consultants. Thomas Ono, a Japanese American attorney, chaired the committee.

The Four Propositions

The plan called for a million-square-foot regional shopping mall on North Atlantic Boulevard; the development of supermarkets, automobile dealerships, and other retail outlets on South Atlantic Boulevard; and a revitalization of the historic Garvey-Garfield downtown district.[1] In the Garvey-Garfield area, buildings would be limited to two or three stories (Proposition A); a section of Atlantic Boulevard could have up to four stories (Proposition B); the extreme northern and southern sections of town could build as high as seven stories (Proposition C);

138

and limitations were placed on the city's authority to issue height-limit variances (Proposition D).

There was only token opposition to this compromise between moderate-development and controlled-growth factions in town. Even RAMP, backed the propositions, and they all passed by four-to-one margins. Though these victories were impressive, the actual voter turn-out in the election was disappointingly low: of the 23,308 registered voters in the town, only 3,113 residents—just 13.3 percent—cast ballots.[2] Calm bordered on apathy.

In April 1988, council incumbents Cam Briglio and Monty Manibog were replaced. The candidate who received the most votes was a Chinese American woman, Judy Chu, a psychologist, college instructor, community activist, and wife of CHAMP co-chair Michael Eng. In second place was Betty Couch, a long-time committed RAMP organizer and wife of former councilman Harry Couch. Both women had run "positive" campaigns focused on controlling growth and using a conciliatory approach to end the strife and vindictiveness that had been so much a part of the city's politics.

A Raucous Prelude

Events leading up to election, however, were anything but calm and conciliatory. One particularly stormy city council meeting in March, exposing the breakdown and re-formation of alliances, was captured by newly installed cable television cameras; Monterey Park viewers were able to watch at home as council members openly fought with each other and with the audience in the City Hall chambers.

The hostilities erupted after Barry Hatch expressed his displeasure with the recent appointment of Steven Tan—the ABC co-chair who had contributed $2,500 to the failed recall effort—to the city's planning commission. Tan was supported by Monty Manibog, historically a RAMP enemy, as well as Cam Briglio and Chris Houseman, former RAMP allies. Briglio called for interracial tolerance: "Let's not look at their eyes or their color or the country that they came from." Houseman (who was mayor at the time) accused RAMP, the group that had endorsed him just two years earlier, of Joseph McCarthy–style tactics. Noting that Tan owned an insurance company, he held up a recent RAMP newsletter that called Steven Tan "a major developer." Houseman labeled the identification "a complete lie" and charged that RAMP wanted to fill the council with "five puppets." RAMP chairman Joseph Rubin—backed by Evelyn Diederich, one of the founders—stood up in the audience and called the mayor a liar. Houseman threatened to eject him from the meeting and, when Rubin refused to sit down, ordered the sergeant-at-arms to remove him. Rubin, Diederich, and a handful of supporters left the room, shouting at Houseman on their way out.[3]

Houseman's hostility toward his former allies that evening stemmed from statements made about him in the newsletter he quoted at the meeting. RAMP had accused Houseman of becoming a "Developer pal," which, it claimed "explains the frequent Houseman-Manibog-Briglio votes on so many recent issues." Steven Tan, the piece continued, was "the LAST man in town to put on the Planning Commission. Who does Houseman have in mind to appoint next?—Fred Hsieh? Kevin Smith?" RAMP also faulted Houseman for naming Mancha Kurilich to the Community Relations Commission. "For those with short memories," the newsletter reminded its readers, "that's the same Mancha Kurilich whose 'Citizens Against Crime' put out the scurrilous phoney 'newspaper' that elected the old Developer team: Chen-Almada-Peralta. . . . What honorable person does Houseman have in mind next? Imelda Marcos?"[4]

Recrimination continued when Barry Hatch said he'd heard that Houseman had met with a group of developers in San Marino, an affluent community not far from Monterey Park. Launching into one of the sermonlike speeches that soon became his trademark, Hatch implied that Houseman had sold out the community for the developers' "pot of gold." Though a clearly agitated Houseman did not respond to Hatch's comments, Manibog lost his patience with "these witch-hunting tactics" and challenged Hatch to present evidence to back up his accusations.[5] It was within such an atmosphere that the city council election was held.

The Election Results

At the polls the following month, Judy Chu finished a strong first with 3,594 votes, followed by Couch with 2,874. RAMP-endorsed candidate, controversial letter writer and planning commissioner George Rustic, came in third with 2,486 votes. Pro-development candidate Fred Balderrama, a business associate of Steven Tan, drew 2,129 votes, and incumbent Cam Briglio 1,489. Other candidates received fewer than 1,000 votes each: Marie Purvis, a former president of the chamber of commerce; official-English proponent Frank Arcuri; and Chinese acupuncturist Victoria Wu. In the race for city treasurer, Louise Davis (also endorsed by RAMP) handily defeated Monty Manibog (who had chosen not to run again for city council) by 4,271 to 3,292 votes. RAMP-endorsed city clerk candidate David Barron easily defeated his nearest challenger, former RAMP supporter John Gerlach (husband of Sonya Gerlach), 3,561 to 1,380.[6]

T A B L E 12

Monterey Park City Council Candidate Preference and Voter Profile by Ethnicity: 1988

	% Chinese (N = 397)	% Japanese (N = 247)	% Latino (N = 216)	% Anglo (N = 266)
Candidate				
Chu	89	75	35	30
Couch	12	28	19	45
Rustic	8	22	15	45
Balderrama	17	21	63	17
Briglio	15	19	19	14
Purvis	1	8	12	14
Arcuri	2	2	8	11
Wu	22	2	1	1
Voter profile				
Female	46	55	56	52
Age 45+	42	71	61	77
Foreign-born	73	6	15	9
College degree	71	42	28	41
$50,000+ income	51	46	31	33
Party affiliation				
Democrat	24	60	80	59
Republican	45	30	16	35
Independent/none	30	10	4	6

Source: Southwest Voter Research Institute, Monterey Park, Calif., Exit Poll, April 12, 1988, for the Asian Pacific American Voter Registration Project. Data cited from John Horton, "The Politics of Ethnic Change: Grass-Roots Responses to Economic and Demographic Restructuring in Monterey Park, California," *Urban Geography* 10 (1989): 578–92; and Laird Harrison, "Voter Survey Gives New Picture of Monterey Park," *Asian Week*, September 23, 1989.

Note: Voters could cast votes for two candidates; hence, percentages add up to more than 100.

This particular election was closely monitored by the Asian Pacific Voter Registration Project in cooperation with the San Antonio–based Southwest Voter Research Institute, along with a team of researchers from the University of California, Los Angeles, led by sociologist John Horton. An exit poll collected 1,390 completed questionnaires, representing 17 percent of the 8,148 residents who voted. The research confirmed the fact that though Asians were approximately 51 percent of the population at the time, they made up only 36 percent of the registered voters. Of registered Asian voters, 58 percent were of Chinese ancestry, and 37 percent were Japanese Americans. Among Chinese respondents to the exit poll, 73 percent were born outside the United States; 51 percent had a family income of over $50,000—a percentage higher than that of any other group (see Table 12).[7]

Not surprisingly, the research also showed a voting pattern that followed ethnic lines for the major candidates: Judy Chu captured 89 percent of the Chinese and 75 percent of the Japanese American vote; defeated candidate Fred Balderrama received 63 percent of the Latino votes. But the most interesting finding was the relatively high percentage of cross-ethnic voting. Chu received 35 percent of the Latino and 30 percent of the white vote. Second-place candidate Couch received 28 percent of the Japanese American vote, 19 percent of the Latino vote, and 12 percent of the Chinese vote. Rustic, who finished in third place, scored 22 percent of the Japanese American and 15 percent of the Latino vote, though only 8 percent of the Chinese vote (Table 12). Horton concluded that the overall political lessons in Monterey Park following the 1988 election were positive. The voters had showed enough unity to set aside racial polarization in order to defeat large developer interests and work toward better ethnic representation.[8]

To many, the poised and articulate thirty-four-year-old Chu was the ideal crossover candidate for Monterey Park. Born and raised in the predominantly black area of South Central Los Angeles, Chu had attended the University of California, Santa Barbara, majoring in mathematics and planning to be a computer programmer. But after taking her first course in Asian American studies, she transferred to UCLA, which offered more such courses and had a larger Asian American student population. It was there that Chu met her husband, Michael Eng. Upon graduating, she moved the focus of her career to community organizing and social services. After earning a Ph.D. from the California School of Professional Psychology, she taught psychology at largely Latino East Los Angeles College and Asian American Studies at California State University, Los Angeles, and UCLA. Chu was one of the founders of the Asian Youth Project, a San Gabriel Valley agency helping immigrant youth adjust to American life. She also served on the boards of the United Way, the Red Cross, the Family Counseling Service of West San Gabriel Valley, and the West San Gabriel Valley Juvenile Diversion Project. Her first step into the political arena was her election to the board of education in the Garvey School District in 1985.

An open city council seat (left by Manibog), a weak field of candidates, and the encouragement of friends persuaded Chu to seek office in Monterey Park. It was not all clear sailing: though supporters called her sincere and dedicated, detractors called her aloof and calculating. Opponents openly accused her of "carpetbagging" because she had lived in the city for only four years and was giving up her position on the Garvey School Board before completing even one term. Nevertheless, Chu's tightly organized campaign relied on a large multicultural cadre of volunteers, and she promoted a controlled-growth and ethnic-diversity platform that appealed to many residents. "The people all around me had the same message," she says. "We had to bring people together and create a positive image for this city and to create a dialogue. We had the ability to bring that message out to the people." Another major part of her strategy was to go door-to-door, introducing herself in as many homes as possible and explaining her support for the Community Design plan as well as her opposition to official English. Her direct approach to residents was effective, she recalls. "When we were talking face to face, the things they would say pertained to nuts and bolts issues: traffic and redevelopment of the city. But underneath I [knew] what was going on. They were checking me out to see if I spoke English, to see if I could relate to them, to see if I was a competent person."[9]

Given the self-destruction of developer interests after the disastrous recall attempt, the lingering distaste for extremist elements advocating official English, and RAMP's infighting, Chu's message was a welcomed breath of fresh air in the gray San Gabriel Valley smog. Chu promised to take no money from developer interests and accepted no campaign donations over $200. Despite these self-imposed limitations, she raised $34,233 from a variety of donors, including many out-of-town Asian American professionals who supported her efforts.[10] She asked for an endorsement from RAMP because of her position on development. Its leaders refused but did agree not to attack her. She was not mentioned in the 1988 edition of the *Record*—which heavily criticized Monty Manibog, Cam Briglio, Fred Balderrama, and Chris Houseman as favoring the developers—but was chided in RAMP's March newsletter for not taking a stand against the recall.

Amid the charges and countercharges of racism and special interests that had monopolized debate in the community for years, the media barely noticed that the election of Chu and Couch and the incumbency of Reichenberger made 1988 the first year in the city's history when women were a majority on the city council. Many hoped that they would constitute a positive force for change.

The Politics of Division

Monterey Park continued to be embroiled in controversy, however, with an increasingly outspoken Barry Hatch adding most of the fuel to the fire.

In July 1988, Hatch sent a message on the city's letterhead to presidential candidates George Bush and Michael Dukakis, advising them to speak out on illegal immigration, which he called "the most serious threat the United States has ever faced. The run-away invasion of this sovereign nation by illegal aliens, drug runners, terrorists and criminals is rapidly placing in jeopardy the safety and quality of life of our citizens. If you, by your silence, allow these hordes of invaders to continue, this nation will cease to exist. . . . Control our borders—preserve our nation. If you cannot support America, we cannot support you."[11] After word of these letters spread, outraged residents castigated Hatch at the September 12 council meeting for using the word "we" and demanded repayment of the tax dollars used for materials and staff time to send the letters. At that, Hatch supporter Clifford Sharp pulled out his checkbook and said he "would deem it an honor" to pay the cost of $101.35. Sharp's offer satisfied that demand, but protesters still wanted Hatch to retract his statements and apologize to the community. He refused to comply.[12]

In September, Hatch reportedly opposed a donation of 10,000 Chinese-language books from the Little Taipei Lions Club to Monterey Park's public library. He was quoted as saying: "I think our library should house mainly English books."[13] This issue was particularly acute because in late 1987 Hatch had successfully spearheaded an effort to replace the library board with a powerless "advisory" commission; the change placed authority over the library's annual million-dollar budget in the hands of the city council. Opponents immediately called the move illegal and charged that the actions were a ploy by Hatch to control book selection.[14]

In early 1988 the Friends of the Library of Monterey Park and three former board members filed a lawsuit challenging the city council's decision. Hatch, Reichenberger, and Briglio, the council members who had voted in favor of the change, cited a consultant's report that had recommended the move for economic reasons. "The City Council doesn't have the time or interest to decide what books will go in there," Hatch said, defending his motives. "That isn't even close to what we have in mind."[15]

But the controversy escalated when a constitutional rights group, People for the American Way, joined the fray and accused the council of using censorship against foreign-language books in the library. The focus of People for the American Way, created by television producer Norman Lear, was on preserving free speech rights. Supporters of the ousted library board pointed to a reduction in the library's budge for the purchase of foreign-language books the following fiscal year as evidence of the council's antagonism toward newcomers. They also provided transcripts from budget hearings during which Hatch told the city librarian he did not think the city should pay for foreign-language books: "If people want a foreign language, they can go purchase books on their own. . . . In spite of demographics, this is the United States of America, and . . . Monterey Park is part of it. Do you read me?"[16]

In the fall of 1988, Hatch and newly elected Betty Couch together worked to reinvigorate the push for more English on Chinese business signs. They wanted an ordinance in Monterey Park similar to the one passed by the neighboring city of Arcadia, which called for a sign to be at least two-thirds English. "I've talked to a lot of people about this, and they want to feel like it's their town, too, not just a Chinese town," Couch said. "Why should Monterey Park be called the Chinese Beverly Hills?" But J. J. Rodriguez, chairman of the city's planning commission, saw no problem: "No one has complained to me," he said. Rodriguez thought the 1985 sign ordinance, whereby each business was to post a sign identifying in English its general nature—"pharmacy," "restaurant," "herb store," "bakery"—was sufficient. Judy Chu, who does not speak or read Chinese, said she was not offended by the existing signs. She also expressed great fear that issue would revive the anti-Chinese animosity and negative publicity of two years earlier.[17]

Chu's fear was realized, especially after Barry Hatch became mayor of Monterey Park. On October 10, 1988, when Hatch was installed in the rotating position, the irony of the situation—a white male favoring official English and limits on immigration as mayor of a city more than half Asian and a third Latino—did not go unnoticed by the media. As one of the most controversial figures in the San Gabriel Valley, Hatch was soon a popular guest on radio and television talk shows across the country. One newspaper called him "the most hated man in Chinese America."[18] Shortly before the installation, Planning Commissioner J. J. Rodriguez, whom Hatch had appointed, resigned in protest. Calling Hatch an "ultra, ultra Republican conservative," Rodriguez said he would be uncomfortable serving the city under such a mayor.[19]

Although his high-profile position brought him media visibility as a front-line defender of "American" virtues and culture, Hatch nevertheless found himself increasingly isolated and unable to push through many of the policies he strongly advocated in the city he was elected to represent. In January 1989 the Monterey Park City Council voted in a new ordinance requiring only slightly more English on business signs; it called for the name and nature of the business to be translated into English but did not mandate the percentage of English words required. Two proposals—one requiring that every sign contain two-thirds English, another that signs be entirely in English except for a small indication that Chinese or Spanish was spoken in the establishment—were both rejected by the Monterey Park Design Review

Board, as well as by the planning commission. Hatch did vote for the new ordinance, but only because "it's all I can get," he said.[20]

In March 1989, Hatch proposed spending $50,000 to replace the existing City Hall sculpture commemorating international brotherhood, which had been built for the 1984 Olympics in Los Angeles, with a statue of George Washington. "Millions" of immigrants entering the United States had no appreciation for America's traditions, values, and hard-won freedoms, he insisted, and the statue would serve as a positive reminder to newcomers and citizens alike how fortunate they were to be in this country.[21] Judy Chu responded, "Then why don't we use the $50,000 to set up citizenship classes?" Betty Couch, a staunch fiscal conservative, wondered how responsible and realistic it would be to spend so much money on a statue when the city was having trouble balancing its books. At this unenthusiastic response to what he considered a paramount issue, Hatch flew into a red-faced rage: "I think you're totally out of line! Why can't we find a few bucks and say thank God we live in America? . . . This country is in more trouble than anytime, other than the Civil War." For half an hour he both berated and pleaded with his colleagues. Eventually, Reichenberger and Houseman voted with him in favor of funding the statue; Couch and Chu voted against it.[22]

But Hatch prevailed only briefly. Two months later the council easily buckled under pressure from residents opposing the expenditure and rescinded its original decision to fund the Washington statue; instead, it set up a committee to seek private donations and, in an apparent move to appease him, appointed Hatch the chair. Hatch cast his vote to rescind the decision with great bitterness, "appalled" by those who opposed the statue.[23]

Just one month after that the California Court of Appeals, following almost two years of legal battles, ruled that the Monterey Park City Council had acted improperly in reducing the library board's authority, and the city council was forced to return the board's administrative power. Hatch lashed out at those who had used the racism charge against him; he called it an "ugly, rotten tactic" intended only to stir up people's emotions and reiterated that his decision had been based solely on fiscal responsibility, not anti-immigrant sentiment.[24]

In July, Hatch once again drew fire after speaking at a meeting of the American Association of Women, a conservative organization dedicated to encouraging more women to become involved in public policy. In his talk he blamed immigrants for causing a variety of southern California's woes, from housing shortages to overburdened medical, social, and educational programs, from overcrowded prisons to overflowing landfills. Locally, he complained, the San Gabriel Valley was "becoming entirely Chinese." Claiming that the attitude of new Asian immigrants was "We don't care about your culture, your traditions, and your history. We're here to make money," he went on to warn, "The American people have to be awakened."[25]

Many in Monterey Park thought Hatch had developed an increased sense of self-importance after the overwhelming defeat of the 1987 recall; he seemed convinced that he had a mandate to speak out. "Instead of getting off those things that would get the town excited and angry at him and concentrate on development," says RAMP leader Joseph Rubin, "Barry Hatch came out of that [recall] a little cocky about how strong he was."[26] Evelyn Diederich agrees. "Barry caused too much dissension," she says. "We told him he should do for Monterey Park and forget about the rest of the world, but he said he wasn't going to let anybody tell him what to do."[27]

Besides creating local divisiveness and unease, Hatch's frequent comments were played up in the media and became an embarrassment for the entire community. As the only Asian American on the Monterey Park City Council, Judy Chu was consistently asked to respond to Hatch's outbursts. "The media kept knocking at the door," she recalls. " 'Barry Hatch said this, what do you say?' They elevated the words of this crazy man . . . and made it seem that that's what everybody was saying. I knew that not to be true." Hatch, a burly and robust man, often verbally bullied the three women on the council when they disagreed with him. Finally, in January 1990, Couch, Chu, and Reichenberger issued a statement warning they would all walk out of the council chambers if he attacked any of them again. He was "sexist, racist, rigid in general, and had poor interpersonal skills," says psychologist Chu. "Barry Hatch would never even look at me, I was such a little cockroach in his eyes."[28]

The 1990 City Council

On all counts, Hatch received heavy criticism from Monterey Park residents for the negative publicity he generated in the media. As a result, many saw the April 1990 city council election as an opportunity to reevaluate the choices they had made four years earlier.

Previously arrogant in their belief that they had been swept into office in 1986 by a mandate of the people, the incumbents were not so secure in 1990. Patricia Reichenberger began to retract her backing of official English in order to gain broader support for her reelection bid. Barry Hatch, the only candidate who did not supply a Spanish translation of his campaign statement, made only a halfhearted reelection effort. Chris Houseman, the leading vote-getter in 1986, quietly let the deadline for filing candidacy papers slip by.

The Defeat of RAMP's Slate

RAMP endorsed just two candidates for the three available council seats: Patricia Reichenberger and David Barron. Though not a member, Barron had been supported by RAMP during his successful bid for city clerk in 1988 and was endorsed for city council on the basis of his position on controlled growth as "basically a property owner and a resident in Monterey Park . . . not a businessman."[29] But Barron made clear that he would not accept RAMP's endorsement if it also endorsed Barry Hatch. The leaders and membership got the message; RAMP decided to cut its losses and actually attacked Hatch in its 1990 version of the *Record*: "On the Council, Hatch voted well on many controlled growth issues—opposing highrises and supporting the moratorium to allow review of construction standards. At times, however, he has behaved like a 'No growth' advocate. He has been stubborn and uncompromising—unwilling to work with other Council members to come up with reasonable solutions in controlled growth matters. His approach, in its excess, threatens us with legal attack, and possible defeat."[30]

The *Record* made no mention of Hatch's comments on official English and immigration; many RAMP members privately agreed with him, though they knew he was not a politically viable candidate. As a result of RAMP's decision, a broader coalition began to form that brought together people who not long before had been avowed political enemies. For example, CHAMP leader Michael Eng openly endorsed and contributed money to both the Reichenberger and Barron campaigns.

Also running for a council seat was Samuel Kiang, a Chinese American engineer and lawyer who announced early in August 1989 that he would be a candidate. Kiang, who had never been involved with electoral politics before, said he made his decision largely because of his dissatisfaction with the performance of Barry Hatch. "Monterey Park is an ethnically diverse city which is more than 50 percent Asian, with many Hispanics and Anglos," he told a reporter from *Asian Week*. "But Hatch . . . made derogatory remarks about [Asian] immigrants, trying to make us the scapegoat for all the problems he could not solve as mayor."[31]

Kiang was strongly supported by the Chinese American Political Action Committee (C-PAC), a group headed by former councilwoman and mayor Lily Lee Chen. With C-PAC's help, Kiang raised $42,844 and spent $43,899, totals well above those of any other candidate.[32] Fluent in English, Mandarin, and Cantonese, he also ran an aggressive door-to-door and absentee ballot campaign. All these efforts were rewarded: Kiang received the highest number of votes among the six council contenders for the three seats available.

Kiang collected 3,880 votes, 1,157 of which came from absentee ballots (out of 1,773 sent out). Fred Balderrama, then president of the Monterey Park Chamber of Commerce, was second with 3,390 votes. Third, in what many considered the election's biggest surprise, was Marie Purvis—the candidate who had fared poorly in the 1988 election—with 2,992 votes. David Barron (2,666 votes) and Pat Reichenberger (2,473) were followed by Barry Hatch, who came in last with only 1,907 votes.[33]

Because Hatch had managed to alienate himself from the community, he also discredited the RAMP group that had helped elect him in 1986 and supported him against the recall attempt in 1987. Despite its refusal to endorse Hatch in 1990, he was still identified with RAMP, and its whole slate lost. But on the same ballot voters overwhelmingly supported RAMP-sponsored Proposition S, an initiative that extended the limitation of new housing units to 100 per year (approved in Proposition K in 1982) for another ten years. The proposition passed by 4,189 votes to 1,014.[34]

The new pro-growth council majority lost little time setting new priorities for the city. Though all the new members campaigned on managing growth, their actions showed them much less restrictive toward development than their predecessors. They passed several variances allowing property owners to build beyond the limits allowed by city ordinances, and whereas the previous council majority was keen on finding "American" stores to come into Monterey Park, the new one entertained proposals to build a large hotel complex and Taiwanese department store in order to lure even more foreign investment into the city.[35]

Intra-Chinese Conflict

With the election of Kiang in addition to Chu, Monterey Park was touted as the first city on the United States mainland to have two Chinese Americans serving concurrently on the city council. But though the emergence of Asian American power and politics in Monterey Park was inevitable, recent events show that calls for ethnic unity are still merely covers for class interests and so continue to be resisted. This was illustrated by the bizarre twist that events took during the summer of 1991 when a group of about a hundred Chinese American seniors—many of whom did not speak English—marched in front of the Monterey Park City Hall demanding a recall of Judy Chu because she was supposedly "anti-Chinese." [36]

The protest stemmed from complaints made months earlier by non-English-speaking residents who wanted the city to provide bilingual emergency services. In May 1991 the city council approved a staff-proposed preferential hiring plan intended to ensure that eventually there would be bilingual emergency 911 dispatchers—fluent in Mandarin, Cantonese, or Spanish as well as English—on every shift. But the plan was rejected in July by the city's personnel board, after it was heavily lobbied by unions representing Monterey Park city workers; the board said the proposal discriminated against people who spoke only English and those who spoke a second language other than the three specified. Angry at the rebuff, newly elected council member Kiang immediately called for a change in the city code which would allow the council to override the personnel board's decision.

While the plan was being considered, Chu voted with Couch and Purvis to fire City Manager Mark Lewis, a supporter of the preferential hiring plan. Ironically, Lewis's dismissal was based on allegations of improper hiring and promotional practices unrelated to the bilingual issue. In addition, Chu had offered her own compromise proposal on the hiring question. But Kiang charged that Chu's vote against Lewis meant that she was opposed to programs Lewis had supported, specifically job preference to bilingual 911 dispatchers. Lewis was popular among immigrant Chinese residents because he had often clashed with Barry Hatch over policy issues and because he encouraged more open economic development planning, supported increased community services programs, and pushed for aggressive affirmative action hiring practices. In fact, one Chinese-language newspaper reportedly dubbed Lewis "the Yellow Savior," whereas others often charged that the American-born Chu was "not Chinese enough." The *Chinese Daily News* cited a "concerned resident" named "Lum" who said that Chu's voting record reflected her desire to broaden her constituency in order to run for statewide office: "Chu needs to support white society issues and laying off the city manager is one of them." [37]

The July protest march against Chu was organized by Abel Pa, president of Southern California Chinese Radio Broadcasting, Inc. Pa acknowledged that the protesters were from "all over Los Angeles County," indicating that the mobilization was not a spontaneous local response. It was rumored, however, that Sam Kiang and former mayor Lily Lee Chen (who had clashed with Chu earlier over development and personal issues) were involved in the effort to discredit Chu with the Chinese community in order to consolidate their own political power base. Chen called such allegations absurd: "If [Chu] understood the Chinese language, she would have been able to listen to the Chinese radio station that claimed responsibility for the protest," she scoffed.[38]

Chu vehemently denied that the firing of Lewis and the bilingual hiring plan were related, reminding reporters that she had tried to save the proposal. "I've always been supportive of the Chinese community," she insisted. "What we see here are distortions that are politically motivated."[39] And indeed, during the August 1 public hearing held at the request of the fired city manager, American-born Asian and Latino CHAMP members, white RAMP members, and proponents of official English—including Barry Hatch—all denounced Lewis and accused him of working with those in the community who were trying to tie his dismissal to the 911 bilingual dispatch issue, thus exciting and dividing the community along ethnic lines. Only a handful of immigrant Chinese activists spoke in his support.[40]

Once Lewis was officially released from his contract, clamor over the bilingual dispatch issue seemed to wane. In fact, when Judy Chu announced her reelection bid for Monterey Park City Council in a formal January 1992 press conference, Abel Pa surprised the audience by apologizing for his actions against her and endorsing her reelection bid.[41]

The 1992 Election and After

While Monterey Park's immigrant Chinese superficially appear to be cohesive because of their overall presence in the city's economic, social, and cultural life, they still do not dominate the city's political life. Many people anticipated that the April 1992 council election would be an important test for Judy Chu's liberal multi-ethnic coalition against a seemingly organized immigrant Chinese voting block that is generally conservative, nationalistic, and ethnocentric. Chu was expected to face stiff competition from Bonnie Wai, who, like Samuel Kiang, is an American-trained attorney born in Hong Kong. Fluent in English, Cantonese, and Mandarin, Wai was strongly supported by Kiang, Lily Lee Chen, and Chinese business interests. Because of Kiang's stunning success in 1990, there were very high expectations for Wai, and speculation that Monterey Park would be the first city in the continental United States to have a Chinese American majority on the city council.

But Chu was reelected and received the highest number of votes in Monterey Park's first city council election utilizing trilingual ballots in English, Spanish, and Chinese. Rita Valenzuela, a political newcomer with long-time ties in the community, came in second, and highly favored Wai finished a distant third. Two other Chinese candidates, Raymond Wu and Charles Wu (no relation), fell eighth and ninth in a nine-candidate race.

Coalition versus Ethnic Politics

That coalition-building rather than polarization seemed to be the dominant theme of the 1992 race was evidenced by RAMP's endorsement of Judy Chu. Despite their previously lukewarm relationship, Chu's consistently moderate positions on growth and development during her four years in office genuinely impressed RAMP members and leadership. Eager to overcome the embarrassment of the 1990 city council election, RAMP very much wanted to move beyond its negative reputation as a "racist" and "no-growth" organization. It also endorsed Rita Valenzuela and threw its support behind Proposition T, a measure that would actually allow an *increase* in the height of commercial buildings.

Joseph Rubin explained that since the 1988 city council election there had been a slowly emerging "realignment" in Monterey Park politics. Judy Chu "got elected without our opposition, but also without our support—how can I not notice that?" he said. "And she came in first! RAMP has to wise up to what is going on now in this city or we risk losing everything we have achieved. We have to be willing to broaden our movement."[42] In the 1992 edition of the *Record*, RAMP had nothing but praise for Chu, telling readers that she had kept her campaign promises to improve development standards and bring the community together. "But there's something else that makes her an unusual politician—Judy is smart," RAMP wrote glowingly. "Sure, she has the university degrees, but that's not what makes the difference— she uses her common sense, and she has the good instincts to do the right thing."[43]

At the same time, RAMP did not deviate from its attack strategy against perceived enemies. The *Record* lashed out specifically at Kiang, citing the bilingual emergency phone service uproar as racially divisive, and was equally harsh to Bonnie Wai, linking her to Lily Lee Chen, the developers, and Sam Kiang and suggesting that "she'll owe some paybacks."[44] Wai did raise more money than any other candidate ($64,238), but RAMP failed to mention that Judy Chu raised the second largest amount ($53,927).[45]

Chu's first-place total of 3,405 votes included 1,220 absentee votes; Valenzuela followed with 2,655 votes and Wai with 1,770. Not far behind was the outspoken official-English advocate Frank Arcuri with 1,341 votes. Though Arcuri toned down his harsh rhetoric, he was the only council candidate who did not submit a Spanish or Chinese translation of his personal statement for the sample ballot and voter information pamphlet sent to all registered voters. His showing indicates that a solid anti-Chinese voting block was still present in Monterey Park. Latino candidate Andy Islas came in fifth, followed by John Casperson, Francisco Alonso, Raymond Wu, and Charles Wu. Monterey Park also passed its first pro-growth initiative, Proposition T, 2,831 to 2,340.[46]

The Native-born versus Foreign-born Split

The 1992 city council election demonstrated that political organizing around race and ethnicity alone is not enough. Though there may well be small "Chinese-only" and "anti-Chinese" voting blocks in Monterey Park, most voters are much more thoughtful and independent about their political choices. Race and ethnicity are significant and obviously the most volatile factors, but a comparative look at other Chinese communities shows that class and nativity have far more influence. Divisions similar to those in Monterey Park have been described by Victor and Brett de Bary Nee for San Francisco's Chinatown and Bernard Wong for New York's.[47] In both studies, the two main factions were the "traditional elite"—predominantly older, China-born merchants associated with the Chinese Consolidated Benevolent Association (CCBA)—and the "social service elite," made up primarily of American-born Asian social service professionals and students.

Generally speaking, the two elites differ considerably in their interactions with the larger society. First, members of the traditional elite have historically been described as isolationists, preferring as little interaction with, and help from, the larger society as possible. If interaction must take place, they choose a low-keyed accommodation over conflict. Members of the social service elite tend more to be conflict-oriented in their interactions with the larger society. Taking their cue from the civil rights movement, they prefer to use direct-action strategies to achieve their goals and assert their power.

Second, members of the traditional elite are described as conservative because of their staunch anti–Chinese Communist position and desire to maintain the status quo in Chinatown communities. Members of the social service elite, mostly American-born and -raised, are much less antagonistic toward the People's Republic of China. In addition, they see themselves as change agents, directly challenging the status quo in Chinatown as well as in the broader society.

Third, members of the traditional elite think of themselves as cultural managers. This means that they maintain strong traditional values of filial piety and support programs—Chinese-language schools, Chinese New Year's parades, Chinese festivals—in the hope of retaining cultural identity and securing community control. Members of the social service elite hold to the larger ethnic identity of Asian American. Their ethnic group identification is intended to promote political and economic solidarity rather than cultural maintenance. In short, the social service elite has taken on the role of an interest group.

Recent work by Peter Kwong on New York's Chinatown and Richard Thompson on Toronto's acknowledge these two polarized camps but add an extra player: a new overseas Chinese "entrepreneurial elite."[48] Both describe the impact of this new group on the Chinatown community, but neither focuses specifically on its relation to the larger society. Events in Monterey Park, however, show that members of the new entrepreneurial elite are a unique hybrid, somewhat fluid in their patterns of interaction with society as a whole. They are *not* isolationists and do not shy away from asserting themselves, economically, culturally, or politically. Though conservative in their anti-Communist positions and with a tendency to vote Republican, they see themselves very much as change agents in the forefront of creating a world financial capital that will serve as the "Gateway to the Pacific Rim." Furthermore, the new elite works in Monterey Park to uphold ethnic group identity for *both* cultural maintenance *and* economic and political ends.

The existence of these different factions helps to explain the rivalries between Lily Lee Chen, Samuel Kiang, and Judy Chu. Chen and Kiang clearly represent the new entrepreneurial elite and their interests. Though Chen is employed as a social service administrator for the county of Los Angeles, her term on the council was marked by several major development controversies and an unabashed ambition for higher office. Since her city council defeat in 1986, Chen has been appointed a member of the California State World Trade Commission, and she made an unsuccessful bid for Congress in 1988. Kiang has positioned himself as a staunch advocate for the immigrant Chinese and has been actively seeking a political issue around which to rally his constituents. His clumsy mishandling of the bilingual services and Mark Lewis episodes, however, failed to generate much excitement among immigrant Chinese residents in Monterey Park and served only to deeply antagonize non-Chinese. The disappointing third-place finish of Kiang's protégé Bonnie Wai revealed his dwindling support base.

American-born Chu, on the other hand, represents a new version of the social service elite. Galvanized into direct political action during Monterey Park's official-English controversy, she was not hesitant to clash with Barry Hatch after she was elected to the city council in 1988. At the same time, when she rotated into the position of mayor in April 1990, one of her priorities was to encourage more interaction among all residents by means of "harmony" programs—among them, a renewed emphasis on Neighborhood Watch, a strengthening of ties with sister cities Yung Ho in Taiwan and Oaxaca in Mexico, and the initiation of a "Harmony Week" of activities promoting an appreciation of ethnic diversity in the city.

Like the traditional elite described above, Chu has tended to follow a low-keyed and accommodating approach when dealing with non-Chinese. But unlike the traditional elite, her primary support is not based on ethnicity. And unlike most other members of the social service elite, Chu has gained support because she is considered a "mainstream" leader rather than a "marginal" outsider. Indeed, when she was installed as mayor of Monterey Park, the oath of office was administered by State Attorney General John Van de Kamp, then a candidate for governor of California. This kind of high-profile attention, of course, helps to enlarge Chu's campaign contributions.

While some may call Chu's positions and strategy co-optation of the highest order, Peter Kwong argues for the same approach. "The working people in [New York's] Chinatown need to participate in electoral politics, but not necessarily along ethnic lines," he writes. "They need to form groups around specific needs and to ally themselves with groups with similar interests. . . . Intercommunity alliances with those in the larger society will enable them to voice their concerns more effectively." The kind of alliance Kwong advocates has been specifically stimulated by uncontrolled land speculation that quickly spread to neighboring communities. "The formation of intercommunity alliances is also taking place on the gentrification issue. Several Chinatown groups have already joined the Lower East Side Joint Planning Council, a coalition of Catholic Church, black and Hispanic tenants' committees, neighborhood artists, homestead groups, and community-development agencies."[49] In Monterey Park, events of the four years from 1988 to 1992 show that the community slowly but surely turned away from the politics of division and isolation symbolized by rigid Barry Hatch and came to recognize calls for ethnic unity as a cover for the class interests of a pro-growth faction. Both the tactics of division and those of false unity were rejected by the community.

It is not clear whether the political and economic future of Monterey Park will be marked by new splits along lines of class, ethnicity, and national origin, pitting development and community interest against each other. It *is* clear that Chinese immigrants are the dominant demographic, economic, social, and cultural force in Monterey Park, but they are not yet the dominant political force—for several reasons. First and foremost, Chinese immigrants who are not yet citizens are ineligible to vote. Second, because Chinese immigrants are constantly moving in and out of Monterey Park, there is no stable population on which to build a political base. Third, since the vast majority of Chinese immigrants are not developers, there should be no reason to expect them to support the agenda of the entreprenurial elite. For now, neither is there reason to expect ethnic solidarity in the political arena, and only time will determine whether the leaders of the new entrepreneurial elite will continue the strategy of ethnic polarization or work toward intergroup coalition.

CHAPTER 8

Theoretical Perspectives on Monterey Park

Immigrant adaptation to life in the United States began receiving scholarly attention early in the twentieth century, in response to the arrival of European newcomers in large numbers. The preeminent theory has been Robert Park's (1950) "race relations" cycle, which posits that immigrants initially clash with natives over cultural values and norms but, over time, do adapt and are eventually absorbed into the mainstream society. This four-part cycle of contact, competition, accommodation, and assimilation, according to Park, is "progressive and irreversible."[1]

Oliver Cox, in *Caste, Class, and Race* (1948), defined a race as "any people who are distinguished, or considered themselves distinguished, in social relations with other peoples, by their physical characteristics."[2] Native Americans, African Americans, Mexican Americans, and Asian Americans have been seen as racially distinct from European Americans on the basis of their physical differences. Even Irish and Italians were referred to as inferior *racial* groups when they first arrived in this country, but with time and intermarriage their physical distinctiveness diminished. It is clear, then, that groupings based on physical characteristics are mutable; they are, in fact, social constructs used to identify persons who are inside or outside the mainstream group as therefore superior or inferior.

Social scientists have distinguished between racial groups and ethnic groups. According to W. Lloyd Warner and Leo Srole, racial groups are defined by their physical characteristics, ethnic groups by cultural differences. In *The Social Systems of American Ethnic Groups* (1945) they claimed that the greater the cultural and physical differences between a group and the dominant society, the slower would be that group's assimilation.[3] Milton Gordon, in *Assimilation in American Life* (1964), defined an ethnic group more broadly as a social group distinguished by race, religion, or national origin: "All of these categories . . . serve to create, through historical circumstances, a sense of peoplehood for groups in the United States."[4] For Gordon, the distinctive characteristics that set ethnic groups apart from the dominant society can be physical *or* cultural; the important factor is a subjec-

tive sense of community based on common descent and an awareness of one's own kind. Scholars have used both concepts of what
constitutes an ethnic group to describe and analyze group experiences throughout the history of the United States. Those who prefer the narrower definition usually conclude that the experience of
non-European groups has been decidedly different from, and harsher
than, that of European groups. Those who accept the broader definition generally argue that the difference is one of degree rather than
of kind.

Attention to the broad field of immigrant, ethnic, and race relations expanded in earnest in the 1960s and 1970s in direct response to
the tumultuous civil rights movement and the changes in immigration
patterns after Congress revised U.S. immigration laws in 1965. In the
1990s there is a revival of scholarly, as well as popular, interest as a
result of the influx of both legal and undocumented immigrants, overwhelmingly from Asia and Latin America, which began after World
War II and increased significantly following passage of the Immigration Act of 1965. Because that influx has radically changed the social,
cultural, and economic landscape of our nation, the body of literature
on ethnic and race relations and immigrant adaptation in the United
States is vast. Five theoretical concepts are useful, in some degree,
to an analysis of the Monterey Park situation: assimilation, structural
discrimination, ethnic solidarity, "ethclass," and racial formation.

Assimilation

The most elaborate discussion of assimilation has been undertaken
by Milton Gordon, who set out to describe the actual adaptation process, not to prescribe what new groups should strive for. Unlike Park,
Gordon recognizes a variety of encounters between different groups
and a variety of possible outcomes. He identifies seven "Assimilation
Variables"; for my purposes his distinction between cultural assimilation, involving a change of cultural patterns to those of the host
society, and structural assimilation, or large-scale entrance into the
cliques, clubs, and institutions of the host society, is particularly important. Gordon departs from a causal relationship between the two;
he acknowledges that cultural assimilation as a generational process
is inevitable for all groups but sees the possibility of complete cultural assimilation without significant structural assimilation—particularly for non-Protestant and nonwhite racial groups. This "structural
pluralism," which challenges the notion of "cultural pluralism" first
proposed in 1915 by Horace Kallen,[5] "is the major key to the understanding of the ethnic makeup of American society, while cultural
pluralism is a minor one."[6]

In *Beyond the Melting Pot* (1964), Nathan Glazer and Daniel Patrick Moynihan support the cultural pluralism concept, concluding that blacks, Puerto Ricans, Jews, Italians, and Irish in New York have largely maintained their distinct identities.[7] Later, as both writers became alarmed at the growing tensions between ethnic and racial groups in urban areas across the nation, Glazer in particular began to speak out for a common value system to help maintain orderly relations.[8] Economist Thomas Sowell argues prescriptively in *Ethnic America* (1981) that every ethnic group that has started at the bottom, worked hard, and quietly assimilated into the mainstream has been rewarded with economic success. He attributes the lack of economic success of certain groups to cultural differences or deficiencies, believing that members of some cultures are just more able and willing to adapt than others.[9]

Most assimilation theorists hold firm to the ideal that integration into a single society and culture ensures social success and economic upward mobility for the individual, and social stability for the host society. In Monterey Park, the extent of the Chinese immigrants' ability or desire to assimilate into the dominant society has been a continuing issue in community relations. Resentful older residents felt that the new immigrant Chinese were not only refusing to assimilate but, more important, were "taking over" the community. Superficially, it's true, there seems to be little evidence that the assimilation process is taking place. Prominent Chinese-language business signs and ethnic restaurants, markets, and shops all provide at least the appearance that the city is quite separate from the cultural mainstream. But the major influx of immigrant Chinese to Monterey Park is barely a generation old, and the self-proclaimed "old-timers" seemed unaware that assimilation into the host country is a generational rather than an individual process ruled by will.

The new immigrants do clearly challenge the pattern of assimilation prescribed by Thomas Sowell and Nathan Glazer; the most affluent and well-educated in particular appear to be achieving economic success without assimilating culturally. Chinese immigrants also caused great consternation by starting alternative organizations such as the Little Taipei Lions Club, the Chinese American Political Action Committee, and to the Chinese Chamber of Commerce. The consequent resentment in the community was testimony to how strongly most long-time residents felt about assimilation. Such resentment manifested itself most clearly in the official-English and anti-immigrant movements in Monterey Park and across the country, reactions to the changing social and cultural landscape brought about by large numbers of immigrants from Latin America and Asia.

Socially, culturally, and economically, Monterey Park is without doubt becoming a Chinese city. Though this seems to be a far cry from Milton Gordon's description of immigrant acculturation, it is apparent upon closer examination that the Chinese people in Monterey Park are a diverse group, the composition of which is constantly changing. Many of the American-born children of immigrants who came in the 1960s and early 1970s are monolingual English speakers, well assimilated and integrated into mainstream American life. For example, Michael Woo, who grew up in the city and worked briefly as a writer for the *Monterey Park Progress*, gained recognition in 1985 as the first Asian American elected to the Los Angeles City Council, and in 1993 he ran a strong though unsuccessful campaign for mayor of Los Angeles. Moreover, the intergenerational cultural assimilation defined by Gordon is exemplified by the many Chinese American immigrants who have relocated to other areas of the San Gabriel Valley after living in Monterey Park for a number of years, and the more recent immigrants who use the city as a way station until they too can move on. It is the continual arrival of new Chinese immigrants to Monterey Park, as well as the presence of Chinese who live outside the city but who choose to shop and eat there, that gives the false impression that *all* Chinese immigrants remain unassimilated, socially and culturally static.

It is necessary, then, to separate the place called Monterey Park from the people in Monterey Park. The city is indeed becoming that "mecca" for the new Chinese predicted by Frederic Hsieh many years ago and a "gateway to the Pacific Rim," as a result of global economic trends and commercial and financial interests pushing in that direction. But though the Chinese newcomers attracted to this community to live, shop, and start small businesses do play a part in changing Monterey Park and the surrounding area, they themselves are also being changed. The entire process is strongly affected by the continuing arrival of Chinese people and capital from Asia. The result is an extremely diverse population that cuts across all levels of cultural and class identification. These divisions are not easily visible to the non-Chinese observer, or even to the U.S.-born Chinese American or Japanese American resident. For this reason, the immigrant Chinese as a whole have been an easy target for blame for all the problems faced by the city. At the same time, it has been difficult to organize them into a consolidated political force to counteract the hostility against them.

Structural Discrimination

Assimilation theory, which assumes that the United States is an open society accepting anyone willing to adapt to the dominant society's norms, has been criticized as not historically applicable to racial minorities. Out of this criticism emerged structural discrimination theories, which argue that racial discrimination is embedded directly in the institutions of society, including corporations, schools, and various levels of government. The term "institutional racism" emerged from this analysis.

Robert Blauner, whose *Racial Oppression in America* (1972) acknowledges structural discrimination in American society, utilizes the concept of "internal colonialism" to explain why some groups make it and others do not. Blauner asserts that racial minorities (African Americans, Native Americans, Chicanos, and Asian Americans) "share a common situation of oppression, from which a potential political unity is inferred." He cites three conditions that differentiate people of color from those of European ethnic background: forced entry (as in slavery), unfree labor (the inability to choose one's relative position in the work force), and cultural destruction (the breaking up of slave families, prohibited immigration by Chinese women, policies against Native American religion, and migratory labor practices that kept Mexican families unstable). Though European immigrants certainly also experienced cultural conflicts, they did not have to face the same institutional or legal oppression. Blauner concludes that all white groups generally benefit from the racial oppression of nonwhites: "In a historical sense, people of color provided much of the hard labor (and the technical skills) that built up the agricultural base and the mineral-transport-communication infrastructure necessary for industrialization and modernization, whereas the Europeans worked primarily within the industrialized, modern sector." [10]

Edna Bonacich, in "A Theory of Ethnic Antagonism: The Split Labor Market" (1972), sees much more contentiousness among three competing interests: businessmen or employers, higher-paid labor, and cheaper labor. Cheap labor, she says, which has always been used by capitalists to keep the cost of production low, and poses a constant threat to higher-paid labor by undercutting wages and displacing the latter from the work force. Bonacich places much of the responsibility for racism on higher-paid white workers and their efforts to protect their economic interests. She cites the 1882 Chinese Exclusion Law in the United States to show how they exercised their power by marginalizing racial minorities and pushing them into the cheap labor market, where they would not threaten higher-paid labor. [11]

Among those who disagree with Bonacich's thesis are segmentation theorists, who emphasize the capitalist ruling class and its members desire to protect their own interests. Within a Marxist framework, Richard Edwards, David Gordon, and Michael Reich all argue that the dominant capitalist class created a two-tiered labor market as a way to fragment the labor force and keep it unorganized: jobs in the primary labor market are well paid, clean, and secure and offer the possibility of advancement; those in the secondary labor market are "dead-end" jobs. Not surprisingly, the primary labor market comprises mostly white men, while nonwhite immigrant workers, native-born workers of color, women, and youth are concentrated in the secondary labor market.[12]

Mario Barrera in *Race and Class in the Southwest* (1979) critiques and synthesizes these models. Developing a theory of racial inequality from a "class-differentiated colonial perspective," Barrera believes that the historical experience of Chicanos (Mexican Americans) can be best described by internal-colonialism theory *plus* class dynamics; Chicanos, he says, have been incorporated into the United States economy as "ascriptive class segments." Barrera sees a class in Marxist terms as a group of people who have a similar relationship to the process of production in society. He recognizes that Chicanos occupy several classes, but whether in the working, petit bourgeois, or professional-managerial class, they are generally found in the lower echelons: "Chicanos in all classes suffer from institutionalized discrimination even though it takes different forms for each class"; as a result, Chicanos supposedly have a group interest based on their common experiences. Barrera acknowledges shifting political patterns, however, in which Chicano class interests sometimes take precedence over racial group interests and vice versa.[13]

Structural discrimination theories have been criticized for being far too deterministic, for depicting people of color as hapless victims, and for not differentiating among historical periods and various non-white peoples. None of the four structural theories—which all focus on what dominant white society has done to racial minorities—can satisfactorily account for the rapid economic, social, and cultural dominance attained by the immigrant Chinese in Monterey Park.

They were not "forced" to come to Monterey Park, as internal colonial perspective posits; nor has cultural destruction taken place against them, despite sign ordinances and official-English propositions; and although some workers and small business owners may still suffer a form of unfree labor, many Chinese immigrants have experienced economic upward mobility. More generally, the internal colonial model underestimates the class differences between and within racial minority groups. Blauner's assertion that a shared history of oppression is more important to people of color than class identity has proved incorrect in Monterey Park. Theoretically, race and cultural symbols should serve as the most effective rallying cries for political mobilization and unity. To a degree this worked for CHAMP in overturning Resolution 9004, but only because the organization focused on harmony and fairness issues. By contrast, when ABC tried to use race and racism to unify people of color against white nativists the recall attempt, it failed miserably.

The split-labor market and segmentation theories both have some applicability in that they locate racial antagonism in economic competition. But in middle-class suburban Monterey Park, competition is not over jobs per se but over much broader economic issues and the direction of change. By underestimating class diversity within and between racial groups, both theories suffer from the same weakness as Blauner's internal colonial model.

The class-differentiated colonial model advanced by Barrera comes closest to addressing the broad class dynamics seen among the Chinese in Monterey Park. Those Chinese however, are not "ascriptive class segments" discriminated against by white capitalists and institutions; indeed, they quickly became the city's capitalist class. In short, structural discrimination theories, though applicable to certain groups in certain periods in American history, do not explain Monterey Park today.

Ethnic Solidarity

What holds the members of an ethnic group together? The large number of Asians living in the San Gabriel Valley region offer an interesting test for ethnic solidarity theories, which emphasize that groups whose attempts to gain entrance into the host society are rejected tend to fall back on the security and protection of their own ethnic communities and start their own businesses in order to advance economically within a hostile environment.

Edna Bonacich developed a "middleman minority" theory to explain the coerciveness that forces immigrant groups into their roles in society. Middleman minorities are, she asserts, independent proprietors who have been rejected by yet cater to the needs of both the elite capitalist class and the working-class masses. In *The Economic Basis of Ethnic Solidarity: Small Business in the Japanese American Community* (1978), Bonacich and John Modell state that the Japanese "became proprietors . . . , because racial discrimination prevented them from finding opportunities for advancement in the general economy. Independent small business was an alternative route to success that did not depend on white goodwill." Middleman groups tend to concentrate in and sometimes dominate economic activities such as trade, petty finance, and money handling, and their typically family-owned firms may prosper; however, "on the whole, these minorities occupy a precarious position in the social structure and may be subjected to outbreaks of antagonism." [14]

The cultural theory developed by Ivan Light in *Ethnic Enterprise in America* (1972) does not dispute the racial discrimination faced by African and Asian Americans but seeks to explain the proportionately small number of black-owned businesses vis-à-vis the high ratio of businesses owned by Chinese and Japanese Americans, relative to their respective populations. Light concludes that among Chinese and Japanese immigrants, ethnic traditions and an effective system of kinship networks enhance business success. In particular, informal methods of raising start-up capital through rotating credit systems—known as *hui* in Cantonese, *ko* in Japanese, and *esusu* among the Yoruba in Africa, Britain, and the West Indies—account in some measure for the differential business success of American-born blacks, West Indian blacks, and Asian American immigrants. According to Light, the reason blacks in the United States lack a tradition of entrepreneurship is that their long experience of slavery and discrimination ruptured the cultural and kinship ties.[15]

Situational theory, a third explanation for ethnic solidarity, is best stated by Pyong Gap Min in *Ethnic Business Enterprise: Korean Small Business in Atlanta* (1988). Although many Korean immigrants are highly educated and often held white-collar jobs in Korea, a majority of those he surveyed had been unable to find similar employment in the United States. This fact and language difficulty, were important reasons for their seeking self-employment; over half had experienced some job discrimination, but only a third called it a major factor in their decision. In short, "Korean immigrants' perception of their labor market disadvantages is much more important than their perception of host discrimination." Moreover, unlike Bonacich and Modell, Min argues that "Korean immigrants' anticipation of economic mobility through business, together with their perception of labor market disadvantages, is the central factor in the decision to start a business in this country." [16] Thus, Min differs also from Light in considering the Koreans' decisions to be economic and rational rather than cultural.

Ethnic solidarity has been most extensively studied by Alejandro Portes and his colleagues in their research on Cubans in Miami.[17] They acknowledge racial discrimination as a driving force but differ from Bonacich in their claim that immigrants willingly choose to enter what they call the "enclave economy" as a viable alternative to assimilation. In "Immigrant Enclaves: An Analysis of the Labor Market Experiences of Cubans in Miami," Portes and Kenneth Wilson show how the Cuban experience contradicts common assumptions about the dual labor market: not only are enclave workers not restricted to the secondary labor market but they share the same degree of human capital returns as workers in the primary labor market. In *Latin Journey: Cuban and Mexican Immigrants in the United States* (1985), Portes and Robert Bach argue that there is a reciprocal relationship within the ethnic enclave. Owners get a steady labor force that can be paid lower wages and is not prone to unionization or agitation, while workers receive employment and promotion opportunities that they cannot possibly hope to find elsewhere. These fulfilled mutual "obligations" stabilize the enclave economy and make it a viable community for all concerned. What makes this theory provocative is the claim that there is no significant negative cost to the enclave's economic and social isolation from the dominant society, that the development of the ethnic enclave is a voluntary act, not a reactive one.

The proponents of all these theories of ethnic solidarity agree that ethnic communities are generally too small in number and too limited in resources to support adequately more than a few ethnic-oriented businesses. In Monterey Park, however, the concentration of Chinese people, capital, and business shows remarkable self-sufficiency and provides an interesting challenge to the ethnic enclave paradigm.

The middleman minority theory well describes the concentration of small businesses, often family-owned and -operated, that is characteristic of Monterey Park. But whereas middleman minority businesses are said to "act as go-betweens, playing the roles of rent collector and shopkeeper to the subordinate population while distributing the products of the elites and/or extracting 'tribute' for them," there is little evidence that the self-employed Chinese are playing this role.[18] Bonacich and Modell could not support the hypothesis that United States and California capitalists benefited from Japanese entrepreneurship; indeed, small Japanese businesses were often regarded as competitive threats that undercut prices.

Light's cultural and Min's situational theories of ethnic solidarity, when applied to Monterey Park, are not so much wrong as incomplete in their view of class dynamics. Light's description of entrepreneurs taking advantage of ethnic investment and credit systems to start businesses and to create ethnic labor markets, consumers, and supply networks is applicable. As Min correctly points out, however, it is well-educated immigrants, often from a professional background but without prior entrepreneurial experience, who tend to start their own businesses in the United States. Yet though he sees class factors rather than the cultural values as key determinants, Min's analysis does not address the even broader class divisions found in Monterey Park because the setting of his study is quite different; he focuses on Kore-

ans who work in black communities but live in white communities in
Atlanta.

The self-sustaining ethnic enclave described by Portes and his colleagues is more comparable to the Monterey Park situation, but their
model does not account for class conflict within an enclave. Although
they acknowledge the existence of exploitation of immigrants by co-
ethnics, they contend that the paternalistic practices of enclave business owners lead to their sharing with workers the same degree of
human capital returns as workers in the primary labor market. Yet
when overseas speculators bought up properties at low prices, with
the intention not of improving them but of reselling them at a large
profit, the resulting rapid increase in land prices brought with it
high commercial rentals that directly and detrimentally affected small
immigrant-owned and -operated businesses. For the many minimal-
profit family entrepreneurs in Monterey Park, high property values
and rent-gouging by ethnic property owners are not conducive to a
symbiotic relationship. In this city we may very well be seeing an enclave economy that is more predatory than supportive, because of land
speculation, too much competition within the enclave, and the inability
of the enclave to reach out to a broader market.

Ethclass

One shortcoming of ethnic solidarity theories is their failure to acknowledge intra-ethnic differences, particularly class differences. The
general assumption is that everyone in the group benefits from ethnic
solidarity, though there is disagreement over whether the dominant
society imposes negative costs. "Ethclass," a term coined by Milton
Gordon, explicitly acknowledges class cleavages within groups which,
as Gordon suggests, may be more important in American society than
ethnic differences.[19]

Stephen Steinberg elaborates this theme in *The Ethnic Myth* (1981).
He argues effectively that the ability of certain European immigrant
groups to enter the mainstream of American life in the late nineteenth
and early twentieth centuries was mostly a social-class phenomenon
resulting from changes in their economic circumstances. To illustrate
his thesis, Steinberg examines the "myth" of Jewish success in business
and education. He explains that it was Jewish immigrants' good fortune to arrive in urban centers at the right time and with the necessary
industrial and entrepreneurial skills. He cites a Russian census of 1897
to show that 70 percent of Jews there were employed in commerce or
manufacturing or were artisans; only 3 percent were in agriculture. In
contrast, 61 percent of non-Jews worked in agriculture. "In a word,

Eastern European Jews were not peasants," writes Steinberg. "This simple fact would have far-reaching implications for their destiny in the United States."[20]

According to Steinberg, Thomas Sowell's argument that Jews possessed positive *cultural* traits is an inaccurate explanation of the relative success of the Jews. Neither does it explain the failure of African Americans to achieve economic mobility in American society; rather, following the Civil War, blacks were systematically kept in low-wage, low-skill agricultural jobs in the South and out of high-paying industrial jobs in the North—destructive experiences of overt discrimination that cannot be explained away by "cultural deficiencies." In *The Declining Significance of Race* (1978), one of the most controversial books published in recent years, William Julius Wilson offers an eth-class analysis of the African American experience. He holds that U.S. race relations went through two historic shifts: from the antebellum period of slavery to the industrial period before World War II, and again to the years after the war. According to Wilson, the last period, given the profound social and legislative changes forged during the civil rights movement, provided opportunities for African Americans in business, government, and the professions never before available to them: "Now the life chances of individual blacks have more to do with their economic class position than with their day-to-day encounters with whites."[21]

Wilson is nevertheless cognizant of the sharp and increasing schism between the well-to-do middle class and the large underclass of African Americans, who overwhelmingly lack educational opportunity, are restricted to low-paid jobs or unemployment, and see little hope. This bifurcation is due to economic restructuring—a shift from labor-intensive manufacturing to a high-technology information and service economy requiring a highly educated work force—which disproportionately hurts the inner-city poor. Wilson recognizes that though the change was not due to any race-conscious policy designed to have a negative effect on a particular group, it posed formidable obstacles for segments of the black population. His follow-up book *The Truly Disadvantaged* (1987) calls for a "universal program" of economic policies designed to help the poor, regardless of race.[22]

David Montejano's *Anglos and Mexicans in the Making of Texas, 1836–1986* (1987) also offers an important race-class analysis. The relationship between "Anglos" and Mexicans in the Southwest has been bitter, but most traditional historical writings about the region have been in the positive terms of a white male perspective. This "triumphalist literature," as Montejano calls it, describes land annexed from Mexico, Indians and Mexicans subdued, and railroads built as "progress" brought to the area with U.S. conquest. Montejano divides the history of Mexicans in Texas into four distinct periods. "Incorporation" (1836–1900) established a "peace structure" in which elite Mexican and Anglo large-scale landowners maintained the quasi-feudal system that had been in existence for generations. With "reconstruction" (1900–1920) came the development of agriculture and bitter political battles between "old-time" ranchers and "newcomer" farmers. During "segregation" (1920–30) the "modern" farm society developed, and experiments in labor control by growers resulted in increased segregation of Mexicans. "Integration" (1940–86), in which an urban-industrial order shifted power from farmers to merchants and consumers, saw the rise of political activism among Mexican Americans which Montejano says represents their political integration and increased influence.[23]

Montejano, like Wilson, argues "that a succession of class societies explains changes in race relations and that the uneven nature of this transformation explains variations in race relations." Class standing helped mitigate the most negative effects of American incorporation for certain Mexicans: to most Anglo pioneers, "Mexican landowners were 'Spanish' or 'Castilian,' whereas Mexican workers were 'half-breeds' or 'Mexican Indians.'" The author concludes: "The well-known aphorism explains the situation—'money whitens.'"[24]

Because the roots of conflict in Monterey Park were indeed economic rather than racial, ethclass theories provide the most plausible explanation for the development of the situation there. The majority of the Chinese newcomers in the early 1970s, well educated and from middle-class backgrounds, were able to adapt, compete, and sometimes excel economically. Those with little or no English-language proficiency often took the highly precarious route of starting small low-profit enterprises, but many bilingual Chinese found a niche in real estate, property management, banking, and other services and thus became "middlemen" for well-financed overseas speculators and developers.

But the key to ethclass theory is the assumption that class factors mitigate or equalize ethnic and racial distinctions. Though this explains the relative harmony in the community when Latinos, Japanese Americans, and Chinese Americans came to Monterey Park in the late 1950s and early 1960s, it falls short of explaining the animosity against the immigrant Chinese who arrived from the early 1970s on. Indeed, their money did not so much "whiten" as heighten racial and ethnic tensions. From broad class cleavages and differing interests emerged both a popular controlled-growth sentiment and an anti-Chinese, anti-immigrant sentiment that crossed ethnic lines. In addition to class and inter-ethnic political conflict, recent events show strong intra-ethnic conflicts within the Chinese community, especially between the American-born and the foreign-born.

More explanatory are two important factors that distinguish the Chinese in Monterey Park from other groups described by ethclass theory. First, the relatively large numbers of the middle- and upper-class Chinese immigrants make them quite different from the small minority of middle-class blacks described by Wilson and the handful of landowning elite Mexicans described by Montejano. Second, the tremendous financial resources available from overseas to some of the newcomer Chinese put them in a situation different from that of the middle-class Jewish immigrants discussed by Steinberg, who brought their skills and education but not actual capital resources. The increasing strength and presence of the Pacific Rim economies, growing economic interdependence between East and West, and the expansion of the global economy have in fact, affected race relations in this country. Though only a minority of Chinese immigrants are developers and speculators who command large financial resources, once growth is associated with them, all Chinese become a suspect homogenous group to non-Chinese.

Racial Formation

The fifth theoretical concept is quite distinct from the other four. In *Racial Formation in the United States* (1986) Michael Omi and Howard Winant argue that previous theories of ethnic and race relations and immigrant adaptation are all flawed by their failure to give enough credence to the centrality of race in American politics and life; race in the United States, they say, should be treated as "a fundamental organizing principle of social relationships."[25] The authors contrast the civil rights era, which profoundly affected race relations as well as legislation and public policies, with the subsequent reactionary backlash led by the "far right," the "new right," and the academic "neoconservative" movements of the 1970s, which gained momentum on the heels of the 1980 presidential election and the Reagan "revolution."

The Ku Klux Klan, the Aryan Nation, the Silent Brotherhood, the Order, and the Posse Comitatus are the best-known white supremacist groups that gained, or regained, prominence following the civil rights movement. These groups, according to Omi and Winant, "constitute an underground network which embraces neo-Nazis, survivalists, and militant tax resisters, among others." Political analysts generally believe that downturns in the economy give rise to such movements, but Omi and Winant see them also as "a political response to the liberal

state . . . reflect[ing] a crisis of identity. . . . The far right attempts . . .
to reassert the very meaning of *whiteness*, which has been rendered unstable and unclear by the minority challenges of the 1960s" (original
emphasis).[26]

The new right—represented by the American Conservative
Union, the Conservative Caucus, the Young Americans for Freedom,
and various fundamentalist Protestant sects and anti-immigration
groups—believes that politicians and bureaucrats have conceded too
many demands of the racial minorities. Its activists attack the liberal
experiments of the Great Society and the political gains of the 1960s:
affirmative action, bilingual education and balloting, busing to achieve
school integration. Unlike the far right, the new right does not advocate violence and—attesting to the lasting moral power of the civil
rights movement—no longer uses explicitly racist language; its criti-
cisms of public policies are instead "rearticulated" into arguments for
individual rights and community control in a conscious strategy to
hook and sway broad public support.[27]

Academic neoconservatism, the new right's intellectual and ideo-
logical base, also depicts itself as opposed to discrimination and supportive of the goals of the civil rights movement, which called for
a "colorblind" society. Omi and Winant identify Nathan Glazer as
the neoconservatives' chief spokesperson. His *Affirmative Discrimination*
(1975) argues that affirmative action programs are unnecessary, ineffective, and offensive to the American ideal of individual rights over
group rights. In his later *Ethnic Dilemmas, 1964–1982* (1983), Glazer
also criticizes cultural pluralism, bilingual education, and ethnic
studies programs.[28]

Racial formation theory has been criticized for its overarching
themes, its broad generalizations, and its lack of a longer historical
perspective.[29] Nevertheless, it does argue usefully that race relations
and adaptation are unstable phenomena that are constantly in flux,
in contrast to the assimilationist theory that minorities are inevitably
absorbed into the dominant society, and to the structural discrimination theory that minorities are fatally marginalized. Moreover, it is an
important attempt to locate "race" at the center of America's social
and political history rather than treating it as a peripheral issue. And
for my purposes, because it does focus on contemporary events, it
provides insights into the Monterey Park situation.

Though one cannot overlook the reality and volatility of *non*racial
boundaries such as those created by cultural (ethnic) and class differences, and though I argue that tensions in Monterey Park are rooted
fundamentally in conflicts over development issues and land-use policies, my analysis does not dismiss the salience of "race" as a political

organizing weapon or the importance of the dramatic ethnic contestation over cultural norms, particularly as they relate to language and assimilation. As Chinese development escalated during the late 1970s, the populist community-control and anti-government messages of the slow-growth movement were taken up by a small faction of nativist, anti-Chinese, anti-immigrant activists who used growth as a "rearticulated" statement of their racial agenda. The overwhelmingly white Residents Association of Monterey Park (RAMP) was slow to distance itself from these nativists. Omi and Winant would explain this in terms of the fear of many older whites that they would become increasingly minoritized and marginalized. Consciously or not, "race" was used as an organizing weapon on this side of the debate.

But racial formation theory is able to address only half the scenario when it focuses on how whites antagonize and fight people of color for political control. My study shows that powerful white *and* Chinese developers exploited race as an organizing tool to further their pro-growth policies. Developers and speculators tried to redefine their class interest as a morally justifiable fight against "racism." In Monterey Park the short-term gains of this tactic were powerful and sensational, but the long-term gains are debatable. The situation is far more complex than just a racial problem.

I believe that a synthesis of ethclass and racial formation theories holds the greatest explanatory power for Monterey Park. The consistent ethclass argument is that broad economic structures and political events have a direct and profound effect on race relations. The national trend in the United States over the last two decades has been a shift from a Western-oriented, manufacturing, and highly bureaucratic economy to a global, high-technology, financial, and entrepreneurial service economy. As the center of the U.S.-foreign economic interaction continues to shift from the European-Atlantic basin to the Pacific Rim, Chinese immigrants are among those best equipped to compete in this dynamic environment, particularly those with capital, connections, education, and bilingual skills. An *inclining* significance of class does not, however, necessarily correspond with a *declining* significance of race. The "rearticulation" of issues into racially tinged politics of resentment did fuel overt anti-Chinese sentiment in Monterey Park, expressed as verbal harassment, physical attacks, vandalism, reactionary anti-growth voting patterns, and white flight. Clearly, the tensions were never just over development issues. But neither were they just over "race." In fact, residents of the city have united steadily to defeat the most uncaring pro-growth, pro-development interests and the most racially reactionary and divisive elements in town.

Close examination of election results in Monterey Park does not reveal consistent racial polarization. For example, Asians were elected to the city council long before they were the majority of the population: Korean American Alfred Song in 1960; Japanese American George Ige in 1970 and 1974; Filipino American G. Monty Manibog in 1976, 1980, and again in 1984; Lily Lee Chen, with the largest number of votes, in 1982. In 1986, the council candidate who stayed away from the official-English issue, Chris Houseman, received the largest number of votes, while the person most identified with official English, Frank Arcuri, received the smallest.

Most telling was the election of Judy Chu to the council in 1988; the significant number of cross-ethnic votes she received indicates that residents were able to stand above the racial conflicts in the community in order to defeat the pro-development interests. In 1990, controversial Barry Hatch decisively lost his bid for reelection, scoring last in every voting precinct in town. Controlled-growth measures have passed unfailingly in Monterey Park since 1981, including the overwhelming passage of one RAMP-endorsed proposition in 1990— paradoxically, the same year that saw the defeat of Hatch and the election of Sam Kiang and two other growth-oriented candidates over the RAMP-sponsored slate.

Yet just two years later, Kiang-supported candidate Bonnie Wai was beaten back by Judy Chu and her moderate-growth, multi-ethnic coalition, which for the first time included support from RAMP. The 1992 election also saw the passage of a pro-growth proposition, a recognition of the city's need to increase its stagnant sales tax base. The dramatic political realignment that began slowly after the 1988 city council election reflects continued instability in this suburban Chinese American community and exposes Monterey Park for what it is: a community very much in a state of metamorphosis.

CONCLUSION

From Marginal to Mainstream

The concentration of large numbers of people of color in urban centers across the country and their impact on the broader U.S. society will continue to be a pressing issue into the twenty-first century. Monterey Park illustrates the social, cultural, and economic intersection of these demographic changes with questions of urban growth and development. Though it has by no means come fully to terms with the resulting dislocations, its history to date may suggest the kinds of realignment and accommodation necessary to a resolution of the issue.

The Metamorphosis of a City

Three prominent changes have taken place in Monterey Park since the early 1970s: the dramatic economic transformation of the community with the influx of Chinese immigrants and capital; the challenge to dominant cultural values and norms posed by immigrant Chinese newcomers; and the complex political controversies that race, ethnicity, and class conflicts combined to create.

Economic Transformation

Long before Chinese immigrants began settling in Monterey Park, civic leaders and residents were debating whether the city should expand its commercial and economic base or remain the small, quiet bedroom community it had been for years. The sentiment against growth was strong enough to stifle most major development projects, and the city began to decline. As commercial development increased in cities surrounding Monterey Park, merchants left because of reduced customer support; the result was a decrease in the city's sales tax volume, and the stagnation of both commercial and residential property values.

By the mid-1960s, pro-growth advocates in the community were desperate for new people and new investment to lift the city out of its economic doldrums. The influx of immigrant Chinese professionals during the early 1970s, coupled with increasing political instability in Asia, brought in a wave of overseas Chinese investors willing and eager to invest in depressed Monterey Park property. At first, these newcomers were welcomed with open arms by both civic leaders and residents. But when the brief but furious, period of land speculation in the late 1970s and early 1980s led to uncontrolled construction and an unprecedented escalation of property values, the initial welcome quickly soured.

As residential property values went up, many new owners found it profitable to tear down single-family homes and replace them with multiple-unit complexes. Monterey Park, quickly gaining a reputation as the "Chinese Beverly Hills" and the "City with a Heart," was increasingly attracting new Chinese immigrants—this time of more modest means—who were looking for a friendly, relatively inexpensive, and less congested alternative to the nearby Los Angeles Chinatown. While the condominium investments turned quick profits, they also created an immediate and unplanned increase in population density, neighborhood traffic, and stress on municipal services. Similarly, as commercial property values went up and new owners compensated by charging higher rents, many of the remaining merchants either sold their businesses or relocated to another community—forcing new owners to divide existing and newly built properties into smaller and smaller units of strip development.

Given this situation, new businesses in Monterey Park now tend to fall into three general economic categories. At one end are small-scale, low-profit operations typically run by immigrant Chinese families who do not have a strong command of the English language: tiny restaurants, curio shops, and specialty stores that rely on free family labor to make ends meet. In the middle range are scores of individual medical, legal, accounting, and real estate offices. These professional services are run primarily by entrepreneurial Chinese immigrants, many of whom have been educated in the United States and are fully bilingual. At the high end are Chinese-owned and -operated banks, savings and loans, and the like. Most new businesses in all three categories cater to an ethnic Chinese clientele, a logical outcome of the influx of Chinese immigrants throughout the San Gabriel Valley and the increased interest in Monterey Park abroad.

The result is an imbalanced, highly competitive service economy that has brought greater density, more traffic congestion, and less open space, parking, and landscaping. Such an economy does little to help the city's treasury, which became dependent on sales tax volume following the passage in 1978 of California's Proposition 13, which reduced property tax revenues by two-thirds. Further, an economy that clearly emphasizes the immigrant and overseas Chinese market tends to create economic, social, cultural, and political consternation throughout the community. As the changes became apparent, they elicited such comments as "This feels like a foreign country" and "The Chinese are taking over." Within a period of just six years, established residents saw their suburban dream turn into what they regarded as an urban nightmare.

The Challenge

Economic and growth issues, often accompanied by out-of-control land speculation, are not unique to Monterey Park; they have been a common source of discontent throughout southern California and across the nation since the 1980s. "Boom to bust" stories in non-Chinese cities such as Denver and Houston are primary examples.[1] But the populist controlled-growth movement in Monterey Park became tainted by nativist elements that exploited the anti-immigrant and anti-Asian sentiments pervasive in the United States for their own ends.

Little wonder that old-timers saw the prominent display of Chinese characters on business signs as an emblem of the newcomers' interest only in their own separate society and unwillingness to assimilate into the American mainstream. Many older white residents in Monterey Park pined for the small-town life they had enjoyed throughout the 1950s and 1960s and welcomed newcomers only if they fell into step with the established social and cultural pace. They saw their way of life threatened when the immigrant Chinese began asserting themselves and their own culture. To some, Western civilization itself seemed to be eroding before their very eyes.

The large number of Latinos and U.S.-born Asian Americans in Monterey Park also felt themselves threatened. Those who had settled there in the late 1950s and 1960s had bought into the American suburban dream, and it was not uncommon for them to confess animosity toward the new immigrants, to fear the loss of the social harmony within diversity that they cherished so much. They also spoke jealously of affluent Chinese immigrants who bought homes, businesses, and expensive cars almost as soon as they arrived. Older Latinos and Asian Americans in Monterey Park prided themselves on having painstakingly—over years or even generations—assimilated into the American mainstream and having "made it" to middle-class status. Not surprisingly, they deeply resented newcomers who seemed able to acquire material goods and status immediately. And even though by no means all the new immigrants were affluent and successful, for many residents the stereotype became the reality.

Negative reactions reached a peak with the emergence of the

official-English movement. Again, Monterey Park was not an isolated example. During the mid-1980s media pundits proclaimed the push to make English the official language the fastest-growing grassroots movement in the country; thirty-seven states had passed or were considering such language legislation. This movement, together with a dramatic upswing of intolerance and violence against foreigners, was symptomatic of the mood of cultural conservativism and insecurity then sweeping the country.

Complex Controversies

Legitimate development and land-use policy issues in Monterey Park became derailed when nativist elements used the rhetoric of slow growth to propel their own anti-Chinese, anti-immigrant agenda. At the same time, powerful developer interests played their own "race card" and positioned themselves as crusaders against "racism" in order to discredit their opponents. Besides these inter-ethnic and class conflicts, recent events show strong intra-ethnic conflict between American-born and the foreign-born Chinese.

The Coalition for Harmony in Monterey Park (CHAMP) originally emerged to confront growing anti-Chinese sentiment in the community, specifically after the official-English movement began to gather steam. But this group of progressive Asian, white, and Latino activists, along with developer interests involved for their own reasons, was a loose union that soon broke apart along class lines. The result was the creation of A Better Cityhood (ABC), which gathered enough signatures to force a racially charged recall election against two standing council members. Because ABC's call for unity against racism was seen by many as merely a smoke screen for developers and speculators, voters rejected the recall attempt by a two-to-one margin.

Again, growth, development, land-use policy, and overcrowding are not issues unique to Monterey Park. When they are associated with Asian developers and with Chinese characters on business signs, however, these "quality of life" issues seem to take on a much higher profile, and the rhetoric becomes harsher. Asked whether things would be different if only white developers wanted to build in Monterey Park, one resident said, "People would still be against too much growth, but they wouldn't know who to blame."[2]

A New Era of Transition

In 1960 the population in Monterey Park was 85 percent white, 12 percent Hispanic, and only 3 percent Asian American. By the year 2000 the population could easily be 80 percent Asian (mostly immigrant and American-born Chinese) and only 3 percent white. In other words, by the end of the century, Chinese immigrants will likely have completed their shift from marginal to mainstream population in the city.

An obvious sign of this transition came on February 8, 1992, when Monterey Park and neighboring Alhambra jointly sponsored the first Chinese New Year parade ever held in the area. An estimated 35,000 spectators showed up to celebrate the Year of the Monkey—smaller than the number who attended the parade in Los Angeles' Chinatown but far larger than the number who attend the annual "Play Days" parade marking Monterey Park's birthday. Over $60,000 in donations from private businesses throughout the San Gabriel Valley was raised for the festive event, including an $18,000 contribution from the long-distance telephone company AT&T.[3] The celebration was also shown live over a privately owned cable television station with commentary in Mandarin.

Though race and ethnicity issues have clearly been used as political organizing tools and weapons, what sets Monterey Park apart are the new class dynamics and the diversity of the Chinese living there, within a rapidly shifting global economy. In short, the changes in race and ethnic relations in Monterey Park can be explained in terms of shifts in the primary sector of the broader economy. The city demonstrates on a community level that race relations have entered an era of transition. More broadly, this transition can be seen in the fluidity of power relations between and among races and classes. Old theoretical dichotomies of black versus white, minority versus majority, do not adequately address the rising inter- and intra-ethnic differences brought about in part by the infusion of highly affluent Asians from Pacific Rim localities since 1965.

Globalization of the economy and long-term U.S. partnership with Asian people and nations are facts that will not go away. The worst-case scenario would be the triumph of economic and social nativism. The challenge in this era of transition is to develop responsible public policy through a better understanding of the international, multiracial, multicultural, and dynamic class reality exemplified by Monterey Park.

NOTES

Introduction

1. U.S. Bureau of the Census, "Monterey Park, City, California," 1990 Census of Population and Housing Summary Tape File 1, May 13, 1991.
2. Kurt Anderson, "The New Ellis Island: Immigrants from All Over Change the Beat, Bop, and Character of Los Angeles," *Time*, June 13, 1983, p. 21.
3. Several newspapers have incorrectly cited this honor as the "All-American" award. According to the official entry form, the term is "All-America."
4. Mike Ward, "Language Rift in 'All-American City,'" *Los Angeles Times*, November 13, 1985; Gordon Dillow, "Why Many Drivers Tremble on the Streets of Monterey Park," *Los Angeles Herald*, July 8, 1985, "English Spoken Here, OK?" *Time*, August 25, 1985.
5. Monterey Park City Council *Minutes*, June 2, 1986.
6. Mike Ward, "Racism Charged over Monterey Park Vote," *Los Angeles Times*, July 15, 1986; Ray Babcock, "'Sanctuary' Resolution Stays," *Monterey Park Progress*, July 16, 1986; Evelyn Hsu, "Influx of Asians Stirs Up L.A. Area's 'Little Taipei,'" *San Francisco Chronicle*, August 1, 1986.
7. See José Calderon, "Latinos and Ethnic Conflict in Suburbia: The Case of Monterey Park," *Latino Studies Journal* 1 (May 1990): 23–32; John Horton, "The Politics of Ethnic Change: Grass-Roots Response to Economic and Demographic Restructuring in Monterey Park, California," *Urban Geography* 10 (1989): 578–92; Don Nakanishi, "The Next Swing Vote? Asian Pacific Americans and California Politics," in *Racial and Ethnic Politics in California*, ed. Bryan O. Jackson and Michael D. Preston (Berkeley: University of California, Institute of Governmental Studies, 1991), pp. 25–54; Mary Pardo, "Identity and Resistance: Latinas and Grass-Roots Activism in Two Los Angeles Communities" (Ph.D. diss., University of California, Los Angeles, 1990); Leland Saito, "Politics in a New Demographic Era: Asian Americans in Monterey Park, California" (Ph.D. diss., University of California, Los Angeles, 1992); Charles Choy Wong, "Monterey Park: A Community in Transition" in *Frontiers of Asian American Studies*, ed. Gail M. Nomura, Russell Endo, Stephen H. Sumida, and Russell Leong (Pullman: Washington State University Press, 1989), pp. 113–26; Charles Choy Wong, "Ethnicity, Work, and Community: The Case of Chinese in Los Angeles" (Ph.D. diss., University of California, Los Angeles, 1979).

8. U.S. Commission on Civil Rights, *The Economic Status of Americans of Asian Descent: An Exploratory Investigation*, Publication no. 95 (Washington, D.C.: Clearinghouse, 1988), p. 109.

9. See Marshall Kilduff, "A Move to Ease Racial Tensions in S.F. Neighborhood," *San Francisco Chronicle*, August 11, 1986; Tim Fong, "The Success Stereotype Haunts Asian-Americans," *Sacramento Bee*, July 4, 1987; David Reyes, "'Asiantown' Plan Taking Shape in Westminster," *Los Angeles Times*, March 22, 1987; "Chinese Enclaves Abound in New York," *Asian Week*, October 3, 1986; Kevin P. Helliker, "Chinatown Sprouts in and near Houston with Texas Flavor," *Wall Street Journal*, February 18, 1983; "$50 Million 'Orlando Chinatown' Features Hotel-Retail Complex and 30 Restaurants," *AmeriAsian News*, March–April 1987; Russell Spurr, "Why Asians Are Going Down Under," *San Francisco Chronicle*, December 7, 1988; Howard Witt, "British Columbia's Anti-Asian Feelings Suddenly Surface," *Chicago Tribune*, February 5, 1989.

10. U.S. Immigration and Naturalization Service, *1989 Statistical Yearbook of the Immigration and Naturalization Service* (Washington, D.C.: Government Printing Office, 1990), p. xiv.

11. In June 1982 Vincent Chin, a Chinese American draftsman, was beaten to death by a Chrysler Motors supervisor and his stepson. One of the assailants was alleged to have yelled, "It's because of you motherfuckers we're out of work." The two men later confessed to the crime, were fined $3,780 each, and placed on three years' probation. Neither spent a day in jail. See Ronald Takaki, *Strangers from a Different Shore* (Boston: Little, Brown, 1989), p. 481.

12. U.S. Commission on Civil Rights, *Recent Activities against Citizens and Residents of Asian Descent* Publication no. 88 (Washington, D.C.: Clearinghouse, 1986), p. 3.

13. Mary Roberts Coolidge, *Chinese Immigration* (New York: Henry Holt, 1909); Alexander Saxton, *The Indispensable Enemy: Labor and the Anti-Chinese Movement in California* (Berkeley: University of California Press, 1971).

14. Stuart Creighton Miller, *The Unwelcome Immigrant: The American Image of the Chinese, 1785–1882* (Berkeley: University of California Press, 1969); Robert McClellen, *The Heathen Chinee: A Study of American Attitudes toward China, 1890–1905* (Columbus: Ohio State University Press, 1971).

15. Gunther Barth, *Bitter Strength: A History of the Chinese in the United States, 1850–1870* (Cambridge, Mass.: Harvard University Press, 1964).

16. E.g., Rose Hum Lee, *The Chinese in the United States of America* (Hong Kong: Hong Kong University Press, 1960); S. W. Kung, *Chinese in American Life: Some Aspects of Their History, Status, Problems, and Contributions* (Seattle: University of Washington Press, 1962); Betty Lee Sung, *Mountain of Gold: The Story of the Chinese in America* (New York: Macmillan, 1967); Francis L. K. Hsu, *The Challenge of the*

American Dream: The Chinese in the United States (Belmont, Calif.:
Wadsworth, 1971); Stanford M. Lyman, *Chinese Americans* (New York:
Random House, 1974); Jack Chen, *The Chinese of America* (San
Francisco: Harper & Row, 1980).

17. Paul C. P. Siu, *The Chinese Laundryman: A Study of Social Isolation*
(1953), ed. John Kuo Wei Tchen (New York: New York University
Press, 1987); James W. Loewen, *The Mississippi Chinese: Between Black
and White* (Cambridge, Mass.: Harvard University Press, 1971).

18. Rose Hum Lee, *The Growth and Decline of Chinese Communities in the
Rocky Mountain Region* (1947; New York: Arno Press and the New
York Times, 1979); Sandy Lydon, *Chinese Gold: The Chinese in the
Monterey Bay Region* (Capitola, Calif.: Capitola, 1985); Sucheng Chan,
This Bittersweet Soil: The Chinese in California Agriculture, 1860–1910
(Berkeley: University of California Press, 1986); and Sylvia Sun
Minnick, *Samfow: The San Joaquin Chinese Legacy* (Fresno, Calif.:
Panorama West, 1988).

19. Victor G. Nee and Brett de Bary Nee, *Longtime Californ': A
Documentary Study of an American Chinatown* (New York: Pantheon,
1972); Chia-ling Kuo, *Social and Political Change in New York's
Chinatown: The Role of Voluntary Associations* (New York: Praeger,
1977); Bernard Wong, *Patronage, Brokerage, Entrepreneurship, and the
Chinese Community of New York* (New York: AMS Press, 1988).

20. Peter Kwong, *Chinatown, New York: Labor and Politics, 1930–1950*
(New York: Monthly Review Press, 1979); Peter Kwong, *The New
Chinatown* (New York: Hill & Wang, 1987).

21. Chalsa M. Loo, *Chinatown: Most Time, Hard Time* (New York:
Praeger, 1992).

22. Min Zhou, *Chinatown: The Socioeconomic Potential of an Urban Enclave*
(Philadelphia: Temple University Press, 1992).

23. Gwen Kinkead, *Chinatown: A Portrait of a Closed Society* (New York:
Harper Collins, 1992).

24. Hsiang-shui Chen, *Chinatown No More* (Ithaca, N.Y.: Cornell
University Press, 1992), p. 263.

25. See Michael Agar, *The Professional Stranger: An Informal Introduction to
Ethnography* (New York: Academic Press 1980); James P. Spradley,
Participant Observation (New York: Holt, Rinehart & Winston, 1980);
James P. Spradley, *The Ethnographic Interview* (New York: Holt,
Rinehart & Winston, 1979).

26. Michael Agar, *Ripping and Running: A Formal Ethnography of Urban
Heroin Addicts* (New York: Seminar Press, 1973); James P. Spradley
and Brenda J. Mann, *The Cocktail Waitress: Women's Work in a Male
World* (New York: Wiley, 1975); Elliot Liebow, *Tally's Corner* (Boston:
Little, Brown, 1967); Nee and Nee, *Longtime Californ'*.

27. See Cullom Davis, Kathryn Back, Kay McLean, *Oral History: From
Tape to Type* (Chicago: American Library Association, 1977);
Ronald Grele, *Envelopes of Sound: The Art of Oral History* (Chicago:
Precedent, 1984); David Henige, *Oral Historiography* (New York:

Longman, 1982); Trevor Lummis, *Listening to History: Authenticity of Oral Evidence* (Totowa, N.J.: Barnes & Noble, 1987); Paul Thompson, *The Voices of the Past* (New York: Oxford University Press, 1988); Jan Vansina, *Oral Tradition as History* (Madison: University of Wisconsin Press, 1985).

28. Berkeley Hudson, "Monterey Park, Star 'Melting Pot,' Getting Fed Up with Publicity," *Los Angeles Times*, April 2, 1989; Berkeley Hudson, "Monterey Park's Mix Lures Researchers," *Los Angeles Times*, October 23, 1988.

29. Berkeley Hudson, "Bare Feet and Buttercups in Monterey Park," *Los Angeles Times*, August 6, 1989.

30. C. Wright Mills, *The Sociological Imagination* (New York: Oxford University Press, 1959), p. 6.

31. Ibid., pp. 218–19.

Chapter 1

1. P. C. Kelly, "Lugo Family Is Closely Linked with Early History of State, Ruled Over Vast Territory," *Monterey Park Progress*, May 6, 1927.

2. On early pioneers, see Richard Dyer's unpublished manuscript "The Growth and Development of Monterey Park, California, between 1916 and 1930" (California State College, Los Angeles, 1961).

3. For more details on Richard Garvey, see H. Russell Paine, ed., *The History of the City of Monterey Park* (Monterey Park: Monterey Park Progress, 1976), pp. 6–7.

4. Erwin G. Gudde, *California Place Names* (Berkeley: University of California Press, 1969), p. 209.

5. "Ramona Acres: Where Located," *Ramona Acres Progress*, August 8, 1919.

6. Paine, *Monterey Park*, p. 8.

7. Monterey Park City Council *Minutes*, June 2, 1916.

8. Monterey Park City Council *Ordinances*, no. 5, July 8, 1916.

9. "Janss Investment Company Gives History of How They Started and Developed Fine Sections of Ramona Acres," *Ramona Acres Progress*, August 8, 1919.

10. Interview with Kenny Gribble by H. Russell Paine, for the Monterey Park Oral History Project sponsored by the Monterey Park Historical Heritage Commission, March–June 1985.

11. Paine, *Monterey Park*, p. 9.

12. Interview with Kenny Gribble.

13. Loftus Land Company advertisement, *Monterey Park Progress*, June 16, 1922; "Local People Buy in Garvey Tract," *Monterey Park Progress*, June 30, 1922.

14. Loftus Land Company advertisement in *Monterey Park Progress*, May 30, 1923.

15. "Big Jump Shown in 6 Months," *Monterey Park Progress*, June 27, 1924.

16. H. Sands, "The Wonderful Growth of Monterey Park," *Monterey Park Progress*, February 22, 1924.

17. "Color Question Agitates the C. of C.," *Monterey Park Progress*, May 2, 1924.

18. "Remarkable Growth of Monterey Park Told by Los Angeles Times," *Monterey Park Progress*, July 18, 1924.

19. "Klan Ceremony Is Seen by 25,000 Spectators," *Monterey Park Progress*, August 22, 1924.

20. Paine, *Monterey Park*, p. 9.

21. "Fundamental Features of Midwick View Estates Are Outlined," *Monterey Park Progress*, June 15, 1928.

22. Quoted in "Monterey Park's Population to Be 20,000 in 1930, Prediction," *Monterey Park Progress*, June 8, 1928.

23. Office of the City Manager, "Monterey Park, California, Community Profile," August 1978, p. 5.

24. Interview with Howard Fry by Tim Fong, for the Monterey Park Oral History Project, sponsored by the Monterey Park Historical Heritage Commission, September 14, 21, and 28, 1990.

25. Interview with Eli Isenberg by Tim Fong, for the Monterey Park Oral History Project, sponsored by the Monterey Park Historical Heritage Commission, October 16, 25, and 30 and November 8, 1990.

26. Monterey Park Community Development Department, *Population and Housing Profile*, September 1987, p. 2.

27. Interview with Alice Ballesteros by Tim Fong, for the Monterey Park Oral History Project, sponsored by the Monterey Park Historical Heritage Commission, August 28 and September 19, 1990.

28. Interview with Eli Isenberg.

29. Interview with Kei Higashi by Tim Fong, for the Monterey Park Oral History Project, sponsored by the Monterey Park Historical Heritage Commission, May 7 and 30, 1990.

30. Quoted in "Discrimination Charge Levelled at Highlands," *Monterey Park Progress*, February 22, 1962.

31. "CORE 'Sitins' Continue Highlands Demonstration," *Monterey Park Progress*, March 8, 1962.

32. Interview with Howard Fry.

33. Quoted in Evelyn Knudson, "Life Back to Normal as Lileys Buy Home," *Monterey Park Progress*, April 12, 1962.

34. "'I Will Sell Liley a Home,' Says Snyder," *Monterey Park Progress*, April 5, 1962.

35. "CORE Sit-in Ends as Snyder Sells New Home," *Monterey Park Progress*, April 5, 1962.

36. Knudson, "Life Back to Normal."

37. Eli Isenberg, "Notes and Comments," *Monterey Park Progress*, April 12, 1962.

38. Interview with Howard Jong by Tim Fong, for the Monterey Park Oral History Project, sponsored by the Monterey Park Historical Heritage Commission, June 25, 1990.

39. Ibid.

40. Ibid.

41. Ibid.

42. Monterey Park Community Development Department, *Population and Housing Profile*, August 1978, p. 2.

43. Ibid.

44. Stanford M. Lyman, *Chinese Americans* (New York: Random House, 1974), pp. 66–85, 111.

45. "Chiang's Last Redoubt: Future Uncertain," in *Time*, November 8, 1971, pp. 32–33.

46. Quoted in Art Wong, "Nixon 'Ping-Pong' Ball Lands in Monterey Park," *Monterey Park Progress*, Sept. 28, 1977.

47. This story, commonly repeated in Monterey Park, has been reported several times. See, e.g., Art Wong, "MP Ethnic Brew Gains Sweet and Sour Flavor," *Monterey Park Progress*, September 21, 1977; Andrew Tanzer, "Little Taipei," *Forbes*, May 6, 1985, p. 71; and Mark Arax, "Nation's 1st Suburban Chinatown," *Los Angeles Times*, April 6, 1987.

48. Wong, "MP Ethnic Brew."

49. Interview with Frederic Hsieh by Tim Fong, for the Monterey Park Oral History Project, sponsored by the Monterey Park Historical Heritage Commission, April 25, 1990.

50. Ibid.

51. Ibid.

52. 1990 U.S. Census. For more detailed tables, see Edmund Newton, "Anglo Enclave Becomes an Ethnic Patchwork," *Los Angeles Times*, March 3, 1991.

53. Edmund Newton, "Anglo Enclave."

54. Interview with Chiling Tong by Tim Fong, for the Monterey Park Oral History Project, sponsored by the Monterey Park Historical Heritage Commission, September 11 and 17, October 1, 1990.

55. Ibid.

56. Ashley Dunn, "East Meets West," *Los Angeles Times*, May 27, 1989.

57. Interview with Chiling Tong.

58. Quoted in Dunn, "East Meets West."

Chapter 2

1. Monterey Park Community Development Department, *Population and Housing Profile*, November 1984, p. 8; 1990 figure from 1990 U.S. Census.

2. Monterey Park Community Development Department, *Population and Housing Profile*, 1973, p. 8.

3. Monterey Park Community Development Department, *Housing Element*, March 1984, p. 7.

4. Charles Choy Wong, "Ethnicity, Work, and Community: The Case of Chinese in Los Angeles" (Ph.D. diss., University of California, Los Angeles, 1979), p. 263.

5. Monterey Park Community Development Department, *Population and Housing Profile*, 1974, p. 17, cited in Wong, "Ethnicity, Work, and Community," p. 290; Monterey Park Community Development Department, *Population and Housing Profile*, November 1984, Table J, App. A.

6. Interview with Howard Fry by Tim Fong, for the Monterey Park Oral History Project, sponsored by the Monterey Park Historical Heritage Commission, September 14, 21, and 28, 1990.

7. Wilsey and Han Company, *Planning Report for City of Monterey Park: 1985 General Plan* (Monterey Park: City of Monterey Park, 1967), p. 4, cited in Wong, "Ethnicity, Work, and Community," p. 262.

8. Monterey Park Community Development Department, *Population and Housing Profile*, September 1987, p. 6; U.S. Bureau of the Census, "Monterey Park, City, California," 1990 Census of Population and Housing Summary Tape File 1, Table 1, May 13, 1991.

9. Art Wong, "Building Boom's Outta Sight," *Monterey Park Progress*, January 18, 1978.

10. Monterey Park Community Development Department, *Population and Housing Profile*, November 1984, p. 8.

11. Interview with Lloyd de Llamas by Tim Fong, for the Monterey Park Oral History Project, sponsored by the Monterey Park Historical Heritage Commission, March 29, April 13, and May 11, 1990.

12. Interview with Cuong Huynh by Tim Fong, for the Monterey Park Oral History Project, sponsored by the Monterey Park Historical Heritage Commission, January 28, 1991.

13. Quoted in Malcolm Schwartz, "Council Rejects Moratorium," *Monterey Park Progress*, July 12, 1978.

14. Ibid.; Monterey Park City Council *Minutes*, July 10, 1979.

15. Schwartz, "Council Rejects"; Malcolm Schwartz, "Moratorium Rationale Offered by Terashita," *Monterey Park Progress*, July 12, 1979.

16. Hal Fiebelkorn, "Kaffee Klatch," *Monterey Park Progress*, July 19, 1979.

17. Joseph R. Blackstock, "Laura Scudder: Southern California's Potato Chip Pioneer" *The Californians* 7, no. 5 (1990): 34, 39.

18. Teresa M. Burrell, "Down Memory Lane with Mrs. Teresa Burrell Reminiscing of Days Gone By," *Monterey Park Progress*, March 27, 1947.

19. Interview with Ed Rodman by Tim Fong, for the Monterey Park Oral History Project, sponsored by the Monterey Park Historical Heritage Commission, October 17 and 24, 1990.

20. Shav Glick, "There Is No Rust on This Iron Man," *Los Angeles Times*, March 7, 1991.

21. Interview with Louis Tripodes by Tim Fong, for the Monterey Park

Oral History Project, sponsored by the Monterey Park Historical Heritage Commission, April 2, 1990.

22. Berkeley Hudson, "Store of Homey Wisdom Is Lost," *Los Angeles Times*, February 11, 1990.

23. Interview with Ed Rodman.

24. Wilsey and Han Company, *The 1985 General Plan* (Monterey Park: City of Monterey Park, 1966), pp. 5-1, 5-2, 2-78. The consultants' retail sales figures estimated that 55 percent of household income was spent on consumer goods. The estimation assumes that (1) retail sales in the state were underreported, and (2) Monterey Park had larger families and a larger middle-income group than the southern California average.

25. Ibid., pp. 2-78 to 2-82.

26. Interview with Ed Rodman.

27. Interview with Lloyd de Llamas.

28. Interview with Frederic Hsieh by Tim Fong, for the Monterey Park Oral History Project, sponsored by the Monterey Park Historical Heritage Commission, April 25, 1990.

29. Ibid.

30. Ibid.

31. Quoted in Mark Arax, "Nation's 1st Suburban Chinatown," *Los Angeles Times*, April 6, 1987.

32. Quoted in Andrew Tanzer, "Little Taipei," *Forbes*, May 6, 1985, p. 69.

33. Ibid.

34. Monterey Park Management Services Department, *Comprehensive Annual Financial Report*, June 30, 1990, p. 77.

35. Wilsey and Han Company, *Economic Development Strategy Element of the General Plan* (Monterey Park: City of Monterey Park, 1980), pp. 8–9.

36. Quoted in Art Wong, "Merchants Reject Chinatown Theme," *Monterey Park Progress*, January 11, 1978.

37. Tanzer, "Little Taipei," p. 71.

38. Quoted in Mike Ward, "Cities Report Growth—and Some Losses—from Asian Business," *Los Angeles Times*, April 19, 1987.

39. Quoted in Joel Kotkin, "The Lessons of Monterey Park," *Inc.*, July 1987, p. 52.

40. Interview with John Weidner by Tim Fong, for the Monterey Park Oral History Project, sponsored by the Monterey Park Historical Heritage Commission, June 16, 1991. For Weidner's activities during World War II, see Herbert Ford, *Flee the Captor* (Nashville, Tenn.: Southern Publishing Association, 1966).

41. Monterey Park Community Development Department, *Taxable Sales in California* (State Board of Equalization), 1980, 1985.

42. Quoted in Ward, "Cities Report Growth."

43. Interview with Lloyd de Llamas.

44. Ibid.

45. Peter Kwong, in *The New Chinatown* (New York: Hill & Wang, 1987),

shows that the effect of a spiraling economic situation on New York's Chinatown was almost identical to what happened in Monterey Park. The only difference is the scale: land speculation in the New York case was so fierce in the late 1970s and early 1980s that by 1987 property rents had risen to $275 a square foot. Only posh Fifth Avenue above 51st Street (at $400 a square foot) could command higher rents in Manhattan. See Albert Scardino, "Commercial Rents in Chinatown Soar as Hong Kong Exodus Grows," *New York Times*, December 25, 1987.

Chapter 3

1. Sheila Carter, "White Cane Days Begin Friday," *Monterey Park Progress*, October 2, 1985.
2. Interview with Joseph Graves by Tim Fong, for the Monterey Park Oral History Project, sponsored by the Monterey Park Historical Heritage Commission, September 12 and 19, October 4, 1990.
3. Interview with Eli Isenberg by Tim Fong, for the Monterey Park Oral History Project, sponsored by the Monterey Park Historical Heritage Commission, October 16, 25, 30, and November 8, 1990.
4. Interview with Norman Lieberman by Tim Fong, for the Monterey Park Oral History Project, sponsored by the Monterey Park Historical Heritage Commission, June 11, 18, and 25, 1990.
5. Eli Isenberg, "A Call for Open Arms," *Monterey Park Progress*, December 7, 1977.
6. Interview with Eli Isenberg.
7. Interview with Joseph Graves.
8. Ibid.
9. Eli Isenberg, "It Seems to Me," *Monterey Park Progress*, February 27, 1985.
10. Fieldnotes from November 20, 1990.
11. Art Wong, "Bilingual Plan Opens Up 'Bucket of Worms,'" *Monterey Park Progress*, June 7, 1978.
12. L. Ling-chi Wang, "Lau v. Nichols: History of a Struggle for Equal and Quality Education," *Amerasia Journal* 2 (1974): 16–46.
13. Wong, "Bilingual Plan."
14. See Andrew Tanzer, "Little Taipei," *Forbes*, May 6, 1985, pp. 68–71; Mike Ward, "Cities Report Growth—and Some Losses—from Asian Business," *Los Angeles Times*, April 19, 1987; and Randye Hoder, "A Passion for Asian Foods," *Los Angeles Times*, June 5, 1991.
15. Malcolm Schwartz, "Monterey Park Is Due for Big Facelift in 1979," *Monterey Park Progress*, January 3, 1979.
16. Interview with Lloyd de Llamas by Tim Fong, for the Monterey Park Oral History Project, sponsored by the Monterey Park Historical Heritage Commission, March 29, April 13, and May 11, 1990.
17. Interview with Ed Rodman by Tim Fong, for the Monterey Park

Oral History Project, sponsored by the Monterey Park Historical Heritage Commission, October 17 and 24, 1990.

18. Mark Arax, "Selling Out, Moving On," *Los Angeles Times*, April 12, 1987.
19. Interview with Joseph Graves.
20. Arax, "Selling Out, Moving On."
21. Interview with David Barron by Tim Fong, for the Monterey Park Oral History Project, sponsored by the Monterey Park Historical Heritage Commission, October 9, 1990.
22. Mark Arax, "Nation's 1st Suburban Chinatown," *Los Angeles Times*, April 6, 1987.
23. Fieldnotes from August 16, 1990.
24. Interview with John Yee by Tim Fong, for the Monterey Park Oral History Project, sponsored by the Monterey Park Historical Heritage Commission, May 31 and June 4, 1990.
25. Ibid.
26. Interview with Kei Higashi by Tim Fong, for the Monterey Park Oral History Project, sponsored by the Monterey Park Historical Heritage Commission, May 7 and 30, 1990.
27. "Second Housing Project for Seniors on Horizon," *Monterey Park Progress*, Sept. 13, 1978.
28. Interview with Dr. Frances Wu by Tim Fong, for the Monterey Park Oral History Project, sponsored by the Monterey Park Historical Heritage Commission, June 22 and July 6, 1990.
29. Mike Weinberg, "Sharp Rise in Crime Rate but Chief Advises Caution," *Monterey Park Progress*, July 16, 1980.
30. Ibid.
31. Mike Weinberg, "Police Reactivate Their Asian Detail," *Monterey Park Progress*, August 20, 1980.
32. Ibid.
33. Helen Wu, "Headline Offends," *Monterey Park Progress*, November 19, 1980.
34. "Now Is the Time to Speak Out," *Monterey Park Progress*, December 10, 980.
35. Interview with Loretta Huang by Tim Fong for the Monterey Park Oral History Project, sponsored by the Monterey Park Historical Heritage Commission, June 12 and July 11, 1990.
36. Sally Sterling, "Task Force Fights Bias," *Monterey Park Progress*, August 14, 1981.
37. Steve E. Yusi, "Why Can't They Drive?" *Monterey Park Progress*, July 29, 1981.
38. Ronnie Katz, "Why Are They Driving"; Norman Lieberman, "No Apology Offered"; Grace Seto, "An Angry Letter," *Monterey Park Progress*, August 12, 1981.
39. See, e.g., Gordon Dillow, "Why Many Drivers Tremble on Streets of Monterey Park," *Los Angeles Herald*, July 8, 1985.

Chapter 4

1. Interview with Alice Ballesteros by Tim Fong, for the Monterey Park Oral History Project, sponsored by the Monterey Park Historical Heritage Commission, August 28, and September 19, 1990.
2. Interview with Eli Isenberg by Tim Fong, for the Monterey Park Oral History Project, sponsored by the Monterey Park Historical Heritage Commission, October 16, 25, 30, and November 8, 1990.
3. Quoted in Eli Isenberg, "It Seems to Me," *Monterey Park Progress*, October 16, 1974.
4. "This One Takes Issue with Us," *Monterey Park Progress*, October 16, 1974.
5. Ibid.
6. Isenberg, "It Seems to Me," October 16, 1974.
7. "Anti-Unification Group Rebuts Editor's Stand, Forecasts 'Nightmare,'" *Monterey Park Progress*, October 23, 1974.
8. "Summary on Prop. G," *Monterey Park Progress*, November 13, 1974.
9. Quoted in Eli Isenberg, "Fear of Added Taxes and Campaign Errors Helped Doom Prop. G.," *Monterey Park Progress*, November 13, 1974.
10. "It Hurts to Smile," *Monterey Park Progress*, November 13, 1974.
11. Malcolm Schwartz, "It Was Her Decision to 'Pick Up the Challenge,'" *Monterey Park Progress*, February 18, 1976.
12. Eli Isenberg, "New Faces at MP City Hall," *Monterey Park Progress*, March 19, 1976.
13. Monterey Park Office of the City Clerk, record of General Election, March 9, 1976.
14. Interview with Louise Davis by Tim Fong, for the Monterey Park Oral History Project, sponsored by the Monterey Park Historical Heritage Commission, May 15 and 21, 1991.
15. "New Civic Center Can Meet Future Needs—de Llamas," *Monterey Park Progress*, January 25, 1978.
16. Malcolm Schwartz, "Couch Campaigns Hard against City Hall Plan," *Monterey Park Progress*, February 15, 1978.
17. Irv Gilman, "Councilmen C3PO and R2D2," *Monterey Park Progress*, March 8, 1978.
18. The March 7, 1978, election results were as follows: George Westphaln, 2,634; Matthew Martinez, 2,268; Harry Couch, 1,986; George Ige, 1,970; Bill Feliz, 1,659; Ernest Wong, 1,065 (Monterey Park Office of the City Clerk).
19. Malcolm Schwartz, "MP Council Opposes Prop. 13 on 4–1 Vote," *Monterey Park Progress*, April 19, 1978.
20. Monterey Park City Council *Minutes*, November 10, 1980.
21. Interview with Louise Davis.
22. Interview with Evelyn Diederich by Tim Fong for the Monterey Park Oral History Project, sponsored by the Monterey Park Historical Heritage Commission, July 11 and August 2, 1990.

23. Mike Weinberg, "Judge Upholds Condo Election," *Monterey Park Progress*, February 25, 1981.
24. Irv Gilman, "Hillside 'Garbage' " *Monterey Park Progress*, February 25, 1981.
25. Benjamin F. (Frank) Venti, " 'Mud-slinging' Charged," *Monterey Park Progress*, March 11, 1981.
26. Quoted in Mike Weinberg, "Mayor Davis Named in New CVJ Lawsuit," *Monterey Park Progress*, March 4, 1981.
27. Monterey Park Recipient Committee Campaign Statement (Government Code Sections 84200–84217), Monterey Park Citizens for Representative Government, March–June 1981.
28. Harold Fiebelkorn, "Why I'm for Prop. A," *Monterey Park Press* (a campaign publication of Monterey Park Citizens For Representative Government), April 1981.
29. George Ige, "Letters to the Editor," in *Monterey Park Press*, April 1981.
30. Mancha Kurilich, "Prop. A and Our Schools," in *Monterey Park Press*, April 1981.
31. Interview with Evelyn Diederich.
32. Monterey Park Citizens against Overcrowding and Sequoia Park Homeowners Association, "Do You Want More Condos in Monterey Park?" (a campaign flyer), April 1981.
33. Monterey Park Office of the City Clerk, record of Special Election, April 14, 1981.
34. Quoted in Mike Weinberg, "Prop. A Gets a Big, Fat NO!" *Monterey Park Progress*, April 15, 1981.
35. "Can We Heal the Wounds?" *Monterey Park Progress*, April 15, 1981.
36. Quoted in Mike Weinberg, "Candidate Calls for Building Halt," *Monterey Park Progress*, April 22, 1981.
37. Mike Weinberg, "Planners Cold to Building Ban," *Monterey Park Progress*, May 6, 1981.
38. E. D. Wright, "We Have Enough," *Monterey Park Progress*, April 15, 1981.
39. Sim Quan, "Look What's Happened!" *Monterey Park Progress*, May 20, 1981.
40. Monterey Park Office of the City Clerk, record of Special Election, June 2, 1981.
41. Monterey Park Recipient Committee Campaign Statement (Government Code Sections 84200–84217), Citizens to Elect Lily Chen, "Consolidated Campaign Statement Form 490," May–June 1981.
42. Monterey Park Office of the City Clerk, record of Special Election, June 2, 1981.
43. Quoted in Mike Weinberg, "Chief Paints a Dismal Picture," *Monterey Park Progress*, June 10, 1981.
44. Quoted in Mike Weinberg, "Council Empty Chair Filled," *Monterey Park Progress*, June 17, 1981.

45. Interview with Irv Gilman by Tim Fong, for the Monterey Park Oral History Project, sponsored by the Monterey Park Historical Heritage Commission, July 10 and 31, 1990.

46. Ibid.

47. Interview with Evelyn Diederich.

48. Sonya Gerlach and Pauline Lemire, "Make Way for R.A.M.P." *Monterey Park Progress*, July 15, 1981.

49. Mike Weinberg, "Anti-Growth Forces Stir Again," *Monterey Park Progress*, November 11, 1981.

50. Mike Weinberg, "Mayor Gives Chin the Nod," *Monterey Park Progress*, January 13, 1982.

51. Eli Isenberg, "It Seems to Me," *Monterey Park Progress*, January 20, 1982.

52. Hal Fiebelkorn, "Kaffee Klatch," *Monterey Park Progress*, January 27, 1982.

53. Eli Isenberg, "It Seems to Me," *Monterey Park Progress*, February 3, 1982.

54. Quoted in Mike Weinberg, "Will No Growth Foes Surface?" *Monterey Park Progress*, February 10, 1982.

55. Quoted in ibid.

56. Joseph Rubin, "Noxious and Divisive," *Monterey Park Progress*, February 24, 1982.

57. Quoted in Mike Weinberg, "Majority Opposes RAMP Initiatives," *Monterey Park Progress*, February 24, 1982.

58. Quoted in ibid.

59. Quoted in ibid.

60. Mike Weinberg, "The Future Could be a Gamble for MP," *Monterey Park Progress*, December 9, 1981; "Will Council Call or Raise?" *Monterey Park Progress*, December 16, 1981; Lily Chen, "The Wrong Signal," *Monterey Park Progress*, December 30, 1981; Mike Weinberg, "Poker Healt a Quick Shuffle," *Monterey Park Progress*, December 30, 1981.

61. Chen, "The Wrong Signal."

62. Mike Weinberg, "De Llamas: 'If You're Sick, Prove It,'" *Monterey Park Progress*, December 9, 1981.

63. Mike Weinberg, "Discord Rocks Police, Firemen," *Monterey Park Progress*, December 18, 1981.

64. Mike Weinberg, "'Signing-up' Controversy," *Monterey Park Progress*, February 17, 1982.

65. Quoted in Mike Weinberg, "Forum Takes On a New Slant," *Monterey Park Progress*, March 31, 1982.

66. Monterey Park Citizens against Crime, *Monterey Park Chronicle* (a campaign mailer), April 1982.

67. Monterey Park Recipient Committee Campaign Statement (Government Code Sections 84200–84217), Monterey Park Citizens against Crime, March–June, 1982.

68. Monterey Park Office of the City Clerk, record of General Election, April 13, 1982.
69. Quoted in Mike Weinberg, "Election Losers Cry 'Foul,'" *Monterey Park Progress*, April 21, 1982.
70. Quoted in ibid.
71. Mike Weinberg, "Election Outcome No Surprise to Police," *Monterey Park Progress*, April 21, 1982.
72. Weinberg, "Election Losers Cry Foul."
73. Eli Isenberg, "It Seems to Me," *Monterey Park Progress*, April 21, 1982.
74. Interview with Lloyd de Llamas by Tim Fong, for the Monterey Park Oral History Project, sponsored by the Monterey Park Historical Heritage Commission, March 29, April 13, and May 11, 1990.
75. Quoted in Mike Weinberg. "Bitter Words Greet New Council," *Monterey Park Progress*, April 28, 1982.
76. Ibid.

Chapter 5

1. "A Different City Council," *Monterey Park Progress*, May 26, 1982.
2. Ibid.; Malcolm Schwartz, "INS Raids Get Official Rebuff," *Monterey Park Progress*, May 19, 1982.
3. Eli Isenberg, "It Seems to Me," *Monterey Park Progress*, May 12, 1982.
4. Hal Fiebelkorn, "Kaffee Klatch," *Monterey Park Progress*, May 26, 1982.
5. Quoted in Mike Weinberg, "Quote Denied by de Llamas," *Monterey Park Progress*, June 2, 1982.
6. Ibid.
7. Monterey Park Citizens for Community Progress, *Monterey Park Times* (a campaign mailer), June 4, 1982.
8. Ibid.
9. Monterey Park Seniors for Safer Environment, "Vote Yes on 'K' and 'L,'" (a campaign mailer), May 1982 (the mailing address of this group was the home of RAMP member Evelyn Diederich).
10. Monterey Park Citizens for Responsible Growth, "Condos Choke the City" (a campaign mailer), May 1982 (the mailing address of this group was the home of RAMP member Joseph Rubin); Resident's Association of Monterey Park, "Stop the Condo Explosion" (a campaign leaflet), May 1982.
11. Interview with Joseph Rubin by Tim Fong, for the Monterey Park Oral History Project, sponsored by the Monterey Park Historical Heritage Commission, July 19, August 1 and 6, 1990.
12. Resident's Association of Monterey Park, "Who Paid for the Developers' 'Newspaper'—'The Times'" (a campaign flyer), June 1982.
13. Monterey Park Office of the City Clerk, record of Special Election, June 8, 1982.

14. Monterey Park City Council *Minutes,* June 30, 1982.
15. "High-Rise MP Hotel Finally Approved," *Monterey Park Progress,*
    July 1, 1982.
16. Mike Weinberg, "Gerlach Snub Sparks Furor," *Monterey Park Progress,*
    January 26, 1983.
17. "Protesters Hit Proposed Mall," *Monterey Park Progress,*
    January 26, 1983.
18. Weinberg, "Gerlach Snub."
19. "Out of Commission," *Monterey Park Progress,* February 2, 1983.
20. Chin's comments were printed verbatim in Harold (Hal) Fiebelkorn's
    "Kaffee Klatch" column, *Monterey Park Progress,* March 2, 1983.
21. Mike Weinberg, "MP Approves $20 Million Mall," *Monterey Park
    Progress,* March 30, 1983.
22. Ibid.
23. "Atlantic Retail Plan Okayed," *Monterey Park Progress,*
    September 28, 1983.
24. Interview with Lloyd de Llamas by Tim Fong, for the Monterey Park
    Oral History Project, sponsored by the Monterey Park Historical
    Heritage Commission, March 29, April 13, and May 11, 1990.
25. "Change For Better," *Monterey Park Progress,* November 9, 1983.
26. Kurt Anderson, "New Ellis Island: Immigrants from All Over
    Change the Beat, Bop, and Character of Los Angeles," *Time,*
    June 13, 1983, p. 21.
27. W.G., "Asian Complaint," *Monterey Park Progress,* November 23, 1983.
28. Interview with Lily Lee Chen for radio documentary on Monterey
    Park (broadcast 1987), October 25, 1986.
29. "Chen Seeking Crackdown on Asian Business Signs," *Monterey Park
    Progress,* February 16, 1983.
30. Mark Arax, "Lily Lee Chen," *Los Angeles Times,* November 11, 1985.
31. Interview with Norman Lieberman by Tim Fong, for the Monterey
    Park Oral History Project, sponsored by the Monterey Park
    Historical Heritage Commission, June 11, 18, and 25, 1990.
32. William Vogeler, "Campaign Winds Down, Election Tension Up,"
    Monterey Park Progress, March 28, 1984.
33. The April 10, 1984, election results were G. Monty Manibog, 2,928;
    Cam Briglio, 1,895; Wesley Ru, 1,324; Gregory Tse, 833; Alfred
    Valdez, 831; Susan Martinez-Vitro, 600; Richard Hart, 584;
    Genevive Dulany, 297; and Victoria Wu, 102. (Monterey Park Office
    of the City Clerk).
34. Eli Isenberg, "It Seems to Me," *Monterey Park Progress,* May 23, 1984.
35. Hal Fiebelkorn, "Kaffee Klatch," *Monterey Park Progress,*
    May 23, 1984.
36. See *Monterey Park Living* (a publication of the City of Monterey Park),
    June–August 1984.
37. Monterey Park Office of the City Clerk, record of Special Election,
    June 5, 1984.

38. Interview with Evelyn Diederich by Tim Fong, for the Monterey Park Oral History Project, sponsored by the Monterey Park Historical Heritage Commission, July 11 and August 2, 1990.

39. Interview with Lloyd de Llamas.

40. Evelyn Diederich, "Wake Up Call"; James Ashley, "Yellow Journalism"; and Irv Gilman, "A Divided City," *Monterey Park Progress*, June 20, 1984.

41. Interview with Lily Lee Chen.

42. Interview with David Almada by Tim Fong for radio documentary on Monterey Park (broadcast 1987), October 23, 1986.

43. Interview with Lloyd de Llamas.

44. Ibid.

45. Interview with Norman Lieberman.

46. Frank Arcuri, "English on Signs," *Monterey Park Progress*, May 29, 1985.

47. "Sign Law Gets Planners' Nod," *Monterey Park Progress*, June 26, 1985.

48. Jon Morris, "Council Passes Sign Law," *News Digest*, July 25, 1985.

49. Quoted in Ray Babcock, "Sign Law Concerns," *Monterey Park Progress*, July 24, 1985.

50. Ibid.

51. See "Legal Notices," *Monterey Park Progress*, August 21, 1985, p. A-8.

52. Quoted in Ray Babcock, "English Use Petition Planned," *Monterey Park Progress*, August 21, 1985.

53. Bill Marticorena, "It Takes Guts," *Monterey Park Progress*, October 2, 1985.

54. Quoted in Mike Ward, "Arcuri Sees Self as 'Rocky' of Politics," *Los Angeles Times*, January 9, 1986.

55. Interview with Frank Arcuri by Tim Fong for radio documentary on Monterey Park (broadcast 1987), October 27, 1986.

56. Quoted in Ward, "Arcuri."

57. Berkeley Hudson, "The World According to Hatch," *Los Angeles Times*, October 9, 1988.

58. Quoted in Patrick Anderson, "Monterey Park's Hatch Lashes Back At Critics," *Asian Week*, September 16, 1988.

59. Ray Babcock, "People Attack Law on English," *Monterey Park Progress*, August 28, 1985.

60. Ray Babcock, "English Issue May Go to Voters," *Monterey Park Progress*, October 23, 1985.

61. Ibid.

62. Quoted in Ray Babcock, "English Debate Carried to City," *Monterey Park Progress*, November 6, 1985.

63. "English Measure Declared Invalid by M.P. Attorney," *News Digest*, November 21, 1985; Mike Ward, "English-Only Initiative Plan Held Invalid," *Los Angeles Times*, November 13, 1985.

64. Mike Ward, "English Issue Backers Amend Ballot Petition," *Los Angeles Times*, November 24, 1985.

65. Quoted in Mark Arax, "Stronger Rules on English in Signs Pushed by Council," *Los Angeles Times*, December 5, 1985.
66. Quoted in Mark Arax, "Further Split Feared over Suit to Force English Vote," *Los Angeles Times*, December 8, 1985.
67. Mark Arax, "Judge Upholds Foes of 'Official English' Vote," *Los Angeles Times*, December 25, 1985.

Chapter 6

1. "State Election Results," *Los Angeles Times*, November 8, 1984.
2. Miles Corwin, "It's Official: In Fillmore, You Have to Habla Ingles," *Los Angeles Times*, May 6, 1985.
3. Quoted in Robert Lindsey, "Debates Growing on Use of English," *New York Times*, July 21, 1986.
4. Interview with Frank Arcuri by Tim Fong for radio documentary on Monterey Park (broadcast 1987), October 27, 1986.
5. Interview with Chris Houseman by Tim Fong for radio documentary on Monterey Park (broadcast 1987), October 24, 1986.
6. Ibid.
7. Interview with Patricia Reichenberger by Tim Fong for radio documentary on Monterey Park (broadcast 1987), November 7, 1986.
8. Ibid.
9. Citizens for Responsible Growth. *Record* (a campaign mailer), April 1986.
10. Ibid.
11. Flyer paid for by Committee to Re-elect David Almada, March 1986.
12. Trini Estrada, "Exploiting Race," *Monterey Park Progress*, April 2, 1986.
13. Recipient Committee Campaign Statement (Government Code Sections 84200–84217), Friends of Lily Chen, March–May 1986.
14. Friends of Lily Chen (campaign mailer), April 1986.
15. Monterey Park Office of the City Clerk, record of General Election, April 8, 1986.
16. Monterey Park Office of the City Clerk. Candidate campaign statements cover period from March through May, 1986. Hatch, the second-place finisher, spent only $2,611, though he had contributions of $4,259. Third-place Reichenberger spent only $2,461 from contributions of $2,964. Arcuri spent his total donations of $3,837—including $1,500 from Manny Ramos, whose popular El Loco restaurant had been forced to relocate because of a redevelopment project. Recipient Committee Campaign Statement (Government Code Sections 84200–84217), Frank Arcuri, March–May 1986; and David Gero, "Landmark El Loco Serves Monterey Park Its Last Taco," *Monterey Park Independent*, March 12, 1986.
17. Interview with Lily Lee Chen by Tim Fong for radio documentary on Monterey Park (broadcast 1987), October 25, 1986.

18. Interview with David Almada by Tim Fong for radio documentary on Monterey Park (broadcast 1987), October 23, 1986.
19. Mike Ward, "Councilman Shelves Official-English Push," *Los Angeles Times*, May 1, 1986.
20. Mike Ward, "Monterey Park's New Council Calls Halt to Building," *Los Angeles Times*, May 1, 1986.
21. "Senior Housing Project Denied," *Monterey Park Progress*, May 7, 1986.
22. Monterey Park Office of the City Clerk, Resolution 9004, June 2, 1986.
23. "Mouth That Roared," *Monterey Park Progress*, January 16, 1985; "Official English Crops Up Again," *Monterey Park Progress*, June 4, 1986.
24. Interview with Patricia Reichenberger.
25. Interview with Chris Houseman.
26. George Rustic, "Seven Out of 10," *Monterey Park Progress*, June 18, 1986.
27. Maxine Vogeler, "Hatch Supporter," *Monterey Park Progress*, June 25, 1986.
28. Marjorie Kemmerer, "Right to Disagree," *Monterey Park Progress*, August 9, 1986.
29. George Rustic, "Anglo Exodus" in "Letters," *Monterey Park Progress*, July 16, 1986.
30. Mike Ward, "Racism Charged over Monterey Park Vote," *Los Angeles Times*, July 15, 1986; Ray Babcock, "'Sanctuary' Resolution Stays," *Monterey Park Progress*, July 16, 1986; Evelyn Hsu, "Influx of Asians Stirs Up L.A. Area's 'Little Taipei,'" *San Francisco Chronicle*, August 1, 1986.
31. Interview with Patricia Reichenberger.
32. Monterey Park City Council *Minutes*, July 28, 1986; Mike Ward, "3 Councilmen Hit by Ouster Effort in Monterey Park," *Los Angeles Times*, July 31, 1986; Ray Babcock, "Q & A: Smith on Recall Petition," *Monterey Park Progress*, August 20, 1986.
33. "Lawsuit Hits Project Decision," *Monterey Park Progress*, August 27, 1986; Mike Ward, "Facing Suit, Council Denies Bias on Housing," *Los Angeles Times*, August 28, 1986.
34. Ward, "3 Councilmen," July 31, 1986.
35. Fieldnotes from October 10, 1986.
36. Lily Eng, "Monterey Park Struggles to Speak with One Voice on English Issue," *Los Angeles Times*, October 30, 1986.
37. "Briglio Shootout," *Monterey Park Progress*, August 20, 1986; Jeff Gottlieb, "Temperatures Are Rising in Monterey Park's Melting Pot," *Los Angeles Herald-Examiner*, June 24, 1987.
38. Monterey Park City Council meeting, October 27, 1986 (audio tape).
39. Mike Ward, "Bolstered by Prop. 63 Vote, Foe of Non-English Signs Renews Attacks," *Los Angeles Times*, November 9, 1986.
40. Monterey Park City Council *Minutes*, November 23, 1986.

41. Mike Ward, "Foreign Flag Ban Set for Passage," *Los Angeles Times*, November 26, 1986.

42. Mike Ward, "Charges Fly in Attempt to Remove 3 Councilmen," *Los Angeles Times*, January 29, 1987.

43. Interview with Joseph Rubin by Tim Fong, for the Monterey Park Oral History Project, sponsored by the Monterey Park Historical Heritage Commission, July 19, August 1 and 6, 1990.

44. Ibid.

45. Jesse Katz, "Monterey Park Fires Its Entire Planning Board," *Los Angeles Times*, February 5, 1987.

46. Quoted in Ray Babcock, "Two Planners Seek Return," *Monterey Park Progress*, February 12, 1987.

47. Irv Gilman, "Monterey Park Under Siege?" *Monterey Park Progress*, January 29, 1987.

48. Larry Landreth, "Position Clarified," *Monterey Park Progress*, February 19, 1987.

49. Ray Babcock, "Recall Goes to Vote June 2," *Monterey Park Progress*, March 5, 1987.

50. Richard Walker, "Chamber Vote Removes Prexy," *Monterey Park Progress*, April 16, 1987; Richard Walker, "Vote Blocking in Chamber Election Alleged," *Monterey Park Progress*, April 23, 1987; Richard Walker, "C of C Studies Policy," *Monterey Park Progress*, May 21, 1987.

51. Mike Ward, "Chamber President Resigns to Protest 'Anti-Asian' Vote," *Los Angeles Times*, May 10, 1987.

52. Richard Walker, "City Manager Lloyd de Llamas Resigns," *Monterey Park Progress*, May 7, 1987.

53. Interview with Lloyd de Llamas by Tim Fong, for the Monterey Park Oral History Project, sponsored by the Monterey Park Historical Heritage Commission, March 29, April 13, and May 11, 1990.

54. Bill Marticorena, "Remove Foreign Signs" *Monterey Park Progress*, May 7, 1987.

55. Committee to Protect Our Children, "Kidnapping Is a Problem . . . But Not to Hatch and Reichenberger" (a campaign mailer), May 1987; Association for Better Cityhood, "We Need Leaders . . . Not Dictators" (a campaign mailer), June 1987.

56. Richard Walker, "Allegations Fly in Recall Campaign," *Monterey Park Progress*, June 11, 1987.

57. Residents Association of Monterey Park, *Record* (a campaign mailer), June 1987.

58. Ibid.

59. "Vote No on Recall," *Monterey Park Progress*, June 11, 1987.

60. Monterey Park Office of the City Clerk, record of Special Election, June 16, 1987.

61. Interview with Alice Ballesteros by Tim Fong, for the Monterey Park Oral History Project, sponsored by the Monterey Park Historical Heritage Commission, August 28 and September 19, 1990.

62. Recipient Committee Campaign Statement (Government Code

Sections 84200–84217), Association for Better Cityhood, May–June 1987.

63. Interview with Alice Ballesteros.

64. Max Millard, "Two Monterey Park Councilmen Face Possible Recall in June," *East West*, March 12, 1987.

65. Mike Ward, "Reforms Urged in Monterey Park after Recall Fails," *Los Angeles Times*, June 18, 1987; Max Millard, "Leaders of Recall Movement in Monterey Park Charge Harassment, Irregularities at Polls," *East West*, June 25, 1987.

66. Monterey Park Office of the City Clerk, record of Special Election, June 16, 1987.

67. Ward, "Reforms Urged."

Chapter 7

1. City Council Community Design Advisory Committee, Sedway Cooke Associates, and Robert La Rocca Associates, *Monterey Park Design* 1987.

2. Interoffice memo from Warren Funk, city clerk, to Lloyd de Llamas, city manager, October 22, 1987.

3. Berkeley Hudson, "Simmering Council Feuds Come to a Boil," *Los Angeles Times*, March 17, 1988.

4. Residents Association of Monterey Park, *Newsletter*, March 1988.

5. Hudson, "Simmering Council Feuds."

6. Monterey Park Office of the City Clerk, record of General Election, April 12, 1988.

7. John Horton, "The Politics of Ethnic Change: Grass-Roots Responses to Economic and Demographic Restructuring in Monterey Park, California," *Urban Geography* 10 (1989): 578–92.

8. Ibid.

9. Interview with Judy Chu by Tim Fong, April 30, 1991.

10. Recipient Committee Campaign Statement (Government Code Sections 84200–84217), Friends of Judy Chu, March–June 1988.

11. Letter from Barry Hatch to Governor Michael Dukakis, July 28, 1988 (copies distributed at council meeting of September 12, 1988).

12. Tina Maria Borgatta, "Hatch Faces 'Barry Bashing' Session Silently, Resident Bails Him Out," *News Digest*, September 21, 1988.

13. Grace Wai-Tse Siao, "10,000 Chinese Books Given to Monterey Park Library," *Asian Week*, September 16, 1988.

14. Monterey Park City Council meeting, September 28, 1987.

15. Mike Ward, "Council Sued in Takeover of Library," *Los Angeles Times*, January 14, 1988.

16. Kim Kowsky, "New War of Words in Monterey Park," *Los Angeles Herald*, November 11, 1988; Berkeley Hudson, "Judge Denies Latest Bid to Reinstate 3 to Library Posts," *Los Angeles Times*, December 8, 1988.

17. Berkeley Hudson, "Monterey Park Grapples Anew with Language Law," *Los Angeles Times*, September 15, 1988.
18. Patrick Anderson, "Monterey Park's Hatch Lashes Back at Critics," *Asian Week*, September 16, 1988.
19. "Planner Quits over Mayor," *Los Angeles Times*, October 20, 1988.
20. Monterey Park City Council *Minutes*, January 23, 1989; Ray Babcock, "Council Adopts Language Sign Code," *Monterey Park Progress*, January 26, 1989.
21. Monterey Park City Council *Minutes*, March 13, 1989.
22. Berkeley Hudson, "Pride or Prejudice?" *Los Angeles Times*, March 31, 1989; Marc Cooper, "Monterey Park Fights Back," *L.A. Weekly*, May 18–25, 1989.
23. Berkeley Hudson, "Monterey Park Scraps Plan to Pay for Statue," *Los Angeles Times*, May 5, 1989.
24. "Library Regains Board," *Monterey Park Progress*, June 22, 1989; Berkeley Hudson, "Library Board Reinstated after Two-Year Struggle," *Los Angeles Times*, June 28, 1989.
25. Berkeley Hudson, "Heavily Asian Town's Mayor Holds Tight to Controversial Views," *Los Angeles Times*, July 16, 1989; "Hatch Honored as Immigration Critic," *Monterey Park Progress*, August 30, 1989.
26. Interview with Joseph Rubin by Tim Fong, for the Monterey Park Oral History Project, sponsored by the Monterey Park Historical Heritage Commission, July 19, August 1 and 6, 1990.
27. Interview with Evelyn Diederich by Tim Fong, for the Monterey Park Oral History Project, sponsored by the Monterey Park Historical Heritage Commission, July 11 and August 2, 1990.
28. Interview with Judy Chu.
29. Interview with David Barron by Tim Fong, for the Monterey Park Oral History Project, sponsored by the Monterey Park Historical Heritage Commission, September 18, October 2 and 9, 1990.
30. Monterey Park Citizens for Responsible Growth, *Record* (a campaign mailer), April 1990.
31. Quoted in Grace Wai-Tse Siao, "Chinese Running against Hatch for Monterey Park Council," *Asian Week*, August 4, 1989.
32. Recipient Committee Campaign Statement (Government Code Sections 84200–84217), Citizens for Sam Kiang, March–June 1990.
33. Monterey Park Office of the City Clerk, record of General Election, April 10, 1990.
34. Ibid.
35. Irene Chang, "New City Council Majority Takes a Softer Line on Growth," *Los Angeles Times*, November 18, 1990; "Proposed North Atlantic 'Gateway' in Sight," *Monterey Park Living*, Spring 1991.
36. Irene Chang, "Embattled Chu Airs Bilingual Hiring Plan," *Los Angeles Times*, July 28, 1991; Edward Cheng, "Councilwoman Judy Chu Draws Ire of Chinese American Community," *Asian Week*, August 2, 1991.

37. Howard Hong, "Chinese Split Signals Power Play in Monterey Park," *Asian Week*, August 2, 1991; *Chinese Daily News*, July 22, 1991 (translated by Susan Chow).

38. Hong, "Chinese Split."

39. Chang, "Embattled Chu."

40. Irene Chang, "Lewis Pleads in Vain to Get City Manager's Job Back," *Los Angeles Times*, August 15, 1991.

41. Howard Hong, "Chu Announces Candidacy for Re-Election, Defends Stance on 911," *Asian Week*, January 17, 1992.

42. Quoted in Marc Cooper, "Monterey Park Fights Back," *L.A. Weekly*, May 18–25, 1989.

43. Residents Association of Monterey Park, *Record* (a campaign mailer), April 1992.

44. Ibid.

45. Recipient Committee Campaign Statement (Government Code Sections 84200–84217), Friends of Bonnie Wai for City Council, March–June 1992; and Friends to Re-Elect Judy Chu, March–June 1992.

46. Monterey Park Office of the City Clerk, record of General Election, April 14, 1992.

47. Victor G. Nee and Brett de Bary Nee, *Longtime Californ': A Documentary Study of an American Chinatown* (New York: Pantheon, 1972); Bernard Wong, "Elites and Ethnic Boundary Maintenance: A Study of the Roles of Elites in Chinatown, New York City," *Urban Anthropology* 6 (1977): 1–22.

48. Peter Kwong, *The New Chinatown* (New York: Hill & Wang, 1987), pp. 25–56; Richard Thompson, "Ethnicity versus Class: An Analysis of Conflict in a North American Chinese Community," *Ethnicity* 6 (1979): 306–22. Thompson sees the "social service elite" as Hong Kong–born rather than Canadian-born; otherwise, his description is virtually identical with Kwong's.

49. Kwong, *The New Chinatown*, pp. 172–73.

Chapter 8

1. Robert E. Park, *Race and Culture* (Glencoe, Ill.: Free Press, 1950), p. 150.

2. Oliver C. Cox, *Caste, Class, and Race* (New York: Doubleday, 1948), p. 402.

3. W. Lloyd Warner and Leo Srole, *The Social Systems of American Ethnic Groups* (New Haven, Conn.: Yale University Press, 1945), pp. 284–86.

4. Milton Gordon, *Assimilation in American Life: The Role of Race, Religion, and National Origin* (New York: Oxford University Press, 1964), pp. 27–28.

5. Horace Kallen, "Democracy versus the Melting Pot," *The Nation*, February 18 and 25, 1915; reprinted in Horace Kallen, *Culture and*

Democracy in the United States (New York: Boni & Liveright, 1924).
6. Gordon, *Assimilation in American Life*, pp. 71, 84–114, 159.
7. Nathan Glazer and Daniel Patrick Moynihan, *Beyond the Melting Pot* (Cambridge, Mass.: M.I.T. Press, 1964), p. 14.
8. See Nathan Glazer, "Blacks and Ethnic Groups: The Difference, and the Political Difference It Makes," *Social Problems* 18 (1971): 444–61; reprinted in Nathan Glazer, *Ethnic Dilemmas, 1964–1982* (Cambridge, Mass.: Harvard University Press, 1983), pp. 70–93.
9. Thomas Sowell, *Ethnic America* (New York: Basic Books, 1981), pp. 295, 284.
10. Robert Blauner, *Racial Oppression in America* (New York: Harper & Row, 1972), pp. 52–53, 62.
11. Edna Bonacich, "A Theory of Ethnic Antagonism: The Split Labor Market," *American Sociological Review* 37 (1972): 547–59.
12. David Gordon, *Theories of Poverty and Underemployment: Orthodox, Radical, and Dual Labor Market Perspectives* (Lexington, Mass.: Heath, 1972); Richard Edwards, *Contested Terrain: The Transformation of the Workplace in the Twentieth Century* (New York: Basic Books, 1979); Michael Reich, *Racial Inequality* (Princeton, N.J.: Princeton University Press, 1981); David Gordon, Richard Edwards, and Michael Reich, *Segmented Work, Divided Workers: The Historical Transformation of Labor in the United States* (New York: Cambridge University Press, 1982).
13. Mario Barrera, *Race and Class in the Southwest* (Notre Dame, Ind.: University of Notre Dame Press, 1979), pp. 214, 212, 216.
14. Edna Bonacich and John Modell, *The Economic Basis of Ethnic Solidarity: Small Business in the Japanese American Community* (Berkeley: University of California Press, 1980), pp. 61, 19. See also Edna Bonacich, "A Theory of Middleman Minorities," *American Sociological Review* 28 (1973): 583–94.
15. Ivan Light, *Ethnic Enterprise in America* (Berkeley: University of California Press, 1972).
16. Pyong Gap Min, *Ethnic Business Enterprise: Korean Small Business in Atlanta* (New York: Center for Migration Studies, 1988), pp. 124–25.
17. See Alejandro Portes and Robert Bach, *Latin Journey* (Berkeley: University of California Press, 1985); Alejandro Portes, "Rise of Ethnicity: Perceptions among Cuban Exiles in Miami," *American Sociological Review* 49 (1984): 383–97; Alejandro Portes, Robert Parker, and José Cobas, "Assimilation or Consciousness: Perceptions of U.S. Society among Recent Latin American Immigrants," *Social Forces* 59 (1980): 200–224; Kenneth Wilson and Alejandro Portes, "Immigrant Enclaves: An Analysis of the Labor Market Experiences of Cubans in Miami," *American Journal of Sociology* 80 (1980): 295–319.
18. Bonacich and Modell, *Economic Basis of Ethnic Solidarity*, p. 14.
19. Gordon, *Assimilation in American Life*, p. 51.
20. Stephen Steinberg, *The Ethnic Myth* (Boston: Beacon Press, 1981), p. 95.

21. William J. Wilson, *The Declining Significance of Race* (Chicago: University of Chicago Press, 1978), p. 1.
22. Ibid., p. 1; William J. Wilson, *The Truly Disadvantaged* (Chicago: University of Chicago Press, 1987), p. 121.
23. David Montejano, *Anglos and Mexicans in the Making of Texas, 1836–1986* (Austin: University of Texas Press, 1987).
24. Ibid., p. 315.
25. Michael Omi and Howard Winant, *Racial Formation in the United States: From the 1960s to the 1980s* (New York: Routledge & Kegan Paul, 1986), p. 66.
26. Ibid., pp. 115–17.
27. Ibid., pp. 118–20.
28. Nathan Glazer, *Affirmative Discrimination* (New York: Basic Books, 1975); Nathan Glazer, *Ethnic Dilemmas, 1964–1982* (Cambridge, Mass.: Harvard University Press, 1983).
29. See reviews of Omi and Winant, *Racial Formation* by Joane Nagel, *American Journal of Sociology* 93 (1988): 1025–26; and Charles Hamilton, *Political Science Quarterly* 103 (1988): 158–59.

Conclusion

1. See Dennis R. Judd, "From Cowtown to Sunbelt City," in Susan Fainstein, ed., *Restructuring the City: The Political Economy of Urban Redevelopment* (New York: Longman, 1983), pp. 167–201; Rick Reiff, "Rocky Mountain Low," *Forbes*, September 5, 1988; Joe R. Feagin, *Free Enterprise City: Houston in Political-Economic Perspective* (New Brunswick, N.J.: Rutgers University Press, 1988).
2. Fieldnotes from September 19, 1990.
3. Irene Chang, "'Other Chinatown' to Usher in Year of the Monkey," *Los Angeles Times*, January 2, 1992; "Chinese Festival Slated," *Monterey Park Progress*, January 23, 1992.

SELECT BIBLIOGRAPHY

Agar, Michael. *The Professional Stranger: An Informal Introduction to Ethnography*. New York: Academic Press, 1980.

————. *Ripping and Running: A Formal Ethnography of Urban Heroin Addicts*. New York: Seminar Press, 1973.

AmeriAsian News. 1987 (March/April). "$50 Million 'Orlando Chinatown' Features Hotel-Retail Complex and 30 Restaurants."

Anderson, Kurt. "The New Ellis Island: Immigrants from All Over Change the Beat, Bop, and Character of Los Angeles." *Time*, June 13, 1983.

Banton, Michael. *Racial and Ethnic Competition*. Cambridge: Cambridge University Press, 1983.

————. *Racial Consciousness*. New York: Longman, 1988.

Barrera, Mario. *Beyond Aztlan: Ethnic Autonomy in Comparative Perspective.* New York: Praeger, 1988.

————. *Race and Class in the Southwest*. Notre Dame, Ind.: University of Notre Dame Press, 1979.

Barth, Gunther. *Bitter Strength: A History of the Chinese in the United States, 1850–1870*. Cambridge, Mass.: Harvard University Press, 1964.

Blackstock, Joseph R. "Laura Scudder: Southern California's Potato Chip Pioneer." *The Californians* 7, no. 5 (1990): 30–39.

Blauner, Robert. *Racial Oppression in America*. New York: Harper & Row, 1972.

Bodnar, John. *The Transplanted: A History of Immigrants in Urban America*. Bloomington: Indiana University Press, 1985.

Bonacich, Edna. "A Theory of Ethnic Antagonism: The Split Labor Market." *American Sociological Review* 37 (1972): 547–59.

————. "A Theory of Middleman Minorities." *American Sociological Review* 28 (1973): 583–94.

Bonacich, Edna, and John Modell. *The Economic Basis of Ethnic Solidarity: Small Business in the Japanese American Community*. Berkeley: University of California Press, 1980.

Breuilly, John. *Nationalism and the State*. Chicago: University of Chicago Press, 1982.

Browning, Rufus, and David Tabb. *Protest Is Not Enough*. Berkeley: University of California Press, 1984.

Calderon, José. "Latinos and Ethnic Conflict in Suburbia: The Case of Monterey Park." *Latino Studies Journal* 1 (May 1990): 23–32.

Chan, Sucheng. *This Bittersweet Soil: The Chinese in California Agriculture, 1860–1910*. Berkeley: University of California Press, 1986.

Chen, Hsiang-shui. *Chinatown No More*. Ithaca, N.Y.: Cornell University Press, 1992.

Chen, Jack. *The Chinese of America*. San Francisco: Harper & Row, 1980.

Cheng, Lucie, and Edna Bonacich, eds. *Labor Immigration under Capitalism:*

Asian Workers in the United States before World War II. Berkeley: University of California Press, 1984.

"Chiang's Last Redoubt: Future Uncertain." *Time*, November 8, 1971.

Coolidge, Mary Roberts. *Chinese Immigration.* New York: Henry Holt, 1909.

Cox, Oliver C. *Caste, Class, and Race.* New York: Doubleday, 1948.

Davis, Cullom, Kathryn Back, and Kay McLean. *Oral History: From Tape to Type.* Chicago: American Library Association, 1977.

Dyer, Richard. "The Growth and Development of Monterey Park, California, between 1906 and 1930." Thesis, California State College, Los Angeles, 1961.

Edwards, Richard. *Contested Terrain: The Transformation of the Workplace in the Twentieth Century.* New York: Basic Books, 1979.

"English Spoken Here, OK?" *Time*, August 25, 1986.

Feagin, Joe R. *Free Enterprise City: Houston in Political Economic Perspective.* New Brunswick, N.J.: Rutgers University Press, 1988.

Fong, Tim, producer. "Emerging Diversity, Changing Values." Radio documentary on Monterey Park. Produced for California Tomorrow, a nonprofit organization, January 1987.

———. "The Unique Convergence: Monterey Park." *California Sociologist* 12 (1989): 171–94.

Gans, Herbert. *Urban Villagers.* New York: Free Press of Glencoe, 1962.

Garcia, Eugene, Francisco A. Lomeli, and Isidoro D. Ortiz, eds. *Chicano Studies: A Multidisciplinary Approach.* New York: Teachers College, Columbia University, 1984.

Gee, Emma, ed. *Counterpoint: Perspectives on Asian America.* Los Angeles: Asian American Studies Center, University of California, 1976.

Gerth, H. H. and C. W. Mills, eds. *From Max Weber: Essays in Sociology.* New York: Oxford University Press, 1972.

Glazer, Nathan. *Affirmative Discrimination.* New York: Basic Books, 1975.

———. *Ethnic Dilemmas, 1964–1982.* Cambridge, Mass.: Harvard University Press, 1983.

Glazer, Nathan, and Daniel Patrick Moynihan. *Beyond the Melting Pot.* Cambridge, Mass.: MIT Press, 1964.

———. *Ethnicity: Theory and Experience.* Cambridge, Mass.: Harvard University Press, 1975.

Goldberg, Michael. *The Chinese Connection.* Vancouver: University of British Columbia Press, 1985.

Gordon, David. *Theories of Poverty and Underemployment: Orthodox, Radical, and Dual Labor Market Perspectives.* Lexington, Mass.: Heath, 1972.

Gordon, David, Richard Edwards, and Michael Reich. *Segmented Work, Divided Workers: The Historical Transformation of Labor in the United States.* New York: Cambridge University Press, 1982.

Gordon, Milton. *Assimilation in American Life: The Role of Race, Religion, and National Origin.* New York: Oxford University Press, 1964.

Grele, Ronald J. *Envelopes of Sound: The Art of Oral History.* Chicago: Precedent, 1984.

Gruver, Scott. "Monterey Park in the Forties." Thesis, California State College, Los Angeles, 1961.

Gudde, Erwin G. *California Place Names*. Berkeley: University of California Press, 1969.

Henige, David. *Oral Historiography*. New York: Longman, 1982.

Higham, John. *Strangers in the Land: Patterns of American Nativism*. New York: Atheneum, 1963.

Hofheinz, Roy, Jr., and Kent E. Calder. *The Eastasia Edge*. New York: Basic Books, 1982.

Horton, John. "The Politics of Ethnic Change: Grass-Roots Responses to Economic and Demographic Restructuring in Monterey Park, California." *Urban Geography* 10 (1989): 578–92.

Hsu, Francis L. K. *The Challenge of the American Dream: The Chinese in the United States*. Belmont, Calif.: Wadsworth, 1971.

Judd, Dennis R. "From Cowtown to Sunbelt City." In *Restructuring the City: The Political Economy of Urban Redevelopment*, ed. Susan Fainstein, pp. 25–54. New York: Longman, 1983.

Kallen, Horace. *Culture and Democracy in the United States*. New York: Boni & Liveright, 1924.

———. "Democracy Versus the Melting Pot." *The Nation*, February 18 and 25, 1915.

Kennedy, Paul. *Rise and Fall of Great Powers*. New York: Random House, 1987.

Kinkead, Gwen. *Chinatown: A Portrait of a Closed Society*. New York: Harper Collins, 1992.

Kotkin, Joel. "The Lessons of Monterey Park." *Inc.*, July 1987.

Kotkin, Joel, and Yoriko Kishimoto. *The Third Century*. New York: Crown, 1988.

Kung, S. W. *Chinese in American Life: Some Aspects of Their History, Status, Problems, and Contributions*. Seattle: University of Washington Press, 1962.

Kuo, Chia-ling. *Social and Political Change in New York's Chinatown: The Role of Voluntary Associations*. New York: Praeger, 1977.

Kwong, Peter. *Chinatown, New York: Labor and Politics, 1930–1950*. New York: Monthly Review Press, 1979.

———. *The New Chinatown*. New York: Hill & Wang, 1987.

Lee, Rose Hum. *The Chinese in the United States of America*. Hong Kong: Hong Kong University Press, 1960.

———. *The Growth and Decline of Chinese Communities in the Rocky Mountain Region*. 1947; New York: Arno Press and the New York Times, 1979.

Liebow, Elliot. *Tally's Corner*. Boston: Little, Brown, 1967.

Light, Ivan. *Ethnic Enterprise in America: Japanese, Chinese, and Blacks*. Berkeley: University of California Press, 1972.

Light, Ivan, and Edna Bonacich. *Immigrant Enterpreneurs: Koreans in Los Angeles*. Berkeley: University of California Press, 1987.

Loewen, James W. *The Mississippi Chinese: Between Black and White*. Cambridge, Mass.: Harvard University Press, 1971.

Loo, Chalsa M. *Chinatown: Most Time, Hard Time*. New York: Praeger, 1992.

Lummis, Trevor. *Listening to History: Authenticity of Oral Evidence*. Totowa, N.J.: Barnes & Noble, 1987.

Lydon, Sandy. *Chinese Gold: The Chinese in the Monterey Bay Region.* Capitola, Calif.: Capitola, 1985.

Lyman, Stanford M. *Chinese Americans.* New York: Random House, 1974.

Mar, Don. 1986. "Chinese Immigration and the Ethnic Labor Market." Ph.D. diss., University of California, Berkeley, 1986.

Marcum, Edward. "A History of Monterey Park, California, From 1930 to 1940." Thesis, California State College, Los Angeles, 1961.

McClellen, Robert. *The Heathen Chinee: A Study of American Attitudes toward China, 1890–1905.* Columbus: Ohio State University Press, 1971.

Miller, Stuart Creighton. *The Unwelcome Immigrant: The American Image of the Chinese, 1785–1882.* Berkeley: University of California Press, 1969.

Mills, C. Wright. *The Power Elite.* New York: Oxford University Press, 1956.

———. *The Sociological Imagination.* New York: Oxford University Press, 1959.

Min, Pyong Gap. *Ethnic Business Enterprise: Korean Small Business in Atlanta.* New York: Center for Migration Studies, 1988.

Minnick, Sylvia Sun. *Samfow: The San Joaquin Chinese Legacy.* Fresno, Calif.: Panorama West, 1988.

Modell, John. *The Economics and Politics of Racial Accommodation.* Urbana: University of Illinois Press, 1977.

Montejano, David. *Anglos and Mexicans in the Making of Texas, 1836–1986.* Austin: University of Texas Press, 1987.

Monterey Park, City of. City Council Design Advisory Committee, Sedway Cooke Associates, and Robert La Rocca Associates *Monterey Park Design,* 1987.

———. City Council *Minutes,* 1916, 1980–87.

———. City Council *Ordinances,* 1916.

———. Community Development Department, *City of Monterey Park Population and Housing Profile,* 1973, 1974, 1978, 1984, 1987.

———. Community Development Department, *Housing Element,* 1984.

———. Community Development Department, *Taxable Sales in California* (State Board of Equalization), 1980, 1985.

———. Management Services Department, *Comprehensive Annual Financial Report,* 1990.

———. *Monterey Park Living* (a publication of the city of Monterey Park).

———. *Municipal Services Program,* 1978–79, 1985–86, 1991–92.

———. Office of the City Clerk, Records of General Municipal Elections, 1976–92; Special Elections, 1981–87.

———. Office of the City Clerk, File of City Council Resolutions.

———. Office of the City Manager, "Monterey Park, California, Community Profile," 1978.

———. Recipient Committee Campaign Statements (Government Code Sections 84200–84217): Frank Arcuri, March–May 1986; Association for Better Cityhood, May–June 1987; Citizens to Elect Lily Chen, May–June 1981; Citizens for Sam Kiang, March–June 1990; Friends of Lily Chen, March–May 1986; Monterey Park Citizens against Crime,

March–June 1982; Monterey Park Citizens for Representative Government, March–June 1981.

Monterey Park Historical Heritage Commission. *Monterey Park Oral History Project*, interview tapes and transcripts. Bruggemeyer Memorial Library, Monterey Park, California.

Nakanishi, Don. "The Next Swing Vote? Asian Pacific Americans and California Politics." In *Racial and Ethnic Politics in California*, ed. Bryan O. Jackson and Michael D. Preston, pp. 25–54. Berkeley: University of California, Institute of Governmental Studies, 1991.

Nee, Victor G., and Brett de Bary Nee. *Longtime Californ': A Documentary Study of an American Chinatown.* New York: Pantheon, 1972.

Omi, Michael, and Howard Winant. *Racial Formation in the United States: From the 1960s to the 1980s.* New York: Routledge & Kegan Paul, 1986.

Padilla, Felix. *Latino Ethnic Consciousness: The Case of Mexican Americans and Puerto Ricans in Chicago.* Notre Dame, Ind.: University of Notre Dame Press, 1985.

Paine, H. Russell, ed. *The History of the City of Monterey Park.* Monterey Park: Monterey Park Progress, 1976

Pardo, Mary. "Identity and Resistance: Latinas and Grass-Roots Activism in Two Los Angeles Communities." Ph.D. diss., University of California, Los Angeles, 1990.

Park, Robert E. "Our Racial Frontier on the Pacific." *Survey* 56 (1926): 192–96.

———. *Race and Culture.* Glencoe, Ill.: Free Press, 1950.

Portes, Alejandro. "Rise of Ethnicity: Perceptions among Cuban Exiles in Miami." *American Sociological Review* 49 (1984): 383–97.

Portes, Alejandro, and Robert Bach. *Latin Journey: Cuban and Mexican Immigrants in the United States.* Berkeley: University of California Press, 1985.

Portes, Alejandro, Robert Parker, and Jose Cobas. "Assimilation or Consciousness: Perceptions of U.S. Society among Recent Latin American Immigrants." *Social Forces* 59 (1980): 200–224.

Purcell, Victor. *The Chinese in Southeast Asia.* New York: Oxford University Press, 1965.

Pye, Lucian. *Asian Power and Politics: The Cultural Dynamics of Authority.* Cambridge, Mass.: Harvard University Press, 1985.

Reich, Michael. *Racial Inequality.* Princeton, N.J.: Princeton University Press, 1981.

Reiff, Rick. "Rocky Mountain Low." *Forbes*, September 5, 1988.

Rieder, Jonathan. *Canarsie: The Jews and Italians of Brooklyn against Liberalism.* Cambridge, Mass.: Harvard University Press, 1985.

Romo, Ricardo. *East Los Angeles: History of a Barrio.* Austin: University of Texas Press, 1983.

Said, Edward. *Orientalism.* New York: Pantheon, 1982.

Saito, Leland. "Japanese Americans and the New Chinese Immigrants: The Politics of Adaptation." *California Sociologist* 12 (1989): 195–212.

————. "Politics in a New Demographic Era: Asian Americans in Monterey Park, California." Ph.D. diss., University of California, Los Angeles, 1992.

Sanders, Jimy M., and Victor Nee. "Limits of Ethnic Solidarity in the Enclave Economy." *American Sociological Review* 52 (1987): 745–73.

Saxton, Alexander. *The Indispensable Enemy: Labor and the Anti-Chinese Movement in California.* Berkeley: University of California Press, 1971.

Siu, Paul C. P. *The Chinese Laundryman: A Study of Social Isolation* (1953). Ed. John Kuo Wei Tchen. New York: New York University Press, 1987.

Smith, Anthony. *The Ethnic Revival.* New York: Cambridge University Press, 1981.

Sowell, Thomas. *The Economics and Politics of Race.* New York: Morrow, 1983.

————. *Ethnic America: A History.* New York: Basic Books, 1981.

Spradley, James P., *The Ethnographic Interview.* New York: Holt, Rinehart & Winston, 1979.

————. *Participant Observation.* New York: Holt, Rinehart & Winston, 1980.

Spradley, James P., and Brenda J. Mann. *The Cocktail Waitress: Women's Work in a Male World.* New York: Wiley, 1975.

Steinberg, Stephen. *The Ethnic Myth: Race, Class, and Ethnicity in America.* Boston: Beacon Press, 1981.

Sung, Betty Lee. *Mountain of Gold: The Story of the Chinese in America.* New York: Macmillan, 1967.

Takaki, Ronald. *Strangers from a Different Shore: A History of Asian Americans.* Boston: Little, Brown, 1989.

————, ed. *From Different Shores.* New York: Oxford University Press, 1987.

Tanzer, Andrew. "Little Taipei." *Forbes,* May 6, 1985.

Thompson, Paul. *The Voices of the Past.* Oxford: Oxford University Press, 1988.

Thompson, Richard. "Ethnicity versus Class: An Anlaysis of Conflict in a North American Chinese Community. *Ethnicity* 6 (1979): 306–22.

Tuttle, William. *Race Riot.* New York: Atheneum, 1970.

U.S. Bureau of the Census. Census of Population and Housing Summary Tape File 1 (STF1): Monterey Park, City, California, 1990.

U.S. Commission on Civil Rights. *The Economic Status of Americans of Asian Descent.* Publication no. 95. Washington, D.C.: Clearinghouse, 1988.

————. *Recent Activities against Citizens and Residents of Asian Descent.* Publication no. 88. Washington, D.C.: Clearinghouse, 1986.

U.S. Immigration and Naturalization Service. 1990. *1989 Statistical Yearbook of the Immigration and Naturalization Service.* Washington, D.C.: Government Printing Office.

Vansina, Jan. *Oral Tradition as History.* Madison: University of Wisconsin Press, 1985.

Wang, L. Ling-chi. "Lau v. Nichols: History of a Struggle for Equal and Quality Education." *Ameriasia Journal* 2 (1974): 16–46.

————. "The Politics of Assimilation and Repression: History of the Chinese in the United States, 1940–1970." Manuscript, Asian American Studies Library, University of California, Berkeley.

Warner, W. Lloyd, and Leo Srole. *The Social Systems of American Ethnic Groups.* New Haven, Conn.: Yale University Press, 1945.

Wilsey and Han Company. *Economic Development Strategy Element of the General Plan.* Monterey Park: City of Monterey Park, 1980.

———. *The 1985 General Plan.* Monterey Park: City of Monterey Park, 1966.

———. *Planning Report for City of Monterey Park: 1985 General Plan.* Monterey Park: City of Monterey Park, 1967.

Wilson, Kenneth, and Alejandro Portes. "Immigrant Enclaves: An Analysis of the Labor Market Experiences of Cubans in Miami." *American Journal of Sociology* 80 (1980): 295–319.

Wilson, William J. *The Declining Significance of Race.* Chicago: University of Chicago Press, 1987.

———. *The Truly Disadvantaged.* Chicago: University of Chicago Press, 1987.

Wong, Bernard. "Elites and Ethnic Boundary Maintenance: A Study of the Roles of Elites in Chinatown, New York City." *Urban Anthropology* 6 (1977): 1–22.

———. *Patronage, Brokerage, Entrepreneurship, and the Chinese Community of New York.* New York: AMS Press, 1988.

Wong, Charles Choy. "Ethnicity, Work, and Community: The Case of Chinese in Los Angeles." Ph.D. diss., University of California, Los Angeles, 1979.

———. "Monterey Park: A Community in Transition." In *Frontiers of Asian American Studies,* ed. Gail M. Nomura, Russell Endo, Stephen H. Sumida, and Russell Leong, pp. 113–26. Pullman: Washington State University Press, 1989.

Zhou, Min. *Chinatown: The Socioeconomic Potential of an Urban Enclave.* Philadelphia: Temple University Press, 1992.

Newspapers

AmerAsian News, March–April 1987.

Asian Week, October 3, 1986–January 17, 1992.

Chicago Tribune, February 5, 1989.

Chinese Daily News, July 22, 1991.

East West, March 12–June 25, 1987.

L.A. Weekly, May 18–25, 1989.

Los Angeles Herald, July 8, 1985–November 11, 1988.

Los Angeles Times, November 11, 1985–January 2, 1992.

Monterey Park Independent, March 12, 1986.

Monterey Park Progress, February 22, 1924–January 17, 1992.

News Digest, July 25, 1985–March 3, 1991.

New York Times, July 21, 1986.

Ramona Acres Progress, August 8, 1919–October 8, 1920.

Wall Street Journal, February 18, 1983.

INDEX

ABC (A Better Cityhood), 130, 133–36, 162, 176
African Americans (also identified as blacks; "negroes"), 18, 26–27, 28, 31, 36, 65–66, 155, 157, 159, 161, 166, 167–69, 177; and businesses owned by, 164
Agajanian, Shant, 52
Agar, Michael, 11
Ai Hoa, 62
Alameda, California, 118
Alatorre, Richard, 121
Alhambra, California, 16, 31–33, 46, 111, 177; High School, 75; and the *Alhambra Post-Advocate*, 69; Unified School District, 70, 74–75, 81, 84
Alkire, I. B., 19
Almada, David, 91–96, 99, 102–3, 109, 112, 121–22, 127, 130
Alta California, 15
American Association of Women, 146
American-born Asians. *See* Asian Americans
Anglos. *See* white(s)
Anglo-Saxon Protestants, 55
anti-Asian, 4–5, 10, 132, 175
anti-Chinese, 4–6, 14, 55, 70, 104–5, 110, 119, 121, 137, 145, 150, 153, 168, 171, 175–76
anti-Communism, 8, 153–54
anti-immigrant attitudes, 5, 14, 124, 159, 168, 170–71, 175–76
apartheid, 4, 60, 126
Arcadia, California, 33, 47, 145
Arcuri, Frank, 111–17, 119, 120, 122, 140–41, 152–53, 172
ascriptive class segments, 162–63
Asia, 35, 49, 114, 158–60, 174
Asian Americans, ix, 6, 62, 65–66, 106, 117, 135, 147, 149, 151, 154, 157, 160, 161, 164, 174, 176. *See also* Asian(s)
Asian American studies, 142
Asian businesses, 111, 132
Asian Detail, 68
Asian immigrants, 6, 32, 70, 118, 147–48
Asian marketplace, 117

Asian Pacific Voter Registration Project, 141
Asian supermarkets, groceries, 34, 62–63
Asian Week, 148
Asian Youth Project, 142
Asian(s), 6, 13, 50, 60, 62, 66, 90, 109, 112, 115, 122, 131, 136, 145, 169, 171, 176; family income of, 36; home ownership by, 36, 38; population, 3, 21, 27, 31, 36, 64, 177; residential patterns of, 36–38; as residents, 62; students, 70; voting by, 133–34, 141–42. *See also* Asian Americans
assimilation, 9, 58, 66, 157–60, 170, 175
Atlanta, Georgia, 164–66
Atlantic Boulevard, vii, 4, 19, 44, 47, 62–63, 65, 69, 71, 81, 101, 103, 106, 138; and North Atlantic Plan, 89, 97, 103–4, 106 (*see also* Proposition Q); South Atlantic Mall, 101–2
Atlantic Square, 45–46, 77

Bach, Robert, 165
Balderrama, Fred, 140–41, 143
Ballesteros, Alice, 21–22, 73, 135
Barerra, Mario, 162–63
Barnes Park, 3, 56
Barron, David, 65, 131, 140, 148
Barth, Gunther, 6
Beijing, 29, 105
Bell Gardens, California, 75, 114
Berkebile, Thomas, 16
Bezaire Electronics, 51, 92
bilingual education, 55, 60–62, 170
bilingual hiring plan, 150–51
bilingual 911 dispatchers, 150–51, 154
bilingual skills, 171
blacks. *See* African Americans
Blauner, Robert, 161, 163
Bonacich, Edna, 161, 163–65
Boston University, 21
Boy Scouts, 23
Brightwood Elementary School, 60–62
Briglio, Cam, 107, 123–24, 127–32, 137, 139–41, 143–44
Bruggemeyer, Nell, 55, 57

Bruggemeyer Memorial Library, vii,
    11–12, 144
Bush, George, 143

Calderon, Charles, 121
California English Campaign, 118
California Tomorrow, vii
California Court of Appeals, 146
California-Japanese American Republi-
    cans, 23
Californian, 55, 57–58
California State University, Long
    Beach, 33
California State University, Los Angeles,
    65, 113, 142
Californio (early settler), 19
capitalism, 109; and capitalists, 9, 161–
    63, 165
Carter, Jimmy, 29, 105
Casperson, John, 153
Caucasians. *See* whites
Chaing Kai-Shek, 28
CHAMP (Coalition for Harmony in Mon-
    terey Park), 115, 124, 127–29, 135, 137,
    148, 151, 163, 176
Chan, Sucheng, ix, 7
Chavez, Cesar, 122
Chen, Anthony, 132
Chen, Hsiang-shui, 9–10
Chen, Lily Lee, 85–86, 90–96, 99, 104–5,
    108, 112, 148, 150, 154, 172
Chicanos. *See* Latinos
Chin, Patricia, 83, 89, 101–2, 131
Chin, Vincent, 5
China, 7–8, 25, 27–30, 66–67, 115, 130,
    153. *See also* People's Republic of China
"Chinatown" theme, 50, 59, 78
Chinatown, 6–10, 112, 153–55; New
    York, 7–9, 31, 153; San Francisco, vii,
    7–8, 31, 153. *See also* Chinese commu-
    nities
Chinese, 4–10, 26, 27–29, 33–35, 41, 51,
    58, 62–65, 67, 71, 84, 90, 92, 104–5,
    113, 115, 120, 127–28, 132, 136, 147,
    152, 160–61, 163, 165, 168–69, 174–
    77; drivers, 4, 71–72; elderly, 3–4, 38,
    126, 150; gangs, 67–69; and intra-
    Chinese conflict, 149–51; population,
    26–27, 31; referred to as "chinks,"
    69, 133; residential patterns of, 38;

residents, 5, 86; students, 61–62, 71;
    voters, 85, 136, 141–42; workers, 6, 28.
    See also Chinese Americans; Chinese
    immigrants
Chinese Americans, 4, 6–7, 9–10, 13, 21,
    24–26, 34, 95–96, 119, 150, 160, 164,
    168; in local politics, 104, 106, 138–39,
    148–49, 151
Chinese Beverly Hills, 29, 33, 71, 86,
    145, 174
Chinese businesses, 43–44, 47, 50, 58,
    62–63, 103, 105, 110, 174; banks, vii,
    49, 63, 121, 174; markets, vii; 43, 62–
    63; professional offices, 43, 103, 174;
    real estate, 43, 174; restaurants, vii, 33,
    41, 43, 63, 128, 174; shops, vii, 43, 174
Chinese business interests, 151
Chinese Chamber of Commerce, 59, 159
Chinese communities, 4, 7–10, 65, 70,
    150–51, 153, 169, 172. *See also* China-
    town
Chinese Consolidated Benevolent Asso-
    ciation, 153
Chinese *Daily News*, 150
Chinese developers, 4, 54, 65, 95,
    119, 171
Chinese Exclusion Law (1882), 27–
    28, 161
Chinese immigrants, viii, 4–5, 13–15,
    27–31, 34–35, 38, 48–49, 51, 55, 60,
    63, 66, 69, 70–73, 78, 91, 94, 114, 116,
    150–51, 154–56, 159–60, 164, 169,
    171, 173–75, 177; and backlash, viii,
    42, 69–72
Chinese immigration, 5, 15, 27–34, 36,
    38, 58–62
Chinese influx. *See* Chinese immigrants
Chinese investors, 35, 43, 47–54, 66–67,
    78, 109, 174
Chinese language, 61, 69–70, 115–16,
    120–21, 129, 145, 151, 175; books,
    60, 144–45; business signs, vii, 51,
    63, 69, 105–6, 110–12, 116, 120, 126,
    129, 145, 159, 175–76; cable television,
    177; characters, 3–4, 69, 110–11, 114,
    120, 122, 175–76; movie theaters, 63,
    69; newspapers, 3, 43, 58, 150; radio,
    150–51; schools, 154. *See also* Chinese
    (language) speakers
Chinese New Year, 59, 154, 177

Chinese Political Action Committee (C-PAC), 148–49, 159
Chinese protesters, vii, 114
Chinese (language) speakers, 3, 51, 62–63, 69, 114–15, 127, 168; in Cantonese, 62, 149–51; in Mandarin, 62, 149–51, 177
Chinese-Vietnamese, 41
Chu, Judy, 139–47, 149–52, 154–56, 172
City Council, Monterey Park, 4, 20, 50, 56, 82, 89, 96, 101–2, 104, 109, 111, 139, 144–47, 154, 172; members of (*see names of individual councilmembers*). *See also* City Council, Monterey Park, elections; *Monterey Park Progress*; moratoriums, Monterey Park; official-English movement; propositions, Monterey Park; Resolution 9004
City Council, Monterey Park, elections: (1976), 73, 76–78; (1978), 73, 79–82; (1980), 82; (1981), 86–88; (1982), 73, 89–95, 104; (1984), 107; (1986), 117–122; (1988), 138–143, 152, 155, 172; (1990), 147–149; (1992), 151–153, 172
City Hall, Monterey Park, 4, 79, 86, 94, 101, 114, 126, 128–30, 139, 146, 150
civil rights movement, 66, 170
class, 6, 35, 153, 155, 162–63, 165–69, 170–71, 176–77; and class conflict, 5, 54, 173, 176; and class interests, 149, 171
Co, Alan, 51
coalition politics, 138, 151–56
Cohen Daniel, 22
Cohen, Edgar, 22
Commissions, Monterey Park; Art and Culture, 91; City Planning, 4, 38, 40, 42–43, 89, 101–4, 111, 123, 131, 139–40, 145–46; Community Relations, 77, 115; Historical Heritage, viii, 12; Recreation and Parks, 91
Committee Against Age and Racial Discrimination, 126
Committee on Economy in Education, 74
Communists, 8, 12, 28–30, 41, 67, 115, 153
Community Design Advisory Committee, 138
condominiums, 35, 38–43, 81–85, 123, 126, 174

Confucius, 64
controlled growth, 4–5, 81, 97–100, 119, 138–39, 143, 148, 168, 172; and slow-growth movement, 81–88
Coolidge, Mary Roberts, 6
CORE (Congress of Racial Equality), 23–24
Couch, Betty, 101, 108, 139–47, 150
Couch, Harry, 79–82, 85, 87, 91–95, 97, 101–2, 107, 139
Cox, Oliver, 157
CRA (Community Redevelopment Authority), 79, 83–84
Crahan, Marcus, 116
Cuban Americans, 115, 118, 164–68
cultural pluralism, 158
CUP (Conditional Use Permit), 123
Cuttrell, Katherine, 85–86, 102
CVJ (developers), 82–85

Danielson, George, 79
Davis, Louise, 76–78, 80–83, 85–86, 96–98, 100–102, 105, 107, 120, 140
de Llamas, Lloyd, 40, 47, 52–53, 63, 78, 80, 89, 93, 97–99, 103, 107–9, 132–33, 134
the Depression, 19–21
Diamond Bar, California, 33–34, 47
Diederich, Evelyn, 82, 84, 88–89, 101, 108, 139–40, 147
Diesing, Ruth, 57
Diho Supermarket, 62, 65
Dukakis, Michael, 143

East Los Angeles Community College, 65, 114, 142
Edwards, Jimmie, 44
Edwards, Richard, 161–62
Edwards Theater, 44, 63
Elder, John, 68, 87
El Loco, 195
enclave economy, 9, 164–66
Eng, Michael, 115, 128, 135, 139, 142, 148
English as the official language, viii, 4, 112–16, 118, 124, 129. *See also* official-English movement
English-only, 112, 116, 122
entrepreneurial elite, 154–56
Erhart, Raymond, 23

ESL (English as a second language), 61–70, 109–10, 114–15
Estrada, Trini, 121
ethclass, 158, 166–69, 171–72
ethnicity, 14, 35, 153, 155, 168–69, 170, 172, 173, 177; and ethnic businesses, 4; and ethnic group, 92, 112, 154, 157–59, 161, 163; and politics, 5, 141–42, 152–56; and property owners, 166; and ethnic solidarity, 135, 163–66; and ethnic traditions, 164; and ethnic unity, 149, 155
ethnography, 11, 13
Europeans, 161; as immigrants, 157–58, 161

far right, 169–70
Feliz, Bill, 91–93
Fiebelkorn, Avanelle, 64
Fiebelkorn, Harold (Hal), 42, 48, 56, 57, 76–77, 83, 85, 89, 97, 107
Filipino (Americans), 4, 26, 76, 112, 172
Filmore, California, 118
Fisher, Montgomery, 23
Fong, Ken, 131
Forbes, 48, 51
Ford, Gerald, 105
Fresno, California, 44
Friends of the Monterey Park Library, 144
Fry, Emma, 20, 64
Fry, Howard, 20–21, 24, 38, 56

Garfield Avenue, 17, 43, 44–45, 47, 109
Garvey Avenue, vii, 14–15, 17, 43–45, 47, 50, 56, 69, 109
Garvey-Garfield, 45–47, 62, 73, 138
Garvey Hardware, 44–46, 52, 63
Garvey Heights, 17
Garvey, Richard, 15–16
Garvey Unified School District, 74, 142
Gay, Bill, 70
Gerlach, John, 102, 140
Gerlach, Sonya, 83, 85–86, 88–89, 90, 92–95, 98, 101–2, 107
Gilman, Irv, 74–75, 80, 82–83, 85–88, 90–95, 97, 101, 107–8, 111, 131
Glazer, Nathan, 159–60, 170
Glendale, California, 25, 126–27
Golden Age Village, 67
Gordon, David, 161–62

Gordon, Milton, 157–58, 160, 166
Graves, Joseph, 56, 59–60, 64
Gribble, John Henry, 16–17
Gribble, Kenny, 17, 56, 75–76

Hacienda Heights, California, 33
Hannigan, P. A., 16
Hartnell College, 30
Hatch, Barry, 112–17, 119–37, 139–40, 143–49, 150–51, 155, 172
Hayakawa, S. I., 112
Haydon, James, 83–85
Higashi, Kei, 22–23, 58, 66
Hispanics. See Latinos
Hollingsworth, Pete, 128
Hong, Francis, 115
Hong Kong, 3, 8, 28–32, 48, 50–51, 114–15
Hong Kong Supermarket, 62
Horton, John, ix, 141–42
Houseman, Chris, 119–22, 125, 129–31, 139–40, 143, 146, 148, 172
Hsieh, Frederic, 29–31, 34, 42, 47–48, 50, 59, 63, 140, 160
Hsu, Evelyn, vii
Huang, Loretta, 70
Huerta, Irene, 134
human capital, 165–66
Human Services Task Force, 70–71
Huynh, Cuong, 41–42

Ige, George, 58, 79–80, 83–84, 172
illegal aliens, 124
immigrants, 157–60, 163, 166; adaptation by, 169; illegal, 143. See also Chinese immigrants
Immigration Act (1965), 28, 158
Immigration and Naturalization Service (INS), 31, 96, 124
Immigration Reform and Control Act (1986), 119
Independent, 58
Indians. See Native Americans
institutional discrimination, 162
internal colonialism, 161–63
intra- and inter-ethnic conflict, 10, 176, 177
Irish, 157, 159
Isenberg, Eli, 20–22, 24, 56–58, 60, 74, 89, 96–97, 107
Islas, Andy, 153

Italians, 157, 159
"It Seems to Me." *See* Eli Isenberg

Jabin, Mark, 82, 92
Jackson, Jesse, 130
Janss Investment Company, 16–17
Japan, 5, 25
Japanese (Americans), 13, 18, 21–23, 42,
    58, 61, 65, 80, 114, 138, 160, 168, 172;
    businesses of, 163–65; as farmers, 17;
    population of, 26–27, 31; residential
    patterns of, 36, 38; as voters, 141–42
Jardin El Encanto, 19
Jewish Americans, 159, 166–69
Jiron, Tony, 68
Johns, Johnny, 56
Johnson, Dave, 50
Johnson, Lyndon, 28
Jong, Howard, 24–26

Kaffee Klatch (group and newspaper
    column), 45, 56, 57, 76, 89. *See also*
    Harold Fiebelkorn
Kallen, Horace, 158
Kawaratani, Yukio, 101–2, 131
Kemmerer, Majorie, 126
Kenneally, William, 102
Kiang, Samuel, 148–52, 154, 172
Kinkead, Gwen, 9
Kiwanis Club, 50
Knight, Goodwin, 57
Ko, Winston, 40, 50, 86
Koetz, Walter, 56
Korca, 164
Korean (Americans), 26, 164–66, 172
Korean War, 112
Kowin Development Company, 40, 50, 63
Kretz, Ed, 45, 52, 56, 63, 121
Ku Klux Klan, 18, 69–70
Kuo, Chia-ling, 8
Kurilich, Mancha, 70, 84, 93, 97–98, 140
Kuwaki, Goro, 17
Kwong, Peter, 8, 154–56

Landreth, Larry, 132
Langley, Arthur, 18
Langley Center, 60
Latin America, 158–59
Latinos (also identified as Chicanos; His-
    panics; Mexican Americans; "Spanish
    Americans"), 3, 4, 12–13, 17–18, 21,

26, 31, 36, 38, 65–66, 70, 73, 96, 115,
    117, 119, 121–22, 127, 131, 133–34,
    135, 136, 141–42, 145, 148, 151, 153,
    155, 161–62, 168, 175, 176
Lau v. Nichols, 61
Lear, Norman, 144
Lee, Rose Hum, 7
Le Kachman, Bill, 44
Lemire, Pauline, viii, 88, 132, 136
Lewis, Mark, 150–51, 154
Li, Johnny, 131
Lieberman, Norman, 57, 71, 106, 110–11
Liebow, Elliot, 11
Light, Ivan, 164–66
Liley, Bob, 23–24
Liley, Helen, 23–24
Lincoln Plaza Hotel, 100
Lions Club, Monterey Park, 20, 56, 59–
    60, 76, 91
Little Taipei, vii, 67, 71
Little Taipei Lions Club, 59–60, 144, 159
Loewen, James, 7
Loftus Land Company, 17
Loo, Chalsa, 8
Los Angeles, California, 16–17, 21, 25,
    30, 106, 160; Chinatown, 21, 25, 30,
    63, 174, 177; City Council, 160; East
    Los Angeles, 21–22; Summer Olympics
    (1984) in, 100, 106; Unified School
    District, 50, 74
Los Angeles County, 36, 46, 57, 105,
    114, 150, 154; district attorney of, 131;
    Superior Court, 82–83, 116
Los Angeles Times, viii, 12, 34, 58, 64,
    113, 132
Lugo, Don Antonio Maria, 15
"Lum," 150
Lydon, Sandy, 7

McCarthy, Eugene, 130
McCarthy, Joseph, 139
McCaslin Industrial Park, 63
McClellen, Robert, 6
Mainland China. *See* China; People's
    Republic of China.
Manibog, G. Monty, 42, 76–78, 80–81,
    91, 96, 99, 101–2, 106, 109, 112, 124,
    131, 137, 139–40, 142–43, 172
Mann, Brenda, 11
Mark Keppel High School, 74, 106
Marticorena, Bill, 113, 133

Martinez, Matthew, 42, 78–79, 81–
 82, 121
Methodist Church, 20, 56
Mexican Americans. *See* Latinos
Mexican American Political Association
 (MAPA), 114
Mexican Beverly Hills, 22, 65
Miami, Florida, 118, 164–66
middleman minorities, 163–66
Midtown Pharmacy, 45, 52, 63
Midwick Country Club, 17
Midwick View Estates, 18–19
Miller, Stuart Creighton, 6
Mills, C. Wright, 10, 13
Min, Pyong Gap, 164–66
Minnick, Sylvia Sun, 7
Modell, John, 163–65
Molina, Gloria, 121
Montebello School District, 74–75
Montejano, David, 167–69
Monterey Bay, 7
Monterey Highlands, 23, 75, 130
Monterey Hills, 75
Monterey Park, City of: Building De-
 partment, 36–37, 53; Chamber of
 Commerce, 18, 23–24, 29, 47, 50, 55,
 58–59, 64, 76, 83, 106, 108, 132, 140,
 149; Community Development Depart-
 ment, 39, 43; Management Services
 Department 49; Police Department,
 67–69, 71, 91, 93, 110, 124
Monterey Park Chronicle (1982), 92–
 94, 136
Monterey Park Citizens Against Crime,
 92–93, 140
Monterey Park Citizens for Community
 Progress, 97–99
Monterey Park Citizens for Representa-
 tive Government, 83
Monterey Park Democratic Club, 91
Monterey Park Design and Review
 Board, 145–46
Monterey Park Library. *See* Bruggemeyer
 Memorial Library
Monterey Park Living, 11, 107, 129
Monterey Park Office of: City Attorney,
 57, 71, 106, 110, 115; City Clerk, viii,
 11, 77, 112, 116, 132, 140 (*see also* Bar-
 ron, David; Lemire, Pauline); City
 Manager, viii, 98 (*see also* de Llamas,
 Lloyd; Lewis, Mark); City Treasurer,

77, 140 (*see also* Davis, Louis; Ige,
 George; Manibog, G. Monty)
Monterey Park Police Officer's Association, 92–93, 132
Monterey Park Press (1981), 83
Monterey Park Progress, 18, 21, 45, 55–
 58, 69, 74; articles quoted from, 50,
 68, 70–71, 76, 81–82, 101, 133–34;
 columnists, 43, 55, 57–58, 76, 96, 107
 (*see also* Fiebelkorn, Harold; Isenberg,
 Eli); editorials/opinions, 57–58, 60, 76,
 85, 96, 102–4, 134; endorsements, 57,
 77, 80, 83, 120; fire at, 70; headlines,
 40, 63, 68; letters to, 68–69, 70–72, 75,
 80, 82–83, 86, 88, 104, 108, 111, 113,
 125–26, 131–33
Monterey Park Taxpayers Association,
 79–80, 87–88, 107
Monterey Park Times (1982) 98–99
Monterey Park Unification Committee,
 75–76
Monterey Views Development Company
 (Monterey Views), 83–84
Montoya, Joseph, 121
moratoriums, Monterey Park: (1978),
 42–43; (1981), 85–86; (1986), 4, 123,
 125, 127
Morillo, Richard, 115
Mountain View, California, 5
Moy, Jones, 68
Moynihan, Daniel Patrick, 159
Municipal League, 110

Nachi Kaatsuura Sister City Associa-
 tion, 33
Native Americans, 15, 157, 161, 167
Nee, Brett de Bary, 7, 11, 153
Nee, Victor, 7, 11, 153
"negroes," 18, 36. *See also* African Ameri-
 cans
Neighborhood Watch Program, 26, 155
Nelson, Alan, 96
"neoconservatives," 169–70
Newmark Avenue 63
"new right," 170
News Digest, 58
New York City, 25, 32, 113, 159; China-
 town, 7–9, 31, 153; Elmhurst, 9; Flush-
 ing, 5, 9, 31–32; Queens Borough, 5, 9,
 31; Manhattan, 5
Nixon, Richard, 29

"no-growth," 108, 148, 152
"No on A," 84

Oakland, California, vii, 44
official-English movement, 4, 112, 116,
    118–20, 122–23, 128, 131, 143, 145,
    147–148, 152, 154, 159, 162, 176
Omi, Michael, 169–71
Ono, Thomas, 138
oral history, 11–13
Orange County, California, 5, 130
Oregon State University, 30
Orlando, Florida, 5
Ornelas family, 121

Pa, Abel, 150–51
Pacific Rim, 49, 154, 160, 169, 171, 177
Paine, H. Russell (Russ), viii, 12
Paris' Restaurant, 45, 56, 63
Park, Robert, 157–58
Pasadena, California, 16–17
Pasadena Rose Parade, 55
Pearlman, Sam, 45
People for the American Way, 144
people of color, 134, 161–63, 173
People's Republic of China, 29, 130, 153.
    See also China
Peppin, Bruce, 81, 84
Peralta, Rudy, 91–95, 96, 99, 121–22
Personnel Board, Monterey Park, 150
Play Days, 56, 177
poker parlors, 91–93
population, Monterey Park: (1919), 16;
    (1940), 20; (1950), 20; (1960), 20, 22,
    176; (1970), 22,25–26, 73;
(1980), 22, 26;
(1990), 3, 22, 31. See also Asian(s), popu-
    lation; Chinese, population; Japanese
    (Americans), population of
Portes, Alejandro, 164–66
Prado Shopping Center, 46
pro-growth movement, 11, 79, 127,
    137–38, 140, 149, 155, 171–73
propositions, California: Prop. 13 (1978),
    79–83, 87, 91, 174; Prop. 38 (1984),
    118; Prop. 63 (1987), viii, 122–23,
    129–30
propositions, Monterey Park: Prop. G
    (1974), 73–76; Prop. A (1976), 76–78;
    Prop. B (1976), 76–78; Prop. A (1981),
    81–85, 88, 90, 92–93, 101; Prop. B

(1981), 86–87, 91–92; Prop. K (1982),
    89–91, 94, 96–101, 119, 149; Prop. L
    (1982), 89–91, 94, 96–101, 119; Prop.
    Q (1984), 106–9; Prop. A (1987), 138–
    39; Prop. B (1987), 138–39; Prop. C
    (1987), 138–39; Prop. D (1987), 138–
    39; Prop. S (1990), 149; Prop. T (1992),
    152–53
PTA (Parent-Teacher Association), 20,
    58, 61, 77, 105
Purvis, Marie, 140–41, 149–50
Puerto Ricans, 159

Quan, Sim, 86
Quang Hua, 113

race, 153, 157, 162–63, 167, 169–71,
    176–77; and institutional racism, 161;
    and racial conflict, 128, 163, 172; and
    racial discrimination 163–64; and
    racial diversity, 65, 168; and racial
    formation, 169–72; and racial group,
    92, 157–59, 163; and racial minorities,
    161–62, 170; and racism, 4, 90, 93,
    109, 123, 126, 134, 136, 143, 163, 171,
    176; relations, 5, 14, 168–71; relations
    cycle, 157; segregation, 15, 23; and
    tension, 168
racist(s), 120, 125, 129, 134–36, 152
Ramona Acres, 15–16
Ramona Homes Garden, 17
RAMP (Residents Association of Mon-
    terey Park), 88–95, 97–99, 107–9,
    119–21, 130–31, 134, 136–38, 140,
    143, 148–49, 151–52, 171, 172
Reagan, Ronald, 89, 96, 169
recall election (1987), 127–38, 143
Record, 121, 134, 143, 148, 152
red and blue flu (1981), 92
refugees, 6
Reich, Michael, 161–62
Reichenberger, Patricia, 119–37, 143–44,
    146–48
Reppetto, Alessandro, 15
Repetto elementary school, 84
Republic of China. See Taiwan
Resolution 9004, 4, 122–32, 137
Ricci, George, 132
Rivera, Fred, 101–2, 131
Rizzo, Frank, 64–65
Rodman, Aaron, 44

Rodman, Ed, 45–46, 64
Rodriguez, J. J., 131, 145
Rosemead, California, 31–33, 47, 123
Rotary Club, 23, 42, 58, 60, 77
rotating credit system, 154–65
Rowland Heights, California, 33–34
Ru, Wesley, 48
Rubin, Joseph, 90, 99, 101–2, 130–31, 139–40, 147, 152
Rubin, Maxine, 130
Rustic, George, 125–26, 131, 140–42

Saint Stephens Church, 56
Salinas, California, 30
San Francisco, California, 5, 32, 130; Chinatown, vii, 7–8, 31, 153
San Francisco Chronicle, vii
San Francisco State University, 105
San Gabriel Mountains, 16, 100
San Gabriel School District, 74–75
San Gabriel Valley, 5, 16, 18–19, 31, 49, 52, 129, 143, 147, 160, 163, 174, 177
San Gabriel Valley Tribune, 58
San Joaquin County, California, 7
San Jose, California, 5
San Marino, California, 33, 47, 140
sanctuary movement, 124
Sands, H., 18
Sands, Kelly, 51
Saxton, Alexander, 6
Scudder, Laura, 44, 63
segmentation theory, 161–62
Sequoia Park Homeowners Association, 82–83
Shanghai, China, 30
Sharp, Clifford, 115, 144
Siu Paul C. P., 7
slow-growth movement, 81–88. *See also* controlled growth
Smith, Gene, 131
Smith, Kevin, 127, 130–31, 133, 136, 140
Snyder, Earl, 24
Snyder, Peter, 18–19, 49
"social service elite," 153–56
sociological imagination, 10, 13–14
"socspeak," 13
Song, Alfred, 24, 172
South San Gabriel, California, 33, 46
South San Gabriel Ministerial Association, 24
South Pasadena, California, 16, 33

Southern California Chinese Radio Broadcasters, Inc., 150
Southwest Voter Research Institute, 141
Sowell, Thomas, 159–60, 167
"Spanish American" vote, 36. *See also* Latinos
split labor market, 161
Spradley, James, 11
Srole, Leo, 157
Star Market, 113
Steinberg, Stephen, 166–69
structural discrimination, 158, 160–63, 170
structural pluralism, 158
Superior Pontiac, 54
Sydney, Australia, 5

TACL (Taiwanese American Citizen's League), 128
Taiwan, 3, 8, 28–29, 31–32, 48, 50, 62, 67, 70, 105; Nationalists, 28–29; and Taiwanese, 4, 9, 28–29, 93, 126, 130; and Taiwanese money, 94
Taiwanese American Affiliated Committee on Aging, 128
Tan, Steven, 130, 139
Terashita, Henry, 42, 86, 123
Thompson, Richard, 154
Thousand Oaks, California, 89
Time, 4, 106
Tong, Chiling, 33–34
Toronto, 5, 154
Townsend family, 121
"traditional elite," 153–56
Treaty of Guadelupe Hildago (1848), 15
Tretter, Richard, 93
Tripodes, Louis, 45
Tripodes, Paris, 45
Tsai, David, 29
Tse, Gregory, 48, 50–51

ultralight airplane, 25
underclass, 167
undocumented immigrants, 158; as workers 96
United Nations, 28, 130
United States Commission on Civil Rights, 5
University of California, Berkeley, viii, 12, 29

University of California, Los Angeles (UCLA), ix, 24, 141–42
University of California, Santa Barbara, 142
University of Washington, 105
USA Today, 4, 110
U.S. English, 112–13

Valenzuela, Rita, 151–52
Vancouver, 5
Van de Kamp, John, 155
Venti, Frank, 83–84, 90, 92
Vietnam, 8, 32, 151
Vietnamese (American), 26
Villa Park, California, 89
Vogeler, Maxine, 125

Wai, Bonnie, 151–52, 154, 172
Walnut, California, 33
Walter, Earl, 33
Wang, Louis, 134
Warner, W. Lloyd, 157
Washington, George (statue), 146
Westphaln, George, 79, 81
white(s), viii, 63, 65–66, 88, 115, 116, 135, 161, 162, 167, 171, 177; city council candidates, 4; communities, 166; family income, 36; flight, 64, 126, 171; goodwill, 163; nativists, 163; population, 3, 21, 26, 64; resident(s), vii, 114, 175; society, 162; voters, 141, 142; and "whiteness," 170; workers, 6

White Cane Days, 56
Widner, John, 51
Wilsey and Han Company, 46
Wilson, Kenneth, 164
Wilson, William J., 167–69
Winant, Howard, 169–71
Winchell, Judy, 76–77
Wong, Bernard, 8, 153
Wong, Charles Choy, 36, 39
Woo, Michael, 160
World War I, 15
World War II, 8, 15, 19–21, 23, 25, 28, 35–36, 51, 55, 113, 167
Wright, E. D., 86
Wu, Charles, 152–53
Wu, Frances, 67
Wu, Helen, 68–69
Wu, Jin Shen, 62
Wu, Li Pei, 126
Wu, Raymond, 152–53
Wu, Victoria, 140–41

Yee, John, 66
Yen, Paul, 123
"Yes on K & L," 98
Ynez Elementary School, 3, 16, 55
"Yokahoma Village," 17
Yung Ho Sister City Association, 130, 155
Yusi, Steven, 71

Zabala, Fernando, 65
Zhou, Min, 9